Economic Instability and Stabilization Policy

Ralf Pauly

Economic Instability and Stabilization Policy

On the Path from Crises to State Directed Economies

Springer

Ralf Pauly
Institute of Empirical Economic Research
Osnabrück University
Osnabrück, Germany

ISBN 978-3-658-33625-7 ISBN 978-3-658-33626-4 (eBook)
https://doi.org/10.1007/978-3-658-33626-4

This Springer imprint is published by the registered company Springer Fachmedien Wiesbaden GmbH part of Springer Nature.
The registered company address is: Abraham-Lincoln-Str. 46, 65189 Wiesbaden, Germany

To Catherine

Preface

This English book is a revised and expanded version of the second German edition from 2018. Before the publication of the first German edition in 2015, I studied the 2008 financial crisis. Re-studying Keynes' seminal work "The General Theory of Employment, Interest, and Money" and reading Minsky's basic publication "Stabilizing an Unstable Economy" contributed to a better understanding. Together with Schumpeter's concept of economic evolution, both books form the foundation for the present analysis of an unstable economy and government stabilization. A retrospective on economic evolution provides a historical perspective for the discussion of state stabilization, the consequences of which are becoming increasingly clear today, and a historical basis for the outlook on future economic developments.

The interaction between the state and the economy no longer stabilizes economic processes for the common welfare as it did in Keynes' time. Traditional state intervention has now reached a dead end: growing instability and inequality weigh on society, distorted markets impair economic efficiency with "evergreening", and high uncontrolled credit expansion upsets together with sluggish growth the intertemporal balance between "much credit" and "fast growth" and reduces society's confidence in the future.

To make the future promising again, the state should realign its policies. In doing so, it can initiate the transition from a market society to a knowledge-based society with autonomous power of initiative. This modern civil society, together with innovative companies, will be a decisive factor for competitiveness in the intensifying international competitive struggle and for new national welfare.

I would like to thank Günter Bamberg and Lothar Knüppel for their critical review of the second edition.

Köln, Germany
December 2020

Ralf Pauly

Contents

About the Author

Ralf Pauly is a professor emeritus for econometrics and statistics at the Institute of Empirical Economic Research, University of Osnabrück (Germany). Until his retirement, he was working on statistical analyses of financial markets, especially on risk analysis and risk management. More recently, his research focused on economic instability and social inequality, as well as on the reorientation of government stabilization policy.

Abbreviations and Symbols

Abbreviations

ABS	Asset Backed Securities
APP	Asset Purchase Programme
ARM	Adjustable Rate Mortgage
BRI	Belt and Road Initiative (China)
BRICS countries	Brazil, Russia, India, China, and South Africa
CAATSA	Countering America's Adversaries through Sanctions Act
CAE	Conseil d'analyse économique
CB	Central Banks
CDO	Collateralized Debt Obligations
CDS	Credit Default Swaps
DB	Deutsche Bank
ECB	European Central Bank
EFSF	European Financial Stability Facility
ESM	European Stability Mechanism
EU	European Union
Fed	Federal Reserve System
GATT	General Agreement on Tariffs and Trade
GDP	Gross Domestic Product
ICT	Information, Communication, and Technology
IMF	International Monetary Fund
IT	Information Technology
MBS	Mortgage Backed Securities
MFT	Modern Fiscal Theory
MMT	Modern Monetary Theory
NA	National Accounts
NB	National Banks
NPL	Non-performing Loans
OMT	Outright Monetary Transactions
P&L	Profit and Loss Account
PEPP	Pandemic Emergency Purchase Programme
QE	Quantitative Easing

SNA	System of National Accounts
TFP	Total Factor Productivity
TSCG	Treaty on Stability, Coordination, and Governance in Economic and Monetary Union (Fiscal Stability Treaty, European Fiscal Compact)
VaR	Value at Risk
WTO	World Trade Organisation
WuT	Wuhan Technical University

Symbols

A_p	Labor Productivity
C	Household Consumption Demand
c	Propensity to Consume
D	Debt Level
DC	Debt Capital
Df	Government Deficit
D_g	Government Debt Level
$de = \alpha \cdot sm$	Mean Income as a Multiple α of Subsistence Minimum sm
EC	Equity Capital
EQ	Equity Ratio
Exü	Export Surplus
F(N, K, TF)	National Production Function
G	Government Consumption
g	National Economic Growth Rate
GK	Gini Coefficient
GK*	Maximum Feasible Gini Coefficient
I	Business Investment Demand
IS	Investment I and Saving S Equilibrium Curve
i	Market Interest Rate
K	National Production Capital, Capital Input
$L_1(Y)$	Household Money Demand for Transaction
$L_2(i)$	Household Money Demand for Liquidity/Speculation
$L(Y, i) = L_1 + L_2$	Household Total Money Demand M^d
LM	Money Demand L and Supply M Equilibrium Curve
M	Central Bank Money Supply
m	Profit Mark-up
N	Number of workers, Labor Input
P	National Price Level
p_Σ	Increase in National Wealth
$r = \Pi/\Sigma$	National Rate of Return
r_p	Project Return
r_e	Return on Equity
rz	Risk Premium

S	Household Savings
s	Propensity to Save
sm	Subsistence Minimum
T	Government Tax Revenues
TF	Technical Progress
Tr	Government Transfer Payments
W	Wage Rate
Ws	Wage Total
v = DC/EC	Debt Leverage
Y	National Income, National Economic Production
Yv	Household Disposable Income
Y_u	National Underemployment Income, Production
Y_v	National Full Employment Income, Production
Z	Interest Payments
Z_g	Government Interest Payments
Δ	Absolute Change
Π	Profit
Σ	National Wealth

Introduction: Views on Economic Crises in the Twenty-First Century

1

Abstract

The book focuses on economic change and the state interventions. The permanently applied Keynesian stabilization policy causes debt to rise. Minsky sees the current heavily debt-financed economy as the source of growing economic instability. The central banks take measures to strengthen the flow of profits and support asset holdings. In doing so, they favor economic inequality. Their massive interventions in economic crises lead to distorted markets and an intertemporal imbalance. In view of these adverse developments, a reorientation of state interventions is urgently needed.

1.1 Financial Crisis at the Beginning of the Twenty-First Century

Let us start with the financial crisis of 2008 and its state stabilization. Central banks supported the private banks to prevent the financial system from collapsing. Therefore, central banks acted as "lenders of last resort". By supporting private banks, central banks wanted to prevent the entire real economy from collapsing. With the bankruptcy of the investment bank Lehman Brothers in 2008, this danger became a realistic threat.

R. Pauly, *Economic Instability and Stabilization Policy*,
https://doi.org/10.1007/978-3-658-33626-4_1

In the following years, the upswing in the real economy remained weak. As a result, central banks around the world intervened massively in economic activity to stimulate greater growth. They now supported the overall economy. The Economist says that, recently, central banks have increasingly acted as "market-makers of last resort". The effects of this are distorted markets with misallocations and moral hazard and an intertemporal imbalance with diminished confidence in the future: economic growth has remained low, in contrast to high and increasing credit. The enormous state interventions triggered by the pandemic crisis are intensifying the damaging effects even further. The economic leverage of government actions is weakening. Traditional government intervention in the economy will be broader and deeper and may have harmful social effects.

Central banks, which have followed in the footsteps of ineffective fiscal policy in the twenty-first century, have been guided by the main motive of making sure the economy flourishes, then society will prosper. After the failure of fiscal policy, it is becoming increasingly obvious that central bank policy will also fail, or at least the risk of failure is very high. The cost of central bank intervention is considerable. It is borne by society in the form of instability and inequality as well as in the form of distorted markets and intertemporal imbalance that weakens trust in the future. It is time for the state to take a different approach. In any case, a new direction is needed.

However, let us put everything in chronological order. First, we will present different views on the financial crisis of 2008, then we will look at the subsequent long-lasting stabilization, which is facing a new and enormous challenge due to the pandemic crisis in 2020. For a better understanding of economic developments in the twenty-first century, we provide a historical review, sometimes in form of narratives in Chap. 2 "A review of the history of the economy and its concepts: change is a constant". In Chap. 3 "Keynes' and Minsky's macroeconomics", we present the main features of Keynesian stabilization policy and explain Minsky's basic ideas on the growing instability in the economy. Chapter 4 "Outlook on the transformation of the market economy and its stabilization" deals with social inequality and other factors, and Chap. 5, "Conclusion: changing economic policies" argues for a reorientation of state economic policy that is less directed at economic growth and more at the common welfare.

The first global economic crisis of the twenty-first century began in the USA in 2006. A longer increase in real estate prices ended with a price slump. Insolvencies of homeowners caused credit default risks to rise and prices of mortgage-backed bonds to collapse. Value adjustments of financial assets in the balance sheets of banks followed and caused their equity ratio to shrink and thus their risk buffer. The real estate crisis spilled over to the American financial market and culminated in the insolvency of Lehman Brothers Bank in 2008. The entire financial system was on the verge of collapse and was prevented from collapsing by the US Federal Reserve applying massive monetary policy measures and significant fiscal policy intervention by the US government. As credit default risks increase, so do the risk premiums for government bonds of less competitive eurozone countries, causing the prices of Credit Default Swaps (CDSs) to rise and bond prices to fall. The

American real estate and financial crisis led to a national debt and euro crisis in Europe, threatening the cohesion of the euro countries and ultimately the entire global economy.

The economic crisis ended a long period of global prosperity, characterized by deregulation in the 1980s and 1990s and a phase of falling market interest rates. The crisis lasted longer than previous crises after the Second World War, and despite drastic state intervention, there are still no signs of a rapid and lasting recovery, especially in Europe, even after many years of crisis. And here we must suffer particularly high youth unemployment.

Numerous economists have commented on economic crises. They usually describe the origins of crises in different ways and often disagree in their advice on how to overcome them. This is partly due to the complexity of the economy—interdependence, dynamics, instability, uncertainty, inequality, and transformation, especially in technology and globalization, that characterize it—and partly to the different perspectives on it.

In 2010, the Indian economist Raghuram Rajan takes social inequality in the United States as his starting point in his highly acclaimed book "Fault lines" on the recent economic crisis. With the subtitle "How hidden fractures still threaten the world economy", he refers to threatening fractures in the world economy, which he wants to see prevented by international cooperation.

Rajan sees the reason for the growing income inequality in the USA over the last 25 years in the American education system. Access to expensive education for highly qualified jobs in industry, commerce, banking, and government is becoming less and less affordable for a large part of the population, which is falling behind in income development. Social advancement is difficult, and equal opportunity is limited.

Increased consumption can mitigate the disadvantage in income development: private US households make less provision for the future and can therefore spend a larger share of their income. Interest rates are low—long-term interest rates have fallen since 1981 from almost 14 to 2% in 2014 so there is less incentive to save, to provide for the future. In addition, high growth rates cause income and share prices to rise, and with them wealth. Low interest rates and higher prosperity—economists speak of the "wealth effect"—generally increase the propensity of US households to consume, making consumption an increasingly important factor in the US economic cycle.

Low interest rates, especially low initial mortgage rates (Adjustable Rate Mortgages, ARMs), also make it affordable to buy a home that requires less savings. Important barriers such as the equity ratio and the debt ratio no longer discourage people from buying a house, namely the 10% equity ratio in the purchase price and the 45% debt ratio of monthly debt repayment on current income. The purchase of a house considerably reduces the compulsion to provide for an uncertain future and ensures the desire for property, for assets, is fulfilled. The increasing income inequality is mitigated in its perception by the fact that households of the lower class can afford more despite relatively low income, and above all a house purchase, a much-desired wish.

American policy has favored home buying, not only through deregulation. The two state financial institutions Fannie Mae and Freddie Mac have also facilitated this development. This policy is intended to ensure that a broad section of the population, which is falling behind in income development, can still participate in the general development of prosperity. This works very well at first. After buying a house, households enjoy rising house prices, which in turn encourages other households to buy. The mortgage loans associated with the purchase are resold to other banks. These banks create new financial securities by bundling mortgages with different risks into so-called Asset Backed Securities (ABS, more generally: Collateralized Debt Obligations, CDOs), which are then marketed worldwide, especially the so-called subprime securities, in a new market for these securities. These bundled bonds, which include high-risk mortgages, are still rated AAA. The rating is based on the assessment that, despite single very high-risk bonds, bundling will lead to a significant reduction in risk for the newly created financial instrument —based on the principle that diversification can significantly reduce risk, but only if the default risks of the bundled mortgage bonds are not highly interdependent; statistically speaking, if they are not highly positively correlated.

This American policy, which aims to reduce inequality in the United States, is based on an alliance of the state, banks, the construction industry, and home buyers. The result is initially impressive: the real estate and subprime markets boom. Until, beginning in 2006, real estate prices fell and interest rates rose. The interest rates are variable, and that is the downfall. As we know from the real estate crisis of 2006–2008, a rise in interest rates causes both markets to collapse with devastating consequences for both house buyers from the lower American income bracket, who were hoping to be better off, and also for financial investors worldwide. In 2008, the real estate crisis quickly turned into a financial crisis with significant repercussions for the global economy. This is because the real economy worldwide is interlocked with the global financial market via high levels of debt financing.

The US government has not so much tried to reduce the growing inequality by means of state education policy but to alleviate wealth inequality by favoring the purchase of the property. In this context, the conditions for purchasing a house were made more favorable, especially for a broad section of the population that lagged behind in income development. This kind of social policy has failed miserably. The innovation of subprime securities, which is closely linked to the purchase of houses, has also proved to be a misconstruction and has discredited other financial innovations. The reputation of the rating agencies, which apparently recklessly rated subprime papers AAA, has also suffered. They may have underestimated the correlation in their ratings.

In 2012, the American Nobel Memorial Prize winner in economics, Paul Krugman, tells the story differently. In his book "End This Depression Now!", Krugman rather defends the state financial agencies and points out that the barely regulated "shadow banking" was primarily responsible for the business with subprime securities. Whatever the case, the alliance between state, banks, construction industry, and house buyers has proved fatal in the USA. Initially, it worked well, but later it did not work anymore, very much at the expense of households with substantial debt financing, but also to the detriment of financial investors, including those from abroad—for instance from China and Germany where, for example, IKB Bank slipped into insolvency through the purchase of subprime securities.

The financial sector has created an ingenious financial innovation with asset backed securities, ABS papers. On the one hand, private banks and commercial and investment banks get rid of both the risks involved in heavily leveraged house purchases and costly local credit monitoring, and on the other hand, they benefit from the securities sold worldwide with the AAA seal of approval of the rating agencies.

In its five review articles on the current economic crisis, which began in mid-September 2013, The Economist pointed out that the long period of prosperity before the crisis, with stable prices and low market interest rates, favored the adoption of risky banking transactions. The low interest rates induce private banks in search of higher returns to invest their money in riskier securities with higher interest rates and to finance these financial investments increasingly with outside capital and thus more risk. This enables banks to increase their return on equity and market value, key targets for bank management. Debt-financed risky transactions increase the vulnerability of private banks in crises. The losses that then occur require value adjustments to be made to the fixed assets in bank balance sheets. This shrinks the equity ratio and, thus, the buffer to absorb further losses. This vulnerability to risk threatens the stability of the financial system and the stability of the real economy. This is because the real economy is closely linked to the financial sector through debt financing. Section 4.5 "Private banks: equity ratio, banking business, risks, and regulation" deals with the banking business in more detail.

The Economist also points out that, in order to stabilize the economy, central banks traditionally intervene in the market via the refinancing rate on the one hand, and in an unconventional way on the other, by buying up bonds and sending signals to market players about their future expectations by setting targets for the unemployment rate and acceptable inflation rates. Central banks buy bonds and thus support their price. By assuming market risks, they protect investors from price losses and thus from asset losses. They thereby favor the wealthy and the emergence of inequality. The Economist's series of overviews begins with the article "The origins of the financial crisis" and ends with the article "Making banks safe", see The Economist (2013a, b, c, d, e).

1.2 Economic Development in the USA: Competitive Advantages Through Innovation

The international macroeconomic situation has also favored the increasing propensity of private households in the United States to spend. In the quarter century before the financial crisis, high American growth rates caused yields in the USA to rise by international standards. The high returns have attracted money from all over the world, especially from Asian countries such as China and Japan. This money has been an important source to finance American investments and has offset the dwindling domestic financial sources due to declining American savings. American deregulation policy, together with American innovation in both the real and financial sectors of the economy, has led to high growth rates in the US and low unemployment. High growth stabilizes capitalist economic development, which tends to be unstable when stagnant.

Over a longer period, the economic situation in the USA has been characterized by high growth rates and yields as well as low unemployment, high consumption, and, the other side of the coin, low savings. As we know, the relatively high yields have attracted foreign money and the purchases of American financial securities are worthwhile financial investments for China and Japan. These investments enable the US, as I have said, to have its domestic investments financed by foreign money and, as we have seen, through the subprime paper, to buy politically desirable homes. Money lacking from domestic savings is replaced by foreign financial investments, and the increased demand for goods at home is offset by an increased supply of foreign goods.

The economic constellation described above is favorable from the American perspective. Over a long period of time, it has enabled Americans to consume more goods than they produce in their own country and to have their investments financed by foreign countries. In short, foreign countries have made goods available for high American consumption through exports and financed American investments through the purchase of American financial securities, both to a considerable extent. This constellation has been advantageous from both an American and a foreign point of view, otherwise, it would not have emerged in the world of trade in supply and demand.

So, what is the basis for this favorable constellation? An essential part of it is to be seen in the American innovative strength, in the dynamism of its economy. It has driven economic development in the Schumpeterian sense through new products and new production processes and has ensured high growth rates and low unemployment. New products and new processes, not only in the areas of information technology and telecommunications, but also in the financial sector, are examples of this. Examples include the high-tech companies Apple, Microsoft, Google, Yahoo, or Facebook and in the financial sector option papers, secured bonds (CDO papers) and Credit Default Insurance (CDS papers). IT technology is giving rise to new market structures, such as online trading and, in this case, Amazon as an e-commerce platform. Thanks to its innovative power, the USA is thus earning a return on investment, which consists of foreign countries voluntarily producing goods for the American market, thus increasing American prosperity. On the other hand, worldwide prosperity is also responsible for the rise of the so-called BRICS states, above all China. Sections 2.13.1 "ICT revolution (Baldwin and Milanovic)", 2.13.7 "Globalization and the international competitive struggle (Marx)", and 2.13.8 "China on the path of globalization to become a world leading economic power" deal in more detail with the increasing global significance of innovation. Section 4.5 "Private banks: equity ratio, banking business, risks, and regulation" deals in more detail with financial innovations.

In the same way that private banks use the CDO securities to sell their risks from the US real estate business, the CDS securities generally enable them to transfer their credit default risk to third parties. The market for CDS innovations has been growing rapidly since 2000, and with the CDS securities for government bonds, this innovation aggravates the Euro crisis. The innovation is an insurance paper. As the risk increases, its price rises, whereas the price of the bond falls. Because of this opposite development, the CDS paper is used to hedge against a price loss. To this end, when subscribing to a bond, the private bank simultaneously buys a CDS paper on that bond. If the credit risk spreads, the risk premium increases, and the bond price falls. The price increase of the CDS paper can compensate for the loss. By purchasing a CDS paper, the bank discharges itself of the market risk and ultimately also the credit default risk. With this hedging, the private bank can take on further risks. The hedging transaction favors moral hazard behavior, see for more detail Sect. 4.5.3 "Risks and risk management".

Even if the individual private bank can get rid of its risk, the risk is in the entire CDS market. This market quickly takes on a life of its own with supply and demand like any other market. If market participants speculate on rising CDS prices in the future, they buy CDS paper, possibly leveraged with debt financing. The CDS innovation is very successful. The market volume grows considerably and with it the risk inherent in it, which can only be borne by the economy as a whole. Furthermore, this new risk market can overstate the risks. The Keynes–Minsky momentum, which we will discuss in detail in Sect. 3.1.8 "Keynes–Minsky momentum", backs this up. If it arises, the functioning of the economy is endangered by rapidly emerging imbalances. Politics must intervene and society may have to bear the costs.

Another essential component for the favorable US–American constellation is to be seen in the interdependence of the USA with foreign countries. As far as goods are concerned, the American "excess demand" is matched by an "excess supply" from abroad, and as far as financial securities are concerned, the "excess supply" from the USA is matched by a foreign "excess demand". Rajan speaks here of "imbalance", we prefer to speak of international interdependence, of international division of labor, which leads to mutual economic dependencies on the world market. For the development of a trouble-free world market, it is important that the "imbalances" in goods and financial titles balance each other out and do not change abruptly over time.

For the economic symbiosis between the USA and China, the American historian N. Ferguson, together with the German economist M. Schularick, coined the word "Chimerica" in reference to the chimera. The Economist sees the two-way relationship between the United States and China changing into a triangular relationship with Europe, see The Economist (2014a).

Recently it has become apparent that the symbiosis between the USA and China is endangered. China is on its way from a developing country to a technological superpower and threatens the dominance of the USA. The global competition for power then turns cooperation into confrontation. The Economist describes the mistrust between the US and China and the danger that this symbiosis, which is a strength for geopolitical stability, can break down and that the forces for returning to national mercantilism can become stronger, see The Economist (2018): “Relations between America and China are built on mutual suspicion”, “It might also shove the world economy back toward mercantilism and competing spheres of economic influence“, and “A world of mutually beneficial trade could turn into one in which there are no winners without losers, and no victory without conflicts“. We discuss the emerging international competitive struggle in Sect. 2.13.7 “Globalization and the international competitive struggle (Marx)”, in Sect. 2.13.8 “China on the path of globalization to become a leading world economic power”, and later in Sect. 4.9 “Globalization: good aspects and bad aspects”.

1.3 Transformation of the Economy

The alliances are subject to change, sometimes abruptly, to upheaval. According to The Economist (2012), China has taken over the preferred position as U.S. trading partner from Japan and Canada. With the BRICS countries, new centers of the world economy are emerging, certainly favored by the low market interest rates worldwide and the globalization of the economy. Logistics enables the profitable networking of worldwide production and the globally operating banks to finance it.

The capitalist economy is also changing. According to Schumpeter, it is developing in thrusts. Innovation processes do not run smoothly. The new displaces the old, which can lead to long-term fluctuations. In addition, there are also fluctuations of an economic nature, which are due to short-term changes in demand. According to J. M. Keynes, a longer-term under-demand on the goods market and labor market can lead to longer-term unemployment. And in order to eliminate this social evil, according to Keynes, the state should increase its expenditure.

In the recent economic crisis, Krugman (2012) has been advocating this Keynesian spending policy. According to Krugman, the American central bank, the Fed, is also to pursue an expansive monetary policy. It should stabilize the financial system. A functioning financial system is a sine qua non for a prospering economy. Krugman also wants to see expansive fiscal and monetary policy combined with debt relief. He confirms that American policy has taken the right measures, but to an insufficient extent. He is certain that economists have the knowledge and the appropriate instruments to overcome this current crisis. The only thing missing is the courage to intervene in the economy to a much greater extent.

Krugman’s confident judgement about the necessary government measures to overcome the current crisis could be expected to be based on sound quantitative economic data analyses. But that is not the case. The numerical–quantitative assessment of state intervention in the economic process proves to be difficult and uncertain. What is the reason for this? On the one hand, the interaction, the interdependence of economic variables, and on the other hand, the time lag, the dynamics of interdependent relationships. Both factors do not allow for a reliable representation of reality in models estimated with data. Moreover, in a constantly changing economy, the structural constancy required for statistical analyses is likely to be lacking. This skepticism is expressed in Keynes' criticism of Tinbergen's empirical economic analysis. The reservations expressed in it are still valid. We will go into this in more detail in Sect. 4.10 "Economic processes and their analysis".

In his remarks on crisis management, Krugman discusses in detail debt-financed expenditure and the associated debt and concludes with discussions on debt by the two American economists Fisher (1933) and Minsky (1986). They point out that under-demand in the goods market and labor market can be triggered and reinforced by the financial market. According to Minsky, under-demand occurs when the payment obligations, arising from debt-financed expenditure, reduce the revenue flows and cause the propensity to spend to fall. A trigger for this can come from the housing market, as in the recent crisis in the USA.

In an expansionary phase leading to a boom, many households buy houses on credit. The situation is favorable: short-term interest rates are low, house prices are rising, and banks are willing to provide follow-up financing when loans fall due. Households feel prosperous despite high levels of debt financing. Many other households do not want to miss out on this situation and want to take advantage of the opportunity to create assets. They also go into debt to fulfill the dream of owning their own four walls. If the situation changes, prices fall, short-term interest rates rise, then debt financing turns out to be risky. Confidence turns into fear. This is the so-called Keynes–Minsky momentum. Rising interest rates raise interest payments, banks refuse to provide follow-up financing when property prices fall—they make it more difficult or even refuse to restructure debt, refinance debt, or continue lending—common practice until then to roll over the debt—and thus curtail the inflow of money to private households, which unexpectedly find themselves forced to curb their spending, reduce their debts, and, if necessary, sell off their assets, thus turning the downward spiral even further downwards.

In his essay "The debt-deflation theory of great depressions", Fisher warns that in an over-indebtedness depression, deflation can cause the real debt burden to rise despite debt reduction. He summarizes his warning in a concise formulation: "The more the debtors pay, the more they owe". The danger of deflation may threaten the USA and Europe. In any case, Fisher's line of argument is interesting. He links a number of economic variables that he considers important by means of his well-known equation of exchange, which relates the quantity of money and its circulation speed to the quantity of goods and the price level, and can use this to structure the mode of action of the selected variables. Minsky takes a similar approach, presenting his idea of the instability of the economy by means of two central relationships. This is discussed in more detail in Sect. 3.2 "Main features of Minsky's macroeconomics".

As already stressed, growth stabilizes capitalist economic development, whereas stagnation threatens instability, which manifests itself in unemployment and insolvencies. Stable growth is the aim of economic policy in every country. But what is to be done if there are no far-reaching and long-lasting innovations in a country?

To promote growth despite the lack of long-lasting innovations, two paths are supposedly open, namely export orientation and the expansion of government spending. Not every country has the innovative power of the USA, which grants this country a privileged economic constellation over a long period of time. Other, less privileged countries nevertheless want to share in the growth.

For some time now, China has been relying on exports, which have been largely absorbed by the USA for years. Here, the American "excess demand" is contrasted with the Chinese "excess supply". The mirror image, as we know, can be seen on the financial market. Here, China is accumulating receivables from abroad to a considerable extent, making it a major creditor for the rest of the world. In the longer term, China will develop into a new world financial center. Unlike in the old financial centers of London and New York, where commercial and investment banks are in charge, the Chinese state bank is the center of power. State and market economy have together written the Chinese success story. In this close alliance, one can certainly speak of state capitalism in the narrower sense. But in western industrialized countries, too, the state is increasingly intervening in economic affairs, be it to stabilize an unstable economy or to secure minimum social standards or assets. The state is becoming a central actor in economic affairs here too.

In the case of China and the USA, one can speak of a voluntary, profitable "imbalance" despite inflexible exchange rates. The export and import interests between China and the USA complement each other and over the years have led to strong economic interdependence. The situation is similar for Japan and for Germany, although here too the export relationship with a particular country is not so extremely one-sided. Japan was successful in the seventies and eighties of the last century with its export strategy, China in the last twenty years up to the present day. The same applies to Germany. However, Japan has been sliding into a phase of stagnation since the 1990s. Despite a continued deficit policy with an enormously high national debt, Japan cannot escape from stagnation.

As is shown in particular in the situation between the USA and China, export orientation is accompanied by strong dependence (dependence according to Rajan, we emphasize interrelation and therefore prefer to speak of interdependence). If the favorable American constellation, from which China also benefits in its rapid economic development, changes, then the "unstable equilibrium" existing for both countries is endangered, both in terms of the exchange of goods and financial interconnections. As the subtitle of Rajan's book says, fracture lines emerge whose distortions can endanger the global economy. Does the call for "Make America great again" have a slight ring of uncertainty about it being the dominant world power in the future?

As far as the favorable economic situation in the USA is concerned, one can only hope that it will last longer, i.e., that it will retain its innovative strength for even longer and that threatening breaks in its interdependence structure can be avoided. However, this hope is reminiscent of Napoleon's mother, who responded to the news of her son's winning streak with the words "Pourvu, que ça dure!" (French: "May it last!"). We know that the streak broke. The series of US innovations is also likely to break at some point, and somewhere else new advantageous economic constellations are creating other advantageous interdependencies.

We take up the topic of economic change again in Sect. 2.13 "Recent transformation in the global economy".

The time of populists is one of change and upheaval, and then one quickly looks for someone to blame and scapegoats. This makes it all the more important to ensure a sober analysis of the realities, to make important connections clear, and to seek fair solutions in international cooperation for the interdependencies in the world economy—the regulative political economist F.H. von Hayek already advocated an international alliance whose central goal should be to prevent states from harming each other. Rajan recommends strengthening international organizations such as the International Monetary Fund (IMF). In Europe, the euro stability system should be more solidly based, i.e., the fiscal framework of the Maastricht Treaty should be reoriented and new institutions should be created and existing ones be reinforced, such as the European Stability Mechanism (ESM), whose task should be to stabilize the euro monetary system and ensure the respect of fiscal commitments. It would be desirable to inform European economic entities better about central economic relations, see Sect. 4.11.2 "Monetary and fiscal policy in the eurozone" and Sect. 4.11.3 "Profits and losses of central banks".

Not every country can play off its export strength to ensure economic prosperity and stability. It is more accessible for every country to increase its government expenditure, which is known to promote growth quickly, but probably not sustainably. Politicians can easily find the justification for an increase in spending in Keynes. They are quick to identify under-demand as being cyclically induced and see increasing government consumption as an apparently effective means of quickly boosting growth. It is debatable whether the large incidence of under-demand identified has really been cyclical in recent years. In any case, this multitude of state interventions leads to public debt, which, according to the assessment of rating agencies and also according to implicit default probabilities of the credit default swaps, makes state insolvencies probable. Whatever one may think of this newer financial product, it should be indisputable that, together with the rise in interest rates on European government bonds, it has revealed unsustainable over-indebtedness in Europe and triggered a change in European fiscal policy.

1.4 Crisis in the Euro Countries

Let us take a closer look at the situation in the eurozone and in Greece in particular. Before the introduction of the euro, differences in competitiveness led to several devaluations, for example against the DM. These devaluations have increased the export opportunities of the countries concerned without seriously reducing prosperity in the interior. By joining the eurozone, the euro countries have decided once and for all to adopt a fixed exchange rate from their national currency to the newly created European currency, the euro. They have thus renounced the flexibility to devalue their currency. With low labor mobility and low fiscal integration, they have fallen into the euro trap, according to Krugman. European politicians saw things differently back then. The euro was supposed to be a tool for European integration. And in the Maastricht Treaty, they considered European fiscal policy to be sufficiently regulated.

Greece is not driven by the innovative strength of the US and cannot achieve growth by making its economy export-oriented like Germany's. By entering the eurozone, it is depriving itself of the opportunity to remain internationally competitive by devaluing its currency. It seems that the Greek state still has one way of generating growth, and that is to increase its government spending. It is making extensive use of this, despite its commitment under the Maastricht Treaty to respect the 3% deficit limit and the debt limit of 60% of GDP. This is possible because banks are initially willing to lend to Greece on favorable terms—for the time being, banks no longer have to price in currency risk. And no euro authority intervenes and imposes sanctions. This is not surprising, because Greece is not an isolated case. The majority of euro countries have maneuvered themselves into a similar situation and do not want to jeopardize this favorable short-term constellation.

While the Maastricht Treaty recognizes the risk of a systematic breach of its rules on public expenditure and believes that the "no bail-out" clause and the possible sanctions will ensure compliance with the rules and thereby keep the euro system stable. High government debt, even well over 60%, need not be serious as long as the associated interest payments, which are the real burden, can be made. In Greece and other euro countries, interest rates are expected to remain at low levels in the longer term, similar to those in Germany.

In their view, Greek governments have seized the opportunity and financed public expenditure to a considerable extent by borrowing, without bothering about the Maastricht fiscal rules. Like private households in the real estate market in the USA and also in Spain and Ireland, the situation tips over after a while, and the Keynes–Minsky momentum sets in. The CDS implicitly indicates a high and rising probability of default for Greece in 2010/2011, which causes interest rates to rise sharply and threatens Greece's solvency, which in turn causes the probability of default to rise further and creates the acute danger of sovereign default. The major rating agencies downgraded Greek government bonds to junk levels. The prices of their bonds plummeted and interest rates rose sharply. Greece can no longer afford the increased interest payments. Can Greece be left alone in this situation and insist on the "no bail-out" clause? No! The "no bail-out" clause turns out to be meaningless. It is unrealistic and not applicable. *The factual breaks the contractual rules.* Too much is at stake if you want to apply it. Its application would have caused a shock on the international financial market and harmed European integration. Despite international support from the EU and the IMF, and despite considerable debt relief, Greece has been forced to cut spending in many areas. As a result, the economy is shrinking and unemployment is rising. Domestically, social tensions arise, the functioning of the market economy is called into question, and there are complaints of paternalism from abroad.

There is an ambivalent relationship between creditors and debtors. It can be illustrated with a sentence attributed to Keynes: “If I owe you a pound, I have a problem; but if I owe you a million, the problem is yours”, see for example The Economist (2011). It makes it clear that quantity can turn into quality and that the creditor–debtor relationship can also change abruptly, for example in a crisis when interest payments and repayments falter. Then you cannot drop a large debtor with nothing to do without this causing shocks. Admati and Hellwig (2013, p. 41) point out that debtors in distress can be particularly demanding: “Specially, they may be excessively reckless, excessively calling for debt reductions and financial aids”. Now Greece owes banks in the eurozone such large sums that insolvency of Greece would have created a banking crisis not only in the European financial system. Greece must therefore be helped. The fact is that the market has overridden contractual rules, the “no bail-out” clause. However, it must be emphasized that European politicians, due to a lack of willingness to sanction, made this possible in the first place. The inadequate functioning of European fiscal policy is one of the causes of the European debt and related financial crisis.

There is a good deal of controversy as to whether the “no bail-out” clause makes sense for a joint project. But when it comes to general rules on public spending, there is no getting away from the demand that politicians interested in short-term growth should not be allowed to decide when and to what extent sanctions should be imposed if these general rules are violated. After all, politicians—and this can be concluded from the growing national debt—often see government spending as an appropriate means of keeping their country’s economy on the growth path, and thus usually consider the violation of rules they have set themselves to be of little importance.

Politicians are in a quandary since they have a conflict of interest. For short-term national interests, they are incapable of making the sanctioning rules provided for in the supranational Maastricht Treaty effective—Rodrik speaks not only of a dilemma, but of a “trilemma” between supranational rules, democratic politics, and nation-state interests, see Rodrick (2011), chapter 9 “The political trilemma of the world economy”, 184–206. The Economist sees the “trilemma” as a source of economic instability, see The Economist (2014b).

In most euro countries, debt is increasing without any sanctions being imposed. As a result, the euro countries have carelessly jeopardized the stability of the euro. The rating agencies and the financial market, especially the CDS market, have sanctioned the misconduct of euro countries. They have made politicians in the euro countries feel that the violation of the debt criteria in the Maastricht Treaty has serious economic consequences. Now they are the driven ones and must react quickly. And how did they react? With prudence? Not a trace! Like frightened chickens! From all sides, the most diverse proposals for solutions and blame for late and insufficient action are fluttering around. As is well known, Berlin and Paris are getting together to draw up a rescue plan, the European Financial Stability Facility (EFSF), in June 2011 for Greece’s acute vulnerability and are organizing debt relief with the participation of European banks and insurance companies in order to bail out Greece and thus avert the danger that an insolvency of Greece could have triggered in the global financial system.

Does this really eliminate the danger? By no means! As we know, Greece is not the only euro country that violates the debt criteria of the Maastricht Treaty. The majority of countries have done so—no wonder these countries are incapable of imposing the necessary sanctions if the debt criteria are violated. The danger of insolvency threatens to spread to all euro countries. The European Central Bank (ECB) is buying Italian and Spanish government bonds after Greek ones. In this way, it wants to avert a feared domino effect. Supported by the power of the facts, it extends its area of responsibility and takes on tasks arising from the misguided European fiscal policy. The question is, however, whether the ECB can provide long-term stability and what the price of its intervention will be. We will investigate this question in Sect. 4.11 "Stabilization policy in the post-Keynesian era".

By purchasing these bonds, the ECB not only further weakens the Maastricht Treaty, but also assumes payment obligations which later—in whatever amount—must be met by the euro countries; for example when the common currency project goes wrong. With regard to ECB losses, see Sect. 4.11.3 "Profits and losses of central banks". The bond purchase can be considered as indirect monetary government financing. According to this, the ECB undermines rights that are primarily reserved for parliaments.

Contrary to what politicians originally led us to believe, financial market players did not have to take the "no bail-out" clause in the Maastricht Treaty seriously. They have been clear: At the crucial moment when the clause would have to take effect, it would be declared null and void. Otherwise, its effect will blow up the euro, undermine the European integration process, and shake up the financial and economic system worldwide.

As far as compliance with the Maastricht debt criteria is concerned, it is clear that a voluntary commitment is not sufficient and that there is also no willingness to impose sanctions in case of violations. This is counterbalanced by the interests of political actors. For, as explained, politicians in many euro countries see government spending as a suitable means of keeping their country on the growth path. This will remain so in the future because Keynesian spending policy is still attractive in many eyes.

As we have seen, debt policy is closely linked to the financial market, and the insolvency of even a small state like Greece can trigger insurance payments via the CDS market, which can exacerbate an acute crisis—no wonder that the then ECB President Trichet, on the occasion of debt relief for Greece, issued a desperate warning against the occurrence of an insurance claim on the CDS market. By buying CDS, a bank wants to hedge against the default of its government bonds, for example its Greek ones. And these hedges are widely traded within the financial system. As Trichet feared, a default on the insurance can trigger payment difficulties in the financial system and, via a domino effect, cause international trade within banks to falter.

1.5 Economic Crises and Stabilization

Unlike the ECB, which is primarily responsible for ensuring price stability in the eurozone, the US Federal Reserve also has to deal with US economic growth, specifically "high growth (sustainable employment) and stable prices (low inflation) as well as financial stability". It sets refinancing rates for financial institutions at virtually zero. At the same time, it indirectly reduces interest payments and thus the deficit of the US budget by buying US Treasury bills at low interest rates via "Quantitative Easing" (QE). In 2014, it reaffirms on several occasions that it will maintain its low interest rate policy for a longer period and that it intends to keep long-term interest rates low; it links the maintenance of its policy to, inter alia, the target of 6.5% unemployment.

The unemployment rate in the US fell below 6% at the end of 2014. However, unlike in previous crises, the employment rate (labor-force-participation rate) in the current crisis fell from over 65 to under 63%, see The Economist (2014c), chart 3 "Many are no longer seeking work", or from 67 to 63%, see The Economist (2014d). Together with the low growth rates of economic output in the US, this may be one reason why the Fed wanted to continue its QE policy in 2015. In his criticism of the Fed's QE policy, the Taiwanese economist Koo (2015) points out that much of the money will flow into asset holdings and less into the current demand for consumer and capital goods. Thus, QE policy stimulates the rate of returns rather than growth rates. And the French economist Piketty (2013) shows that inequality increases in phases where the rate of return exceeds the growth rate. Thus, QE policy is likely to be at the expense of inequality.

Deregulation in the USA has not only boosted the housing market, but also facilitated the expansion of the financial market there. There, as in the UK, financial innovations have led to the creation of new products which, according to Rajan, have an *asymmetric characteristic*. They initially yield high returns and only later do the major risks—the so-called "tail risks"—become apparent. In the case of financial institutions, therefore, *the creators of new products take precedence and have priority over the risk controllers*. The asymmetry also makes government regulation more difficult, be it national or international. After all, it is precisely new risks that emanate from unknown sources that are not fully identifiable and thus not fully regulable at the outset. However, this newness drives the innovation process, and on the other hand, innovations are again the basis for prosperous economic development.

The shockwave on the international financial market triggered by the USA has led to a rethink of European fiscal policy. In order not to lose any further creditworthiness, European countries are increasingly rethinking their fiscal policy and endeavoring to accelerate debt reduction. However, concrete implementation is proving to be protracted and full of obstacles. Moreover, the QE policy of central banks takes a lot of pressure of politicians to introduce economic structural reforms. This confirms Rajan's skeptical assessment (2010, pp. 208–210) of the international coordination of national policies: "Politics are always local, there is no constituency for the global economy". "Change will come only when countries are forced to change, or decide it is in their best interest to do so, but that process may be too costly, or too slow, for the global economy".

The economic crisis has led to innovations. The G7 has been expanded into a G20 conference. Economic problems can now be discussed internationally, and economic policy measures coordinated globally. But long-term prospects are not to be expected. Skepticism about international coordination of national interests stands in the way of this. In Europe, the temporary EFSF has been followed by a new institution, the permanent ESM. It can be expanded into a Euro Stability Fund with the task of ensuring Euro stability in accordance with the Maastricht Treaty. On the one hand, it can, in coordination and in competition with the IMF, continuously analyze the situation of the world economy and explain its analyses to the general public. On the other hand, it can tie its financial support to conditions and provide targeted support for projects that can promote a reorientation of European economic policy—away from an agricultural policy focus toward an innovative orientation—and strengthen competitiveness in the euro countries. The European parliaments concerned would have to vote on the development of the overall fund, so that the parliaments would ultimately retain their full budgetary rights. To this end, the new Stability Fund can act flexibly and in a targeted manner to stabilize the eurozone through a deeper European fiscal policy. The recent crisis has revealed weaknesses in the European construction. But it has also created the ESM, a supranational institution that can promote European integration. In the future, this may prove to be a cornerstone in the European edifice that has been lacking until now.

The ECB can then concentrate, as it should, on its own simple objective of price stability. Europe would then have two institutions with clearly defined competences and simple objectives: the ECB as the guarantor of price stability and the ESM as the agency for stabilizing the euro and the eurozone. Both institutions, the ECB and the ESM, can be regarded as regulatory bodies in the sense of Hayek because their actions are subject to general rules. Regulators will argue that in times of crisis, the ECB acquires powers that it does not have per se. Indeed, its self-imposed mandate to buy up unlimited amounts of eurozone government bonds on the secondary market cannot be derived from its primary objective of price stability. From a regulatory point of view, it can be argued that the ECB is extending its powers arbitrarily when it justifies its Outright Monetary Transactions (OMT) program on the grounds that the divergence of interest rates in the euro countries is contrary to its interest rate policy. In doing so, it admits that, like the Fed, it also feels responsible for growth. In addition, it is taking the right to exert pressure on economic reforms and fiscal consolidation and on the consolidation of the banking sector through bond purchases. In this way, the ECB combines its actual task of ensuring price stability with a European restructuring and fiscal policy. The German Constitutional Court laconically stated in connection with its ruling on the European stabilization mechanism for maintaining financial stability in Europe ("euro rescue package") 2011 regarding the ECB: "The ECB also allowed itself to be included in the new approach—meaning the rescue package—by adopting a 'program for the securities markets'" (Bundesverfassungsgericht 2011, p. 6).

Interestingly, it does not say a word about whether the ECB is thereby undermining the budgetary rights of parliaments in the long term. However, the Constitutional Court now sees the situation differently and speaks of 2014 as an "ultra vires act" of the ECB, an arbitrary assumption of competence by the ECB, see Bundesverfassungsgericht (2014). We discuss this in more detail in Sect. 4.11.2 "Monetary and fiscal policy in the eurozone".

1.6 Keynes' and Minsky's Economic Approach

Economists, as we have seen, take different perspectives on economic events and differ in their economic policy recommendations. Many refer to Keynes. He is considered revolutionary in that he has shown that market forces can fail in the short term. Market failure can lead to under-demand in the market for goods, resulting in socially unacceptable unemployment, as was dramatically demonstrated in the Great Depression of the early last century. According to Keynes, the state should therefore intervene in the economic process to correct the situation and close the demand gap. It should increase its spending and increase the spending effect on aggregate demand by credit financing. Credit financing also pumps money into the economic cycle and thus stabilizes the financial system. With his deficit spending approach, Keynes introduced a new paradigm into economic policy at the time: Keynesian state interventionism. This concept has gained worldwide acceptance—no wonder, it is tempting for politicians, because they can spend money and, unlike with tax-financed spending, do not have to justify themselves to the voters—and it is not only used to overcome cyclical market failures. As permanent deficit spending, politicians use it to promote national economic growth. However, with their externally financed spending policies, they accumulate considerable amounts of debt over the years, which in turn, as the current crisis has shown, can trigger and intensify economic crises. This negative effect reveals, as the ordoliberal economist Hayek—Keynes' counterpart in England at the time—could argue, if he were still alive, the danger of interventionist economic policy constantly interfering with the economic process. The price of state intervention is, thus, a greater vulnerability of the economy to crises.

Through the accumulation of debt, the permanent deficit spending policy has turned the fiscal policy into a blunt weapon in the fight for a stable economy with full employment. It must increasingly leave the field to monetary policy. However, monetary policy can only have an indirect and delayed impact on employment through its policy of low interest rates. According to Keynes, the employment effects of monetary policy are small, as we can see in Sect. 3.1 "Main principles of Keynesian macroeconomics". The objective also becomes more modest. It is now limited primarily to stabilizing the financial system and rescuing assets from decline. According to the motto "If the economy is to function, traffic and electricity must flow and, in the modern economy, also communication and money", the central bank ensures the flow of cheap money. No state can do without cheap money these days. Cheap money is supposed to stimulate domestic banking, promote lending, and support securities prices. The purchase of government bonds is intended to make public finance cheaper—in the eurozone it also ensures the cohesion of the euro states—and the purchase of mortgage-backed securities is intended to reduce uncertainty on the real estate market. Monetary policy takes risks and protects against asset losses. It also protects against deflation and promotes inflation, and indirectly it increases export opportunities through falling currency parities. The policy of cheap money is thus also a "beggar-my-neighbor policy", the name being derived from the British economist Joan Robinson.

Moreover, it can be argued that a sustained deficit spending policy not only piles up debt but also, to the same extent, claims that it generates substantial interest income. Government bonds are not bought by the poor, who barely make ends meet. Interest accrues to the richer, and this source of money would not exist for them in tax-financed spending. The permanent deficit spending policy thus increases inequality in income and wealth. And this endangers social consensus and thus the very foundation of the market economy. Poorer people are no longer able to make adequate personal provision for themselves, and the state is increasingly assuming responsibility for basic care in sickness and old age.

Strongly leveraged expenditure is not limited to the government alone; consumer and investment expenditure, whether real or financial, is also heavily leveraged. Fisher and Minsky see the resulting debt as a threat to economic stability. It is no wonder that in the current crisis, the Keynesian Krugman not only argues that the state should close the private spending gap and stabilize the financial system, but also that it should provide debt relief.

The world economic crisis after the First World War with its prolonged unemployment finds its theoretical expression in Keynes' work "The General Theory" (Keynes 1936). In it, he formulates the underemployment equilibrium with *flow variables*. He sees the economic system as *fundamentally stable*. However, the economic equilibrium can be disturbed. The low flexibility in the labor market can mean that under-demand in the goods and labor market can last longer, with the result of persistent unemployment, which is socially unacceptable and can also endanger the social acceptance of the free market economy. Nor must unemployment be accepted as natural. The state can solve the problem of "unemployment". To do so, it must close the demand gap arising on the goods market only by additional government demand in order to eliminate unemployment; a debt-financed expenditure policy, the so-called deficit policy, is particularly effective.

In the course of time, economic processes have changed fundamentally, but the prevailing economic theory has changed less. The Keynesian approach of 1936, which was new at the time, is largely outdated. It is no longer relevant today. Starting from Keynes, Minsky (1986) has created a new, more sustainable macroeconomic paradigm.

Minsky sees the economy as *fundamentally unstable*. The instability results on the one hand according to Schumpeter from the dynamics of economic evolution, in which the new constantly displaces the old, and on the other hand from the debt financing of the economy, which private banks and commercial and investment banks are constantly trying to expand out of profit interests. Debt financing links the financial market with the real economy and thus the instability of the financial system can easily spill over to the real economy. Minsky's main focus is on the discussion of instability. He sees himself as the successor to Keynes. However, he is reshaping his approach. He develops two central economic relationships for the real economy and devotes considerable attention to debt financing and the role of private banks.

He directs the IS relationship from the ISLM model, which emphasizes the correspondence between Investment I and Saving S in the goods market equilibrium, forward into the future with his profit–investment dynamics. With this reorientation, expectations about future economic events come into play, which are also essential for the so-called Keynes–Minsky momentum of instability. The second central relationship is its price mark-up hypothesis. With it, he departs from the traditional thesis that money supply M controls inflation. Furthermore, the Keynesian LM concept is not viable for him on the money market. According to Keynes, the money supply of the central bank M meets the money demand of private households L(Y,i), which depends on the income Y and the interest rate i. According to Minsky, money comes from the central bank, but private banks channel it into the economic cycle, making them key players in the economy. In their own interest, they do everything they can to promote debt financing, which increases risk and instability.

Private banks are yield-oriented and risk-conscious in their lending. Their objectives do not necessarily have to coincide with those of central banks. Cheap loans will only be passed on by private banks to companies and private households after careful yield and risk calculation.

Commercial banks as well as investment banks are usually absent from macroeconomic approaches, although their activity is increasingly shaping modern economic processes. Admati and Hellwig (2013) focus on banking activities and their impact on the economy. They attribute the instability emanating from banks to the insufficient equity base, in other words to the high level of debt financing, to the high leverage ratio. They argue for a significant increase in the equity ratio, which increases risk liability and thus leads to less risky decisions in their own interest. In their balance sheet considerations, they focus on stock figures such as assets and liabilities, whose values can change dramatically and rapidly during the economic process. The opportunities for high returns on equity in an upswing—"bright side of debt financing"—are abruptly transformed into risks in a downturn—"dark side of debt financing". This turnaround has already been dubbed "Minsky momentum". We speak of the Keynes–Minsky momentum because Keynes has already discussed the impulse for a change in economic assessment and the resulting decisions in detail in his central work "The General Theory". As far as *stock variables* such as assets and liabilities are concerned, they are symptomatic of a change in economic theory. They are becoming increasingly important. On the one hand, they reflect the growing debt financing with its instability of economic processes and, on the other hand, they are the source of rising inequality. Instability and inequality both threaten the acceptance of the capitalist market economy and make the public increasingly call for state intervention.

1.7 Traditional Economic Policy in the Crisis

1.7.1 Economic Policy in an Impasse

With his economic paradigm, Keynes gave the government options on how it could lead its national economy out of a recession for the benefit of the general interest. In doing so, he attributes the decisive impact to fiscal policy and a rather supportive role to monetary policy; we discuss the modes of action in detail in Chap. 3 "Keynes' and Minsky's macroeconomics". There we also explain that the fiscal policy applied over the years has become ineffective. Governments have permanently used debt-financed expenditure policy to achieve increased growth. The result has been less real growth and more debt. According to Minsky, this has made the economy more unstable, putting it in riskier waters. The risk was then revealed in the 2008 financial crisis. In Chap. 3 "Keynes' and Minsky's macroeconomics", we also discuss in detail the development of the economy after Minsky toward instability.

During the financial crisis, central banks, with their monetary policy, entered the stage of economic policy as key players. They endeavored to make the economy work at a considerable cost to the economy and society. They thought they could achieve this by buying up risky securities in enormous quantities and keeping their interest rates at historically low levels for a long time. In doing so, they were intervening massively in the market economy. They were suspending the price mechanism on the central financial market, they were taking on market risks—in a market economy this is typically part of entrepreneurial decisions—and thereby they wanted to prevent impending losses for companies.

Public authorities are getting more and more into debt and are pumping more and more money into the economic cycle. The central banks are buying enormous quantities of government bonds and increasingly financing government spending. This spending increases the money supply outside the banking sector, as the government pays for pay rises for its employees, pension increases or additional construction contracts, or even the purchase of additional shares of less profitable airlines. The money later flows to private banks, which will further increase the quantity of money, cf. the comments on credit money creation in Sect. 2.8 "Economic evolution through innovation and credit creation (Schumpeter)" and there especially Harari's comments on the creation of credit money. Private banks seek the most profitable investments worldwide. Much of the money from the eurozone can be channeled into the Singapore real estate market, for example. Some research shows *that large sums are invested in highly profitable but unproductive financial assets*. The growth effects of the newly created money will therefore be small locally. One indication of this is that countries in the eurozone have low growth despite high levels of debt. Moreover, to safeguard jobs, the state often supports unprofitable companies. *The "evergreening" is flourishing, i.e., unprofitable companies are kept alive artificially.* In crises, they are then threatened with insolvency. Instability increases.

The desired impact on growth is likely to be small. The increase in money supply has a strong impact on markets where stocks are traded. For example, on the rise in house prices. This inflation tends to benefit richer people, thereby increasing social inequality. Contrary to theoretical expectations, however, inflation in the circular flow economy will not occur, possibly only for the time being. If it did, the central bank would be in a dilemma, as explained in Sect. 4.11.3 "Profits and losses of central banks".

Central banks continue to promote instability by fostering the "evergreening" of the private banking system, leading to "moral hazard" and social inequality. They weaken citizens' initiative, self-reliance, and personal responsibility, which we discuss in detail in Chap. 4 "Outlook on the transformation of the market economy and its stabilization"; see also The Economist (2020a). There is a short definition of "moral hazard", and it also assesses its importance at the present time: "Moral hazard describes situations in which the costs of risky behavior are not entirely borne by those responsible for that behavior, so encouraging excessive risk-taking in the future" and further: "Rarely has the scope for moral hazard seemed as massive as now. To slow the spread of COVID-19, countries have shuttered much of their economics. And in order to prevent lost sales and jobs from translating into spikes in bankruptcies and poverty, governments have pumped huge amounts of aid to households and firms", The Economist (2020a).

"Moral hazard" favors people who can take risks, rich people. And so it promotes inequality.

The Economist magazine also points out that central banks run the risk of incurring losses and losing their independence through their enormous purchases of high-risk securities. In view of the increased risk of losses during the Corona pandemic, the British Treasury has already promised to support the Bank of England: "Britain's Treasury has already promised to compensate the Bank of England for losses that result from today's bond-buying" and further "Central banks face a dilemma: make policy independently and invite government interference, or preempt political meddling by minimizing losses", The Economist (2020c). Losses incurred by a central bank are dealt with in Sect. 4.11.3 "Profits and losses of central banks".

Now the corona pandemic has once again plunged the global economy into crisis. Countries will emerge from the crisis differently and this will have consequences for their prosperity, especially if international competition intensifies in the future. Countries that practice too much "evergreening" will fall behind. "Evergreening" consists of banks renouncing repayment of the capital they have lent out as long as the borrower pays interest. Minsky refers to "evergreening" as Ponzi finance, which makes the economy unstable, see Sect. 3.2.5 "Finance market: private banks, debt financing, and instability". *"Evergreening" keeps unprofitable firms alive and prevents them from disappearing in a process of creative destruction.* The evolutionary self-regulation process no longer works in the Schumpeter sense. It is weakened, to a considerable extent by central bank policy, and thus also the international competitiveness of the countries concerned. "Evergreening" leads to particularly endangered companies, to so-called "zombies". Zombie companies are companies that have been on the market for at least ten years and have not been able to cover their interest payments for three years. The share of zombie companies on the stock market is increasing noticeably. Almost every eighth listed company is a "zombie", see https://boerse-ard.de/aktien/hilfe-immer-mehr-zombie-firmen-an-der-boerse.

Meanwhile, the ECB is concerned about "evergreening", as it may burden the EU banking system and thus the entire EU economy. A "bad bank" is proposed to relieve the burden, see Enria (2020): "ECB: the EU needs a regional 'bad bank'" and also Sect. 4.11.3 "Profits and losses of central banks".

Share prices, which reflect the assessment of many market participants, indicate that the ICT revolution will accelerate. Prices worldwide fell by 15 to 25% in the first quarter of 2020. But not share prices of the technology companies Google, Apple, and Facebook. The Amazon price rose by as much as 25%. This development indicates that technological progress will continue to drive globalization. Globalization is becoming an international competitive struggle which, in turn, will accelerate innovation worldwide and make it even more important. Increasing worldwide competition will be the next economic challenge. Karl Marx has already pointed out the global competitive struggle and the Israeli–American economic historian Joel Mokyr has recently agreed with him. Section 2.14.2 "State, democracy, economy, society,and ecology" deals with this; see also the article in the newspaper Le monde, "Coronavirus: le monde d'après selon Wall Street", 2.05.2020. The Economist paints a similar picture in "The stock market rally. Uppers and downers", see The Economist (2020b).

1.7.2 Reorientation of Economic Policy in Democratically Constituted States

The failure of previous macroeconomic concepts for governmental economic management is becoming increasingly obvious. The lack of a supporting concept calls for a reorientation, for a novel solution, see The Economist (2020e): "Free money. Government can now spend as they please. That presents opportunities—and grave dangers", and also The Economist (2020f): "Starting over again. The pandemic has accelerated a rethink of macroeconomics. It is not clear where it will lead". *A new paradigm for democratic states is emerging: the close connection between state and economy—strengthened over the years by massive lobbying—must be loosened and the bond between state and society strengthened.* In this way, the state can contribute to a manifold society of citizens with their own initiative and self-responsibility, to a powerful civil society. The central bank has a key role to play in this reorientation, and approaches to this are outlined in Sect. 5.3 "Reorientation of government economic and social policy".

This is where democratic states can gain long-term advantages over autocratic states that want to keep control of their citizens in an ideologically oriented way—with all the means modern technology provides them. Means that even George Orwell did not suspect. According to Iversen and Soskice (2019), a knowledge-based society in cooperation with innovative companies contributes to the prosperity of a country. Innovation is an open process that can thrive in a free society. *The knowledge-based society with free initiative, together with innovative companies, not only contributes to the prosperity of a country, but also to its global competitiveness, which will be increasingly in demand in the future.*

For a knowledge-based society, the state is expanding its education system. Starting with day-care centers and schools, it ultimately supports universities. It is strengthening independent science centers to make them attractive to the world's best minds in a wide range of disciplines. More money must flow here, directly from the central bank. The direct flow of central bank money into social projects is part of the program that focuses the state more strongly on society.

The democratically constituted state gives society more scope for initiative and influence. *One guiding principle here is to strengthen the trust of and in the people.* This can begin at the local level in order to expand active participation in political life in the sense of a civil society and can be continued in Europe at the supranational level by giving the European Parliament increasing powers in central decision-making processes, for example in the election of the EU Commission President. Strengthening the local level increases cooperation and the quality of life at the local level and strengthening the supranational level increases identification with Europe.

European institutions have a central role to play in this reorientation, first and foremost the ECB but also the ESM. The ESM can be expanded so that it can become an essential cornerstone in a cooperative Europe, see Sect. 4.11.2 "Monetary and fiscal policy in the eurozone".

In its new role, the CB is moving away from the private banks and the economy toward society. The aim is to increase equal opportunities right from birth, to extend the protection of older citizens, and to cushion risks in crises in working life that are not the fault of the individual. *In this new role, the CB assumes less business, market, and credit risks from companies and more social risks from civil society.*

To improve equal opportunities, for example, the ECB can give each new born child in the eurozone countries a substantial starting balance in the cradle, which will later allow the child to finance its education in the first few years, irrespective of the parents' economic status. The protection of the elderly is about protecting them from the need in old age and enabling them to live in dignity. Support in crises is aimed not so much at securing jobs as at supporting the working population so that they can reorient themselves in a financially secure manner in times of upheaval—crises are also upheavals for working people. This orientation strengthens the confidence of the citizens and makes the unstable economy more robust. The mode of support can be organized in the form of built-in stability. Margarete MacMillan sums up the social significance of trust: "Without trust societies are vulnerable", The Economist (2020d).

A new orientation of a different kind can benefit science and the environment. Promoting science means furthering future prosperity and moving away from the fatal "evergreening" and generally away from harmful state intervention in the market economy. Continental Europe lacks a tradition in foundations as is known in the Anglo-Saxon world. This is where the ECB can step into help create a productive research landscape. Another fund can be dedicated by the ECB to the environment to improve the local quality of life. This supports an important pillar that is vital for a prosperous society, see also Rajan: "The third pillar. How markets and state leave the community behind" (2019). The reorientation may provide the ECB with a second pillar. It can also become a central bank for social and community projects. This addition can save it from a dead end into which its ambition to correct economic failures with insufficient means has let it slip. This is discussed in more detail in Chap. 4 "Outlook on the transformation of the market economy and its stabilization" and in Chap. 5 "Conclusion: changing economic policies".

1.8 Key Theses

Economic processes change over time and with them the theoretical concepts used to explain economic interactions. This is indicated by the differences in views on the recent economic crisis. Koo explains in his foreword: "The wide discrepancy in the views of purported experts suggests we are experiencing not only an economic crisis but also a crisis in economics", Koo (2015, p. XX). Piketty is specifically skeptical about marginal productivity, cf. Piketty (2013, pp. 52–524). We will discuss basic economic concepts and critically comment on their sustainability in Sect. 4.10 "Economic processes and their analysis".

We begin with a review of the history of the economy and its concepts, which provides a longer historical perspective. Then we come to the Keynes-inspired macroeconomic ISLM model. We introduce Minsky's novel pattern of thinking that replaces the common but outdated macroeconomic ISLM concept. We discuss in detail Minsky's discussion of stabilizing unstable economies and expand on Minsky's approach. Here, instability and inequality in the transformation of economic processes and their state stabilization come to the fore. In the case of state stabilization, it is generally apparent that its short-term successes are offset by serious consequential costs. In the long run, it increases instability and inequality and has a lasting negative impact on the functioning of the market economy. It leads to distorted markets and misallocations in the economy.

The ISLM model provides the formal framework for discussing Keynesian deficit policies to stabilize the economy. Under the conditions then prevailing, it shows that the market can fail and create a prolonged underemployment equilibrium with socially intolerable unemployment. *In the first thesis on state intervention, we can note: The market can fail and the government can fix it. It can correct the market failure in the goods and labor market, not so much through monetary policy as through fiscal policy. The state can manage national economies for common welfare, for public interest.*

Minsky is moving away from the ISLM model. In his new macroeconomic thinking pattern, he replaces the goods market equilibrium "Investment I = Saving S" with the investment–profit dynamic directed toward the future. Future profit expectations ultimately support today's investment decisions. With the profit orientation, the causal complex for investing changes. The profits Π result from the sales revenues minus the variable labor costs resulting from the demand for less qualified employees N. Thus, the profits Π also include the high fixed costs for highly qualified workers. Minsky's distinction between less and higher qualified workers is similar to Rajan's, pointing to educational inequality.

With the profits Π, Minsky not only draws attention to economic inequality. He is thus also moving away from the traditional monetary quantity-based approach to explaining inflation. According to Minsky, companies secure profits through a profit mark-up $m = \Pi/WN$ on the variable labor costs WN, and it is a major determinant of the price level P and thus of inflation as explained in Sect. 3.2.3 "The mark-up approach and price levels".

Minsky also moves away from the Keynesian equilibrium condition LM in the money market. This is because private banks channel the central bank money M into the economic cycle. They are central actors in Minsky's approach. They intervene in the economic process in a variety of ways, and in doing so they push forward the debt financing of the economy. According to Minsky, this causes instability in the financial system and, through its interdependence with the goods market, instability in the economy as a whole.

Less favorable than in the ISLM model is the conclusion on state intervention in a world that has now changed dramatically. *The less advantageous second thesis is that continued fiscal policy expands debt financing and thus promotes instability*: *It has lost much of its impact on the stabilization of the goods and labor markets through its permanent deficits. The public debt built up by the long succession of deficits restricts the ability of fiscal policy to act and makes it dependent on the central bank. The financial assets and interest income resulting from the debt increase economic inequality.*

The central bank remains the main player. Its attention is focused on the financial market and its stabilization. It considers the functioning of the financial market to be a "sine qua non" for the functioning of the economy as a whole. Central bank policy also increases inequality. Indeed, during the crisis, its actions are aimed at supporting assets at risk and strengthening the weakening flow of profits so that current investments can pay off in the future.

Like fiscal policy, central bank policy strengthens debt financing, which, according to Minsky, is the source of instability. Recent market interventions by the central bank overshadow traditional Keynesian market interventions. The central bank, with its massive buying-up programs and drastic interest rate cuts, is undermining the open market economy with free competition. It is the decisive determining factor in the financial market. It allows private banks to market the risk and it allows it to become a systemic risk, which ultimately must be borne by society. It structures future market expectations. Signals that usually come from the market are increasingly sent by the central bank. The central bank is also the determining factor for the development of values in the capital markets. It supports assets in crises. And by supporting securities prices, the central bank promotes economic inequality.

We can draw a third thesis: The free market economy shows obvious weaknesses. It can no longer function without state support. State intervention—above all, central bank policy—increases instability and inequality. They cause distorted markets with misallocations and deepen the interdependence between market and state.

The features of state directed economies are unmistakable. The state will continue to be called upon to intervene in a stabilizing way in economic affairs, in a dynamic and interdependent economic process in constant change. But where is the leverage to intervene in a targeted manner? It does not exist! The state would have to be able to assess the possible consequences of its interventions, for example on instability and inequality, if it does not want to be surprised by unintended effects. Quantitative, statistically sound estimates would be desirable. There is no basis for this. Keynes' fundamental objections to quantitative macroeconomic analysis, as he expressed in his article "Professor Tinbergen's Method" (Keynes 1939) against the econometric analysis of the Dutch Nobel laureate Jan Tinbergen, are still valid despite considerable progress in econometrics, as outlined in Sect. 4.10 "Economic processes and their analysis".

Despite the uncertainty as to how it will operate, the state's management of the economy is under pressure from the public expectation that the state can quickly take effective measures to stabilize the economic situation in the goods and labor market and to stabilize the unstable financial market. However, the desired successes do not have to come quickly. It is uncertain how the measures will work. And in the long run, it cannot be ruled out that they will further promote instability and inequality. State stabilization is a risk, and it is itself full of risks. And in the longer term, it will lead to greater interaction between business and government. Central banks are the main actors of government. They are increasingly taking on the private sector and fiscal risks, in particular the ECB. As they assume more risk, they socialize potential losses, see Sect. 4.11 "Stabilization policy in the post-Keynesian era".

The central bank, the main actor of state intervention, is now confronted with the instability of the financial market and, because of its close links with the real economy, with the instability of the economy as a whole. The central bank is taking several stabilization measures, the short-term success of which is not assured. The long-term costs are becoming apparent. The central bank is intervening so massively in the financial markets that it is effectively overriding the open market economy with free competition. By taking private sector and fiscal risks, the central bank restructures the market economy, making it the mainstay of the economy. The central bank is further increasing instability through debt financing. And by supporting asset holdings, it embellishes the solvency of private banks and increases economic inequality. Its measures alter the mechanisms of the market economy and, in the longer term, may jeopardize the social acceptance of the capitalist economy.

In the aftermath of the world economic crises at the beginning of the twentieth century, Keynes created, as we know, a new paradigm that has guided economic policy for many decades. The Keynesian narrative states that the market can fail in a short time and that failures can generate huge social damage but the government—first and foremost fiscal policy rather than monetary policy—can fix it and provide for the common welfare in national economies.

States are now massively using monetary policy for economic management. As expected after Keynes, it is not very effective. It can hardly contribute to public welfare. On the contrary, it increases instability, favors inequality, and significantly undermines the market mechanism and the price mechanism, with considerable misallocations. These are reflected in large profits, in an increase in moral hazard and "evergreening". It prevents a promising self-regulated evolution of national economies for the upcoming international competitive struggle. Traditional economic policy leads to a dead end.

Now we come to our fourth and last thesis: Economic policy is at a crossroads. It must reorient itself and be innovative. In a changing world it must find a new way. Major changes are emerging in international trade and in the imbalance between today's debt-financed expenditures and tomorrow's required revenues.

The change in international trade will be less about the comparative advantages of nations, as David Ricardo pointed out, and more about the lead in technological development. Karl Marx speaks of an emerging international competitive struggle in globalization. *The promising basis for this is innovative companies and a knowledge-based society.* By supporting both, the state becomes the supporter of international competitive struggle. In contrast to China, which relies on a wide-ranging state power center to generate innovation, democratically constituted industrial countries can increasingly promote the knowledge-based society and allow market forces to develop to the full with competition.

Another new path is opening for a democratically constituted state. *It consists in loosening its traditionally close ties with the economy and weaving the bond with society more closely. In this way, it will take on social risks rather than business, market, and credit risks.*

Central banks can support this reorientation by opening up to private economic entities, thereby strengthening the development of civil society. This can take the form of a state bank for social and civil projects. In this opening, there is a great opportunity for Europe in particular. Its rich diversity can develop more effectively if European states cooperate and face the challenge of international competitive struggle. The reorientation of government policy is discussed in more detail in Sect. 2.14 "Realignment of government economic and social policy" and in Chap. 5 "Conclusion: changing economic policies".

Globalization is currently the subject of criticism, and tendencies of national interests are increasingly coming to the fore. According to Rajan, further fault lines in the world economy will open up. Section 2.13.7 "Globalization and the international competitive struggle (Marx)", Sect. 2.13.8 "China on the path of globalization to become a world-leading economic power", and Sect. 4.9 "Globalization: good aspects and bad aspects" deal with the new development in world trade.

A reorientation is also necessary because the *intertemporal balance between today's credit-financed expenditure and tomorrow's returns is increasingly disturbed.* There is an imbalance between today's credit-financed expenditures and tomorrow's revenues needed to cover the credit costs for yesterday's expenditures. The state has played a major role in this development into imbalance. It favors the expansion of credit and supports artificially unprofitable firms before insolvency. This is the case, for example, of the so-called "evergreening firms", which are hardly profitable. The state is creating a dilemma with serious consequences for their national economies. On the one hand, it stimulates credit expansion—it expands current spending possibilities—and on the other hand, it supports unprofitable firms by "evergreening"—it shrinks tomorrow's revenues. The state is about to jeopardize the intertemporal balance between today's expenditure and tomorrow's earnings, and thus society's vital confidence in the future. We will discuss this in Sect. 4.12 "Consequences of economic change and state stabilization: instability and inequality, distorted markets, and intertemporal imbalance".

In view of the widening discrepancy between today's debt-financed expenditures and future income for this debt financing, some economists are calling for debt reduction. Debt relief can help in the short term, but it does not generally cure the problem of intertemporal imbalance. To do so, central banks would have to change their previous course in the long run. In their reorientation, they could support private economic subjects in the civil society with grants rather than with credit. In this way, they can ensure that a strong knowledge-based civil society can emerge, which can be a trump card in economic evolution in the long run. As I said, we will discuss this in more detail in Sect. 2.13 and Chap. 5.

One more word about the text. Newly included in the second edition is the second chapter "A review of the history of the economy and its concepts: change is a constant". In this English edition, Sects. 2.3 "Invisible hand, market, profit, division of labor, productivity, and international trade (Smith and Ricardo)" and Sect. 2.13 "Recent transformation in the global economy" as well as Sect. 2.14 "Realignment of government economic and social policy" have been added. The reading of this chapter provides the reader with a condensed insight into essential stages of economic history up to the current development in globalization. This will help the reader to better understand the explanations in the third chapter "Keynes' and Minsky's macroeconomics" and in the fourth chapter "Outlook on the transformation of the market economy and its stabilization".

The text in both Chaps. 3 and 4 is also accessible without the formal parts Sect. 3.1.2 "Commodity market and equilibrium curve IS in the ISLM model", Sect. 3.1.3 "Money market, equilibrium curve LM, and underemployment equilibrium in the ISLM model", Sect. 3.1.4 "Government intervention to stabilize the goods and labor market: fiscal and monetary policy" as well as Sect. 3.2.2 "Interdependence between profit and investment", Sect. 3.2.3 "The mark-up approach and price levels", and Sect. 4.1 "Interest rate effect on Minsky's profit–

investment dynamics, on inequality, and on monetary policy". These help to deal with the topic in depth. The reader can skip the formal parts for the time being and, if interested, deal with them later.

1.9 Summary

Economic processes change over time, and so do the theoretical concepts that explain them. According to Schumpeter, innovation is the decisive factor for change in economic processes. Innovations generate competitive advantages and growth in the international market. Innovations are not equally distributed among competing countries. Yet everyone wants to share in the growth. Politicians in many countries see the Keynesian deficit policy as a way of promoting growth in their country. Their permanently applied deficit policy causes the national debt to rise and increases debt financing. Minsky sees the now heavily debt-financed economy as the source of growing economic instability. Weakened fiscal policy must increasingly leave the field of stabilization to monetary policy. The central banks are taking measures to strengthen the flow of profits and support asset holdings. In doing so, they favor economic inequality. Their massive interventions in economic crises lead to distorted markets and an intertemporal imbalance with "High credits", "Sluggish growth", and "Low trust in the future". With the emerging international competitive struggle, the intertemporal imbalance is becoming more accentuated in countries with pronounced "evergreening". A re-alignment of state interventions is urgently needed.

References

Admati, A.A., Hellwig, M.: The Bankers' New Clothes, Princeton (2013)
Bundesverfassungsgericht: Urteil des Zweiten Senats vom 7. September 2011, 1–28
Bundesverfassungsgericht: Hauptsacheverfahren ESM/EZB: Urteilsverkündung sowie Vorlage an den Gerichtshof der Europäischen Union, 7. February 2014, 1–5
Enria, A.: ECB: The EU Needs a Regional 'Bad Bank'", Financial Times October 26 2020
Fisher, I.: The Debt-Deflation Theory of Great Depressions. Econometrica 1 (1933), 337–357
https://boerse.ard.de/aktien/hilfe-immer-mehr-zombie-firmen-an-der-boerse, 03.11.2019
Iversen, T. and Soskice, D.: Democracy and Prosperity. Reinventing Capitalism through a Turbulent Century, Princeton (2019)
Keynes, J.M.: The General Theory of Employment, Interest, and Money, New York (1936)
Keynes, J.M.: Professor Tinbergen's Method. The Economic Journal XLIX (1939), 558–568
Koo, R.C.: Escape from Balance Sheet Recession and the QE Trap, Singapore (2015)
Krugman, P.: End this Depression Now! New York (2012)
Minsky, H.P.: Stabilizing an Unstable Economy, Yale (1986)
Piketty, T.: Le capital au XXIe siècle, Paris (2013)
Rajan, R.G.: Fault Lines. How Hidden Fractures Still Threaten the World Economy, Princeton (2010)
Rajan, R.G.: The Third Pillar. How Markets and the State Leave the Community Behind, New York (2019)

Rodrik, D.: The Globalization Paradox, New York (2011)
The Economist: Default Options, June 25th 2011, 38
The Economist: Going up in the World. Special Report, November 24th 2012, 1–16
The Economist: The Origins of the Financial Crisis. Crash Course, September 7th 2013a, 56–57
The Economist: The Dangers of Debt. Lending Weight, September 14th 2013b, 66–67
The Economist: Monetary Policy after the Crash. Controlling Interest, September 21st 2013c, 62–63
The Economist: Stimulus v Austerity. Sovereign Doubts, September 28th 2013d, 68–69
The Economist: Making Banks Safe. Calling to Accounts, October 5th 2013e, 68–69
The Economist: Trading Places, April 5th 2014a, 28
The Economist: Three's a Crowd. The Instability that Stems from Trilemmas, July 5th 2014b, 63
The Economist: The Woes of the Average Joe, September 27th 2014c, 38–39
The Economist: The Budget. Deficit? What Deficit?, December 6th 2014d, 39–40
The Economist: Trading Peace for War. Sino-America Interdependence has been a Force for Geopolitical Stability, June 23rd 2018, 66
The Economist: Tough Love. How to Think About Moral Hazard during a Pandemic, April 25th 2020a, 65
The Economist: The Stock Market Rally. Uppers and Downers, May 9th 2020b, 57
The Economist: Unprofitable Arguments. Losses by Central Banks are nothing to Fear, May 9th 2020c, 61
The Economist: The Pandemic is a Turning Point in History, May 9th 2020d, 71
The Economist: Free money. Governments can now Spend as they Please. That Presents Opportunities – and Grave Dangers, July 25th 2020e, 7
The Economist: Starting over again. The Pandemic has accelerated a Rethink of Macroeconomics. It is not yet Clear where it will Lead, July 25th 2020f, 13–16
www.lemonde.fr/economie/article/2020/05/02/coronavirus-le-monde-d-apres-selon-wall-street

2 A Review of the History of the Economy and Its Concepts: Change Is a Constant

Abstract

This chapter gives a review of the economic history. Today, the ICT revolution unbundles national production processes and, with globalization, further drives economic change. Globalization has recently led to an international competitive struggle. A new perspective in their intervention policy is opening up for states. They can turn their attention more towards society: A strong knowledge-based society, together with innovative local companies, can bring new prosperity to the national economy from the bottom up.

2.1 The Agricultural Revolution

As mentioned in the transition from the Keynesian inspired ISLM model to Minsky's approach, the *time aspect in the economic process has changed*. In Minsky's approach with increased borrowing and indebtedness, expectations come into play and as a result, economic players *increasingly focus their actions on the future*. Nowadays, *confidence in the future is dwindling*. This is because the intertemporal balance between today's credit-financed expenditures and the revenues to be generated tomorrow in exchange for these expenditures is at risk. In the early days of human history, the past and its outcomes still largely determined ongoing economic activity.

If we look far back in history, we see large migrating families that are mainly self-sufficient. For their subsistence, they hunted game, caught fish, and collected wild plants. Not everything was intended for immediate consumption. Some of these could be stored, such as cereal grains. The grains that they did not eat they could pick and store. This gave them supplies for seasons when nature offered little to harvest. When it comes to the grains they collected, the large family decided how much they wanted to consume immediately and how much they wanted to store for

R. Pauly, *Economic Instability and Stabilization Policy*,
https://doi.org/10.1007/978-3-658-33626-4_2

tomorrow. This precaution gave them more security for the future. Figure 2.1 explains the decision-making situation behind provision.

According to Fig. 2.1, after current consumption C_h, a stock of S remains from the collected grain Q, which can be consumed later, $S = C_m$.

The families cooperate in collecting, hunting, and provisioning. Together they could hunt more game. The cooperation is beneficial. Families are largely self-sufficient; they offer only a small portion of the grain they collect to other families, primarily in exchange for other goods, such as grain for livestock.

In the agricultural revolution, gatherers and hunters became farmers and cattle breeders. The name revolution is misleading. The change is only gradual. It takes centuries and decades. Harari (2011, p. 94), puts it like this: "A band of *Homo sapiens* gathering mushrooms and nuts and hunting deer and rabbit did not all of a sudden settle in a permanent village, plowing fields, sowing wheat, and carrying water from the river. The change proceeded by stages, each of which involved just a small alteration in daily life".

Significant stages in the development of mankind are noted in Fig. 2.1 "Timeline: From fire to cuneiform" in Scott (2017, p. 4):

- 12,000 BCE Scattered evidence of sedentism
- 9,000 BCE Scattered evidence of domesticated plants and livestock
- 6,000 BCE Evidence of permanent towns
- 5,000 BCE Strong evidence of agrarian villages relying on planted crops and livestock
- 3,000 BCE Walled, territorial statelets (3,100) and proto-cuneiform for record keeping (3,200).

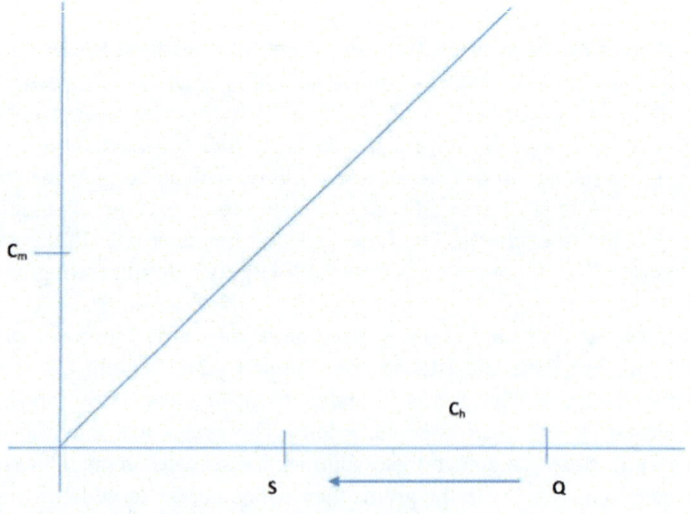

Fig. 2.1 Precautionary decision-making when collecting

The discovery of a fascinating building in Turkey, which researchers date back to around 12,000 BCE, is extraordinary. The site is a place of worship, built by gatherers and hunters who must have already settled in the area. Temporarily settled hunters and gatherers had already baked bread and brewed some kind of beer before growing grain. This is evidenced by a find of 14,000-year-old dough-pumps, see The Economist (2018c). The domestication of wild plants was gradually leading to agriculture. The transition to agriculture has taken place gradually over many centuries.

More and more people were settling down with agriculture and cattle breeding. They built huts, houses, and storerooms where they could store their crops more safely. They improved their tools to work the soil and thus increased the harvest yield. They grew wheat, millet, and rice and, in addition to cereals, they grew pulses such as lentils, beans, and peas. As they settled down, local communities based on the division of labor developed. Communities with markets and legal systems were emerging as were smaller urban settlements. In peasant civilization, people's economic living conditions changed fundamentally, albeit, as I said, very slowly.

The change is formally expressed in the yield function in Fig. 2.2. Of the quantity of grain Q harvested, the quantity S remains after consumption C_h for sowing. Compared to stockpiling, it produces an additional yield, $C_m > S$. Figure 2.2 indicates that, compared to the previous stockpiling, people can increase their yield for the coming period by sowing on well-treated soil. Sowing and tilling the soil increases the yield for the next period. The yield function is above the bisector. According to this, arable farming increases the yield compared to pure storage.

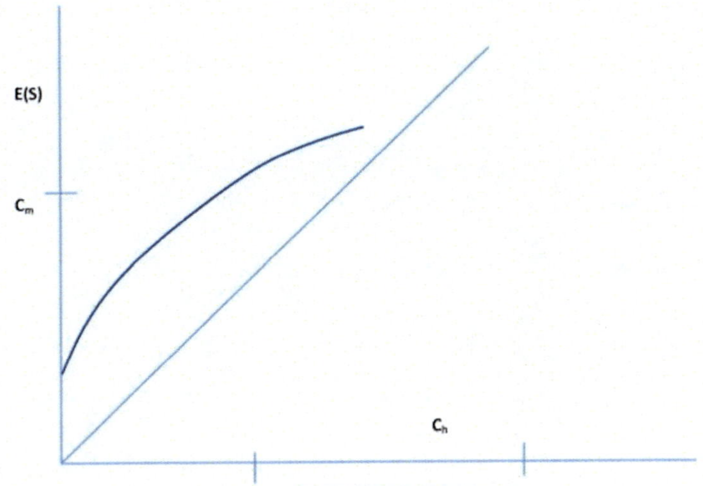

Fig. 2.2 Yield function E(S) in arable farming by sowing

With the building of houses and the production of tools, craftsmen's trades were emerging. And the craftsmen constantly refined their techniques, thereby continuously contributing to an increase in production output. Technological development took place from the cultivation of digging sticks to hoeing and plowing. This change goes hand in hand with progress in knowledge. Knowledge and its technological application are still the driving forces of economic progress today. Today, the process of change is accelerated. Information can be stored comprehensively, retrieved, and exchanged between interested parties. Today we can rather speak of a revolution, a permanent revolution. In large-format advertising, the car manufacturer Hyundai, for example, sums this up in big letters with "Change is an attitude". According to Karl Marx, technological change, innovation, is entering a decisive new phase with globalization, which is the subject of Sect. 2.13.7 "Globalization and the international competitive struggle (Marx)".

Formally, the change in economic conditions brought about by the ongoing agricultural revolution was reflected in an upward shift in the yield function, cf. Figure 2.3. According to this, progress further increases the additional yield in arable farming. As the arrow in Fig. 2.3 indicates, technical progress, innovation, pushes the yield function upwards. According to this, working the soil with better tools produces a further additional yield, which is above C_m.

The increased use of products that farmers bought from craftsmen sometimes made it necessary for them to finance their purchases with external funds. To finance these purchases, a family was often able to draw on its own financial reserves. However, these were usually not sufficient. If they lacked money, they could borrow it, for example from other, usually richer families who were increasingly specializing in financing—they acted as banks. The royal clan acted

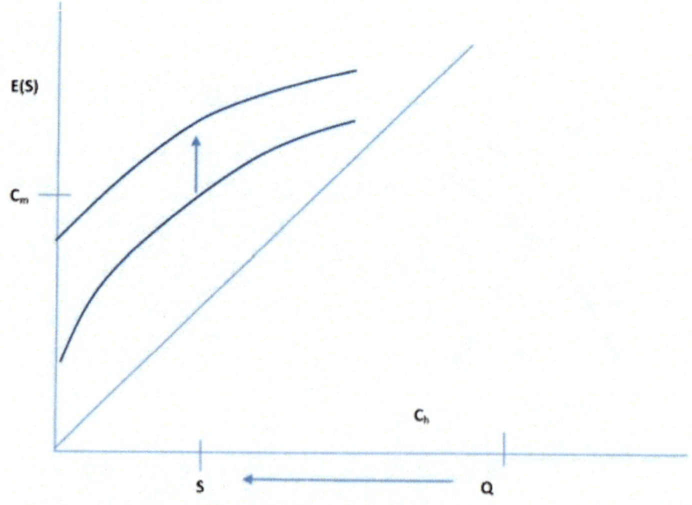

Fig. 2.3 Yield function E(S) in arable farming with technical progress

less as a financier. Rather, it regulated the interests of society. The royal clan exercised legal sovereignty and regulated the money business, the relationship between creditors and debtors.

The additional yield from more intensive farming was to increase the future decision-making scope for families. They could use it to consume more cereals tomorrow than before or to exchange more cereals for other goods. They could also sell the extra cereals on the market for money, for example silver or gold coins, and keep them for their future needs as a reserve and security, a function of money.

Bad weather could spoil some of the stock, and pests could also decimate the stockpile. Cereals were perishable despite well-protected storage. The situation was different for silver and gold. This non-perishable money fulfilled its function as a store of value better. Since it was accepted by all parties, it also had the function of a medium of exchange because it simplified the barter business. Furthermore, the value of goods could easily be expressed in units of silver and gold coins, which means it also functioned as a unit of account. Over time, the volume of market transactions with money increased. This is because money promoted exchangeability. It also strengthened cooperation since it also provided the basis for people to be able to work together effectively in trade and manufacturing, cf. Harari (2011, p. 207). According to Harari, money is based on the two universal principles of exchangeability and trust. He elaborates on this: "Money is based on two universal principles:

a. Universal convertibility, with money as an alchemist, you can turn land into loyalty, justice into health, and violence into knowledge.
b. Universal trust: with money as a go-between, any two people can cooperate on any project.

These principles have enabled millions of strangers to cooperate effectively in trade and industry". Then he points out that if everything is exchangeable, these advantages also have their downsides. We will come back to this in connection with Polanyi's market society in Sect. 2.5 "Market economy and market society (Polanyi)".

A transformation of the economy began to develop, with production gradually becoming more market-oriented and increasingly being sold for money. The economy gradually transformed as self-sufficiency declined in favor of market production. With the transformation, the economy became more specialized. *Self-sufficient people become consumers and producers.* Baldwin (2016) speaks here of the first "unbundling", see Sect. 2.13.1 "ICT revolution (Baldwin and Milanovic)". The division of labor in production was the key factor in increasing labor productivity. The use of machines drastically increased production and gradually led to a new type of economic process, the circular flow economy with the players, consumers, producers, and the state.

2.2 Capital Accumulation, Economic Growth, and Industrial Revolution (Smith)

According to Smith (1776, p. 109), "Book One, Of the causes of improvement in the productive power of labor, and of the order according to which its produce is naturally distributed among the different ranks of people, Chap. 1, Of the division of labor", it is the division of labor that significantly increases labor productivity. The increase in productivity was due to the fact that, with the specialization of the entrepreneurs, the latter made better use of the individual skills of the workers (specialization effect) and in doing so were able to coordinate work processes more and more effectively (networking of work processes, cooperation). Above all, however, entrepreneurs could increase production by using new machines (innovation) since in this way they could make the work process more effective. However, the increasingly finely tuned work processes were based on a pronounced willingness to cooperate on the part of all those involved in the company. According to Tomasello (2010), "Warum wir kooperieren", the willingness to cooperate is evident in people at a very early age. Whether it is inherited must nevertheless remain open. In any case, it is the basis for people to specialize more and more and still be able to cooperate fruitfully. The question arises, however, whether this willingness to cooperate is not increasingly strained by growing inequality, especially in terms of pay. With the industrial revolution, the use of machines in the production process has become increasingly widespread and has transformed people's working conditions.

Let us continue to follow Adam Smith. According to Book Two, "Of the Nature, the accumulation, and employment of stock, Chap. 3. Of the accumulation of capital, or of productive and unproductive labor", the increased use of machines and the accumulation of capital lead to an increase in productivity and thus economic growth. Although output is increasing as shown in Fig. 2.4 "Production function F (k) and growth", it is increasing with decreasing margins.

The macroeconomic production function F(K), as we will learn about in Sect. 4.8 "Capital, growth, and sluggish growth", depends, in addition to capital K, on labor input N and technical progress TF. For simplicity's sake, we do not account for the last two factors.

With the accumulation of capital, the economy is now increasingly oriented toward the future. Whether the accumulation to date is worthwhile will only become apparent in the coming periods. *The view into time is changing. In contrast to Figs.* 2.1, 2.2 and 2.3, *the arrow pointing to the right is now directed toward the future.*

The production function F(K) increases with increasing capital accumulation, F (K2) > F(K1). But as we can see from the growth in K1 and K2, marginal productivity decreases. The marginal return of capital decreases and so does the profit rate.

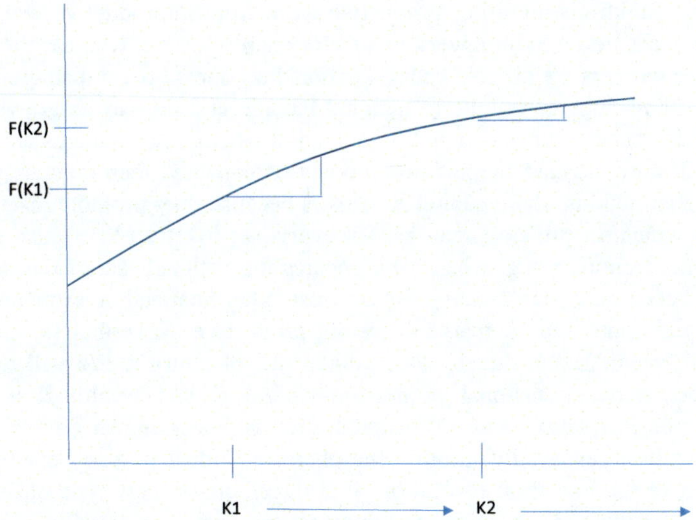

Fig. 2.4 Production function F(K) and growth

Schumpeter's approach with the innovative economy, where old is constantly being replaced by new, no longer has room for a stable production function. The new can also lead to substantial profits and increasing returns.

Before the accumulation of capital, according to Adam Smith, the products of labor basically belong to the worker. Afterward, he has to share them with the owner of the capital stock K, because the investment of capital has to be paid for. Thus, the income from the sale of goods is divided between the workers' wages and the profits of capital, which we will discuss in Sect. 4.2 "Inequality of income and wealth".

In practice, however, even before the accumulation of capital, the population engaged in agriculture and crafts does not receive the full value of goods as income. They pay levies to the big landowners from whom they have borrowed land and taxes to the royal clan which protects them. The clan wants to finance its army and lead a feudal life. So, it is not surprising that even before the accumulation of capital, inequality in income and wealth was already considerable, as pointed out by Scheidel (2017), "The Great Leveler. Violence and the History of Inequality from the Stone Age to the Twenty-First Century". We present more of his theses in Sect. 4.4 "Scheidel on inequality". J.S. Scott also points out right at the beginning of his book, in the words of Claude Lévi-Strauss, that exploitation began very early in human development with the hierarchical form of society, see Scott (2017), "Against the Grain". Rousseau (1754) already argues in a similar way, cf. Rousseau (1992, p. 232) and also The Economist (2018d, p. 55).

Adam Smith distinguishes productive work from unproductive work. Roughly speaking, according to him, work in a factory is productive, whereas the services of domestic workers are not. Nowadays, national accounts do not distinguish between the two; both jobs contribute to national income and thus to its growth. We will distinguish later in the accumulation of capital whether investments are productive or not. If they increase the national production capacity, then they are productive. And we are talking about capital K. This is because they promote macroeconomic growth which, in principle, can benefit everyone; Piketty (2013) also emphasizes this in his formula $r > g$, where he compares the national rate of return r with the national economic growth rate g. By contrast, other financial investments, primarily in the real estate and art markets, are not productive. Nevertheless, they increase national wealth Σ and thereby the national rate of return r. We will return to the difference between national production capital K and wealth Σ in Sects. 4.3 "Piketty on inequality" and 4.8 "Capital, growth, and sluggish growth".

Agriculture, especially through the chemical industry, also benefits from the progress of the industrial revolution. It is developing a new type of fertilizer, the artificial fertilizer. Its use further increases the crop yield; in Fig. 2.3, the yield function shifts further upwards. More and more farmers are using artificial fertilizers. Its purchase proves to be profitable. It is worth taking out loans and going into debt for it today, *as the future additional yield will be higher than the current costs.* This means that the future is increasingly being accounted for in today's calculations. The view is increasingly directed toward the future. Credits are becoming an essential part of the modern economy, compare Harari (2011), Sect. 16 "The capitalist creed", 341–373.

The focus on the future has paid off over hundreds of years. Confidence in the future has been built. It favors the raising of loans. In economic terms, the current expansion of loans is based on expected future growth. Harari (2011, p. 344) expresses this as follows: "Credit enables us to build the present at the expense of the future. It is founded on the assumption that our future resources are sure to be more abundant than our present ones. A host of new and wonderful opportunities open up if we can build things in the present using future income". According to Harari, our modern economy is based on three pillars: "High growth", "Much credit", and "Great trust in the future". This intertemporal balance is at risk today as explained in Sect. 4.12 "Consequences of economic change and state stabilization: instability and inequality, distorted markets, and intertemporal imbalance"

Progress is evident in many areas. It is revolutionizing textile production. The invention of the steam engine completely opens up new transport possibilities on land with the railway and drastically improves shipping. Urban centers are created, attracting more and more people, first with high-rise buildings and then with even higher skyscrapers. The earth is becoming connected. It is the first step into a new world of communication, which will be followed by many more to come. And the networking of the earth continues at a rapid pace to this day. Today, it is technology companies like Google and also state economies like China that are investing massively in international networks. Back then, it was a daring venture that Zweig (1964) described as one of mankind's great moments. With his story, he sets a monument to a courageous entrepreneur, namely C. W. Field. He also vividly illustrates the novelty of industrial progress in human development.

At the beginning of his narrative "The first word about the ocean", pp. 154 and 155, he writes the new rhythm that begins with the industrial revolution as follows: "During all the thousands and perhaps hundreds of thousands of years since the strange creature called man walked the earth, no other means of earthly locomotion had been used than the running of the horse, the rolling wheel, the rowing or sailing ship". "Only the nineteenth century fundamentally changed the measure and rhythm of earthly speed. In its first and second decades, peoples and countries moved closer together more quickly than in thousands of years before". Here he emphasizes the achievement of the railway and the steamship. They accelerate the movement on our planet. People can travel at unprecedented speeds and goods can be transported in large quantities faster and cheaper. According to Stefan Zweig, however, this enormous progress pales in comparison to the discovery of electricity. Its performance brings about something previously unimaginable. People can talk to each other across oceans in real time. Wiring makes it possible. And with further advances, cabling is often superfluous. Nevertheless, today enormous amounts of data are transported at an undreamt-of speed.

Stefan Zweig tells of the first laying of an underwater cable from America to England, of the daring enterprise of C. W. Field. Despite enormously adverse circumstances and against the advice of experts, he begins laying the cable in 1857 and ends it after setbacks in 1866. A new era of international communication began through him. Today it is based on an extensive network across the earth. Without it, modern life would be unthinkable, including major projects such as the networking of things, under the heading of Industry 4.0, as well as the 5G mobile phone standard, which is intended to further advance the networking of the world, keywords such as smart cities, networked automatic traffic, and intelligent energy management. C. W. Field can be imagined as the prototype of an entrepreneur whom Schumpeter later celebrates as a pioneer of economic evolution. Section 2.13 "Recent transformation in the global economy" presents the latest developments.

2.3 Invisible Hand, Market, Profit, Division of Labor, Productivity, and International Trade (Smith and Ricardo)

Narratives essentially shape our ideas, as can be read in Wikipedia. Narratives are meaningful stories that influence how we perceive our environment. Narratives are legends that provide orientation for people and enable people to live together in larger societies, according to Harari (2011). A narrative is the story of the "invisible hand"; here we can also speak of Smith's narrative.

The market, price formation, and competition together form the foundation of the capitalist market economy. It is open to innovation, and expected profits promote the division of labor and productivity. Profits are expectations that drive economic activities, which in turn increase the division of labor and the productivity of the economy, thus generating growth and prosperity. Competition ensures that profits are temporary and disappear again. This effect is at the core of Smith's narrative "invisible hand". The market mechanism is explained in more detail in Sect. 2.6.1 "Market equilibrium, price mechanism, competition, and profit".

As outlined in Sect. 2.2 "Capital accumulation, economic growth, and industrial revolution (Smith)" according to Smith (1776), the division of labor is central to the productive market economy. According to him, productivity leads to more growth and greater prosperity. Both are of general advantage, for the prosperity of a nation, for the nation's wealth. Markets promote the division of labor and markets open up opportunities for profits for producers who are innovative and competitive. Division of labor and specialization and innovation go together in the market economy. *With competition, the market ensures that profits, the drivers of productivity, disappear again. And prosperity remains. In this sense, the market enables the self-interest of companies striving for profit to create common welfare*. In this context, the market economy benefits from the willingness to cooperate that is inherent in human nature and that is manifested at an early age, see Tomasello (2010).

Let us take a look at the everyday life of an economy that is not yet highly developed, in which the handicraft determines the economic production conditions. It is not worthwhile for a tailor to make his own shoes, and vice versa for a shoemaker to make his own suit. It is always advantageous to buy the other person's product. The other one has specialized. With their special knowledge, they each have comparative advantages, so that they can sell their products at a profit. The market is the platform for their business and their successful initiatives. In the market, the shoemaker competes with others. And he can only make profits if he proves to be competitive. His goods must therefore attract the demanders, the consumers, in terms of quality and price.

The tailor and the shoemaker make great efforts to be able to produce their goods profitably. The same applies to other craftsmen such as butchers and bakers. The pursuit of self-interest drives them to risk initiatives for new things. The economic self-interest is focused on profit. The profit is the reward for their efforts. They claim it for themselves and want to secure it in the long term. Profit is the driving force for offering competitive goods on the market, which, as already mentioned, convince the demanders, the consumers, both in terms of quality and price. Craftsmen, traders, and entrepreneurs strive to secure profits in the long term. It is therefore the role of the state to keep the markets open, to ensure competition, and thus contribute to the common interest. In this sense, the state is a servant of the market and indirectly contributes to the common welfare.

Indirectly, the state also lays the foundations for the prosperity that the market economy creates by providing education, training, and research, thus forming a knowledge-based society. It also ensures social cohesion and cooperation through its various social policy activities, especially in the area of social security—unemployment, pension, health, and long-term care insurance. Cooperation is another side of specialization. It would be fruitless if it were not complemented by cooperation.

In a competitive market, the "invisible hand" transforms self-interest into the common welfare. Individual profits are the driving force for growing productivity, which benefits the general public in the form of a richer supply of goods. The market is also the place where talent and specialization can flourish and where exchange—money for goods—takes place, between people, between producers and consumers, an economic cooperation. In other words, where the plans of a multitude of suppliers and consumers are coordinated.

Bakers have bread and cakes and other sweets in their assortment and can specialize in baking cakes. Some of the bakers discover their talent for making chocolate products. With his fine chocolate products, a baker can then become a successful chocolatier. This development from baker to confectioner or chocolatier is easier to achieve in the city than in the village. The city with its large number of consumers and its high purchasing power favors specialization. And with more opportunities for specialization, talents of different kinds can develop more easily. This makes the city more attractive, a trend that continues to this day and can now be observed worldwide. The city enables people not only to pursue their own interests, but also to pursue their social interests in a variety of social exchanges and thus benefit from their local quality of life.

The metropolitan areas are currently threatened by the environmental pollution caused by unbridled industrialization. The ecological and social basis of the market economy is under threat. Recently, economic inequality and instability have been growing, placing a burden on the traditional economy, which according to Smith is based on the division of labor, the expansion of markets, and increased productivity and national wealth, ultimately for the benefit of the general public. In fact, in the past, Smith's "invisible hand of the market" has over a long period of time transformed self-interest into the common welfare. But the question arises whether this story will persist.

International trade carries on the division of labor. The advantages of the division of labor for the productivity and prosperity of a nation were described in detail by the Scottish economist Adam Smith (1723–1790). Another British economist David Ricardo (1723–1823) developed this idea further. He shows that international trade increases the prosperity of trading nations. Trade leads to specialization in production and thus to higher production. This international division of labor increases the prosperity of trading nations. This positive effect occurs even if one country can only produce goods with lower labor productivity, with more effort than the other. This country also contributes to the increased total production of both countries. In the words of the 2019 Nobel Prize winners Banerjee and Duflo, Ricardo's argumentation reads as follows: "Based on this argument, Ricardo concluded that even if Portugal was more productive than England at producing *both wine and cloth*, once trade between them opened up, they would nonetheless end up specializing in the product for which they had a *comparative advantage* (meaning where their productivity was high *relative to their productivity in the other sector*: wine for Portugal, cloth for England). And the fact that both countries make the goods they are relatively good at making and buy the rest (instead of wasting resources producing a product ineptly) must add to the Gross National Product

(GNP), the total value of goods people in each country can consume", see Banerjee and Duflo (2019, p. 53). *Thanks to Ricardo, we can state that the invisible hand of the market is global.* The magazine The Economist concisely expresses Ricardo's idea as follows: "David Ricardo showed in 1817 that a country could benefit from trade even if it did everything better than its neighbors". The Economist: "An inconvenient iota of truth", August 6th 2016d.

2.4 Globalization Versus National Mercantilism

The industrial revolution is spreading worldwide, and international trade is leading to an international division of labor, roughly speaking to industrialized countries with high development potential and to countries that mainly supply raw materials for local production. The road to globalization is paved, albeit from different regional perspectives; see Rodrik (2011), "The Globalization Paradox". Globalization leads not only to a regionally different development, but also to differences in social development in the industrialized countries.

According to Smith (1723–1790), the *size of the market* favors the division of labor and thus the productivity and growth of an economy. The larger the market, the greater the division of labor, the greater the chances of growth in an economy. Rodrik (2011) praises multilateral agreements that replace national mercantilism, which in imperialism showed the naked power politics of industrial nation states.

According to Milanovic (2016), globalization has produced many winners in developing countries. The middle classes in China and South-East Asia have benefited from international trade. They no longer need development aid. In global terms, economic inequality has been reduced.

The downside is that low-skilled workers in industrialized countries lose touch with the prosperity in their country and see themselves as losers of globalization. More than 50 years ago, the Stolper–Samuelson theorem already pointed out that the win-win situation in international trade, as outlined by Ricardo (1772–1823), does not necessarily apply to everyone in global trade. There are losers, and if they are numerous, tensions can arise in the dichotomy between politics and the market described by Polanyi (1886–1964). In the political sphere, ideas of national mercantilism may regain ground in those who are critical of and wish to restrict the exchange of goods in open markets. This dark side of globalization is currently under criticism, and tendencies to emphasize national interests are increasingly coming to the fore worldwide.

Markets cannot function without mutual trust between market participants. *Trust and cooperation are the foundations of economic activity*. Cooperation is the basis for the division of labor and thus ultimately for economic prosperity. With open markets, cooperation can develop worldwide and continue to contribute to the well-being of all people. The question arises as to how this development can be further secured despite current resistance. An international compensation fund could help here by estimating the losses of certain population groups in the form of a cost–benefit analysis and by providing financial support for the disadvantaged. We discuss globalization in detail in Sects. 2.13 "Recent transformation in the global economy" and 4.9 "Globalization: good aspects and bad aspects".

2.5 Market Economy and Market Society (Polanyi)

In an economy based on the division of labor, innovation, capital input and money are becoming increasingly important. And another transformation is emerging: the transformation of time. For gatherers and hunters and, in the first phase, for farmers and cattle breeders, the past determines to a great extent their current economic activities. Yesterday's stocks of grain are the basis for today's consumption. Accordingly, in the case of arable farming, the grain saved and sown in the past is the basis for economic activity in the next period. With innovation and future additional yield as well as with credit financing, the economic process over time is increasingly oriented toward future expectations. In addition, the time span for economic decisions is shortening and the economic circumstances are changing more and more. These transformations are changing people's living conditions to a great extent, and with them their social lives.

Polanyi (1944) traces the transformation of economic–social systems in a long historical analysis. According to this, after centuries of history, the transformation of economic systems with the Industrial Revolution leads to a market economy that shapes social life; cf. Polanyi (1944), "The Great Transformation, Part Two, Rise and Fall of the Market Economy, 6. The Self-Regulating Market and Fictitious Goods: Labor, land, and money". In the self-regulating market economy, goods are now produced primarily for the market, and the prices that can be obtained there give rise to the expectation of profits, to which the production of goods is ultimately geared. The concept of the self-regulating market is central for microeconomics, perhaps the basis of microeconomics. It is associated with the economists L. Walras and G. Debreu, who received the Nobel Prize in Economics in 1983 for his elegant mathematical foundation. The constitutive elements of microeconomics are discussed below.

Not only goods are subject to the price mechanism of the self-regulating market, but also the labor needed in production. The market thus turns labor into a commodity, as well as land and money—goods that are inauthentic according to Polanyi. Goods are used and ultimately consumed, and as long as their production promises profits, they can be multiplied. The price of labor, the wage, is for the worker the basis for his existence and his family. His wage must be sufficient to feed himself and his family, to cover his housing costs, and to finance his provision for health and pensions. However, in a market economy, his life and that of his family become increasingly dependent on the market. And here, unemployment threatens those with few qualifications in a recession. Soil, and more generally nature, is a limited resource. Its exploitation threatens people through the environmental crises that are becoming increasingly evident. The private banks multiply money by creating credit and loans and creating markets for it, where they make loans and thus risks tradable. Nowadays, the market for land and money has developed into a weighty real estate and financial market, which has now triggered numerous economic crises. The risks there make the entire economy unstable. We will discuss this in detail in connection with Minsky's remarks on instability.

The market creates a market society. Polanyi sees in this and not in the industrial society a weakness for society, see Polanyi (1944, p. 331). The self-regulating market represents a weighty autonomous unit in society. Compared with the political sphere, it forms an independent economic sphere, cf. Polanyi (1944, p. 106). This results in a social dichotomy. On the one hand, there is the market and market power, money and wealth, and on the other hand, there is political power, in democracy legitimized by elections, the will of the people. Tensions between the two sides continue and are currently reflected in the euro crisis and in other fields such as ecology.

Below we compile the constitutive elements of a self-regulating economy.

2.6 Basic Elements of Microeconomics (Walras and Debreu)

2.6.1 Market Equilibrium, Price Mechanism, Competition, and Profit

Microeconomics is one of two pillars of the market economy theory that students of economics learn worldwide. It involves two main actors, namely households and firms. There are many of these in each case. Each of them draws up their economic plans independently of the other according to their own interests. Demand for goods and services results from maximizing the individual utility of households and supply from maximizing the profits of firms, which involves minimizing the costs of producing goods. In this context, variable costs in the form of marginal costs determine supply in relation to the price of goods and are central to the price mechanism. Microeconomics deals with the optimal use of scarce resources from the perspective of individual households and firms.

The general costs, the fixed costs, only play a minor role in the theory. They only determine the actual beginning of the supply curve via the average costs, namely in Fig. 2.5 the beginning of the supply curve at point (p_0, q_0). The supply curve results from the marginal costs. This curve shows in a bold line schematically the quantity q offered as a function of the price p. The quantity q equals zero up to the price p_0 and jumps to the quantity q_0 at the price p_0, and then rises steadily with p.

In Fig. 2.6, the increasing branch of the supply function is taken from Fig. 2.5, and the demand function resulting from the utility calculation is added. The point of intersection of both functions results in the equilibrium price p_a with the equilibrium quantity q_a. If the supply curve shifts to the right, as shown in Fig. 2.6, then the old price p_a causes excess supply, which causes the price to fall, so that after an

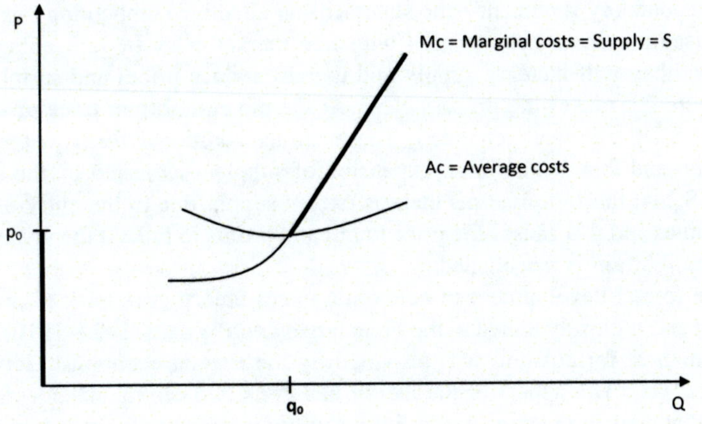

Fig. 2.5 Average costs and marginal costs = supply

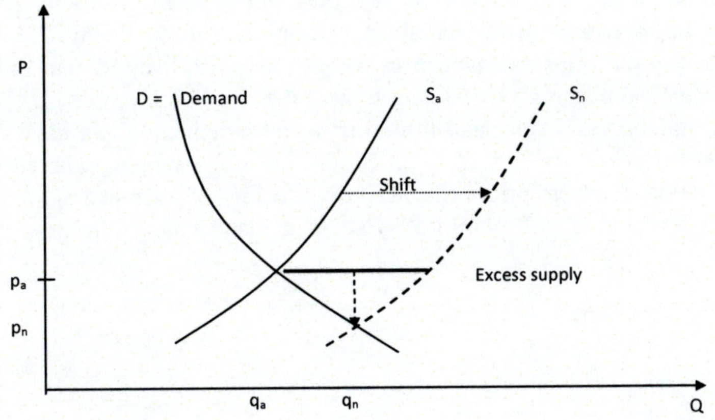

Fig. 2.6 Supply and demand with equilibrium price p_a and shift in the supply function with new equilibrium price p_n

adjustment process, a new equilibrium price p_n with a new equilibrium quantity q_n results.

Figure 2.6 illustrates one of the main statements of microeconomics for the market economy: the equilibrium statement. This states that there is a price constellation in the markets where the independently generated demand and supply plans correspond to each other. So, there is an equilibrium on the commodity market, and in that balance, none of the players has any interest in changing their plans. In equilibrium, everyone is satisfied with the result, there is therefore a balance of interests.

A second key statement—the statement on effective competition—is that profits will disappear in an open market with free market entry by new entrants. This is because they will increase supply and thereby reduce prices and shrink profits.

Figure 2.6 makes the process clear. At the old equilibrium price p_a with the old supply S_a, profits are generated. These attract additional firms to the market in question and this results in an expansion of supply—indicated by the new supply curve S_n. At the old price p_a, there is excess supply due to the entry of additional companies and this causes the price to fall and profits to fall. At the lower price p_n, a new equilibrium is established.

The formal development of economic micro-theory goes back to the Lausanne School and is closely linked to the Frenchman Léon Walras (1834–1910). Its general mathematical formulation was provided by the French economist Gérard Debreu (1921–2004). The appeal of the theory lies in its two central statements. Firstly, it states that there is a market equilibrium: a price system coordinates a large number of demand and supply plans that are drawn up separately. There is therefore no need for a central coordinator to collect information on plans from a wide range of economic entities in order to bring them into line in any way. Secondly, as Fig. 2.6 shows, free competition leads to an expansion of supply in the event of profits. The resulting excess supply causes prices to fall and profits to shrink. In Fig. 2.7, the arrows indicate that the price mechanism in the case of excess supply and in the case of excess demand ensures a movement toward the equilibrium price p_g.

With the excess supply and the resulting price reduction, we have addressed a process that can, in turn, lead to an equilibrium. The same applies in the case of excess demand, where prices rise according to Fig. 2.7. An example of this is the wine "Chateau Lafite Rothschild". Excess demand causes the price to increase

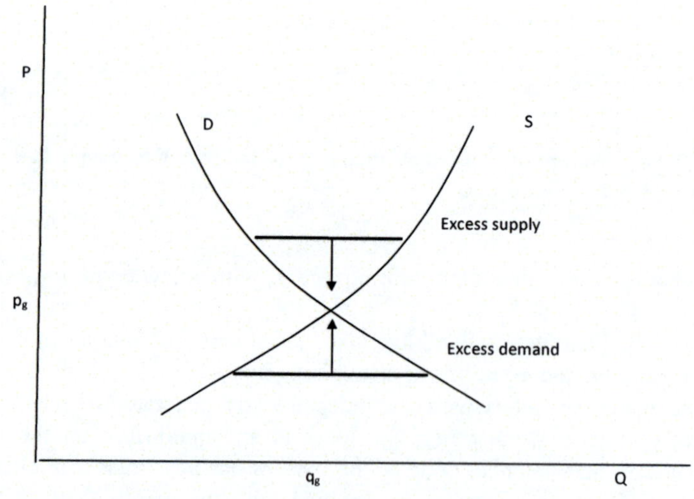

Fig. 2.7 Excess supply and excess demand with equilibrium price p_g

several times over within ten years from 2000 to 2009. The reason for this lies in particular in the increased demand from China. It pushes the demand function strongly upwards. The winery still wants to offer its wine in the highest quality and does not increase production, so the supply remains constant. The old equilibrium price creates considerable excess demand. Wine becomes scarce and the shortage causes the price to skyrocket. Among the wines, the wine "Chateau Lafite Rothschild" is a product with special characteristics. They give the product an additional attractiveness. The special image turns the product into a brand, protects it from the competition, and ensures the winery's profits. The brand image generates the profits.

The price mechanism is a central element of a market economy. Open markets with free market access and a functioning price mechanism are the mainstay of a market economy. However, the price mechanism does not have to produce equilibrium in reality.

In a situation of longer-lasting serious imbalance, it will be impossible to avoid talking about market failure and discussing external state intervention in the market economy process which seems appropriate to stabilize it. Historically, the name of the British economist John Maynard Keynes (1883–1946) is associated with market failures. In an underemployment equilibrium, as it became apparent at the beginning of the twentieth century, Keynes proposed a so-called "deficit spending policy" to stabilize the market economy, i.e., to prevent underemployment in the labor market and to stimulate growth by stabilizing the economy. As a result of a permanent deficit spending policy, politicians pile up government debt, the financing of which, however, jeopardizes financial market stability in the long term and also promotes income inequality. We will come back to this issue later, as it reveals a serious asymmetry in time: The initial stabilization of the commodity and labor market is followed with a long delay by financial market instability and growing economic inequality.

The increased intervention of the central bank in the market has recently increasingly disturbed the central price mechanism in the market economy, as the third thesis in Sect. 1.8 "Key theses" explains. This is a high price for traditional economic stabilization.

2.6.2 Constitutive Elements of Microeconomics and Their Critical Evaluation

Before the transition to macroeconomics—the second pillar of market economy theory—we take a critical look at constitutive elements of micro-theory. The goods on the markets are well known for their characteristics, and competition works there. Innovations, the engine of dynamism in modern economic activity, are not accounted for. Companies do not develop new goods with previously unknown properties that change household demand. Free market access is guaranteed. Companies do not have a law department here which watches over their patent rights and, if necessary, defends their market position, nor do they have a marketing department that stylizes a product into a brand in order to protect it from the competition. Moreover, innovations do not replace established production processes, they do not change the cost structure and thus the range of products on offer. Ongoing innovation does not allow a company to stay one step ahead of the competition. The state plays only a subordinate role; it provides the economic framework and does not intervene in the economic process, in the market.

Microeconomics is, as can be seen from the graphical analysis, a comparative-static theory. It isolates the price mechanism. Time does not play a significant role. Within a fixed framework of supply and demand, we imagine a price movement toward equilibrium. Although time passes, it has no influence on the economic decisions of households and firms. These are fixed in the demand and supply functions, and both remain unchanged. In the constant supply and demand patterns, the price mechanism works as shown in Fig. 2.7. No single household or firm has the power to influence the market in its favor.

The fixed pattern changes with continuous innovation. New products change the utility calculation and thus the demand structure, new production processes change the cost structure and thus the supply structure. This raises serious doubts as to whether the market mechanism that adjusts from excess supply or excess demand to equilibrium price works in a dynamic economy.

The economic dynamics are based on innovations. Innovation means change, it holds opportunities and risks at the same time and generates profits and losses. The Austrian economist Joseph Schumpeter (1883–1950) placed innovative processes at the center of economic analysis. In a process of creative destruction, innovations cause the old to be replaced by the new and thus drive economic evolution, economic dynamism, whether goods with new characteristics are offered or obsolete production processes replaced by more efficient ones or logistics ensures an international division of labor and networking in production.

Schumpeter explains the economic evolution by the fact that the new takes the place of the old. This has direct consequences for the concept of the supply function in microeconomics. He argues: "What should be said is that the old total or marginal cost curve is destroyed and a new one put in its place each time there is an innovation", see Schumpeter (1939, p. 89).

Profits do not have to shrink despite free market access if innovative companies with novel goods are constantly one step ahead of the competition and if marketing experts manage to stylize goods into brands and thus seal them off from the competition.

The impact of innovation on future profits, the driving force behind investment in new goods and production techniques, is uncertain. Faced with this uncertainty, entrepreneurs have no choice but to base their decisions on expectations and be prepared for changes that may render their current calculations obsolete by future cost and revenue streams. As a result, every business decision involves risk and must be constantly adapted to new circumstances. Keynes (1936) and Minsky (1986) argue similarly. We will come back to this later in Sect. 3.1.8 "Keynes–Minsky momentum".

The American economist Hyman Minsky (1919–1994) moves away from the price mechanism that is central to the market economy theory. Less marginal cost than average cost is more important. In his dynamic approach, Minsky emphasizes the profit–investment relationship. It is ultimately the core of the capitalist market economy. Investment drives its dynamism, and companies do it in an uncertain environment in order to make profits in the future. And in Minsky's profit–investment dynamics, it is not so much the variable production costs that play a central role in the economic process as the general costs, such as the costs of the development, IT, logistics, advertising, and law departments and, one can add, above all the costs of managing a company. The Economist takes a similar view: "Most jobs will not be on the factory floor but in the offices nearby, which will be full of designers, engineers, IT specialists, logistics experts, marketing staff, and other professionals", cf. The Economist 2012, p. 13. Thus, general costs are becoming increasingly important compared to variable costs. According to Minsky, entrepreneurs set the price by adding a profit mark-up to variable labor costs. The price mark-up secures profits for the entrepreneurs, which they can hope for by offering new products. According to Minsky, these profits are ultimately the decisive motive for investment. And investment and profits are the foundation of capitalist economic evolution. Later more on the profit–investment interdependence and the price mark-up hypothesis, which explains inflation differently from traditional money supply approaches.

If we summarize the essential elements that theoretically ensure the optimal functioning of markets with decentralized decision-makers, we can highlight:

- Complete information for market participants about the goods traded on the markets
- Competition that controls the supply of goods and makes profits disappear as new firms enter the market
- A tendency toward equilibrium when markets become unbalanced.

If Keynes still relied fundamentally on market forces toward equilibrium, Schumpeter questions them in his economic evolution process with innovations; so does Minsky, who emphasizes the economic instability caused by the rampant debt financing of business banks. After the financial crisis at the beginning of this century, the central banks dominate the financial markets and override market forces there. We present the basic ideas of Keynes and Minsky in Sects. 3.1 "Main principles of Keynesian macroeconomics" and 3.2 "Main features of Minsky's macroeconomics" and discuss current central bank policy in Sect. 4.11 "Stabilization policy in the post-Keynesian era".

Schumpeter highlights the profits as a result of the innovation process and points out that innovators will do everything possible to maintain the profit streams in the long term. According to him, companies use a variety of means such as product differentiation and advertising and do not shy away from aggressive actions against competitors themselves. Schumpeter (1939, pp. 98–99) comments on this: "… the struggle to conserve the stream of profits itself. Secrecy regarding processes, patents, judicious differentiation of products, advertising, and the like, occasionally also aggression directed against actual and would-be competitors, are instances of a familiar strategy …"

Milton Friedman even propagates that the achievement of profits is a social responsibility of companies, cf. Friedman (1970). And recent developments show that companies are making profits that were unimaginable for a long time. Peter Thiel, the co-founder of PayPal, is credited with saying that competition is for losers, cf. The Economist (2016e, p. 5). We will discuss profits in more detail in Sects. 2.13.3 "Inequality, blitzscaling, and monopoly formation" and 4.9 "Globalization: good aspects and bad aspects", where we will also show their impact on inequality.

Akerlof (1970) questions that market participants are equally well informed about the quality of goods; see also The Economist (2016b). He illustrates the asymmetric information among suppliers and consumers by means of a fictitious market for used cars. A used car can be of good or bad quality. The seller knows the true condition, but the buyers do not. They distrust the price signal of the seller who offers cars in good condition more expensively than in bad condition. They do not buy the more expensive cars, and the seller remains stuck with them. Here the seller has disadvantages. Usually, it is the other way round. This is ensured by experts such as product designers and marketing specialists. In recent times, many financial products have been offered whose quality is not easy to understand for consumers, even for specialists in rating agencies. Below we will address the growing importance of experts at several points in the modern economic process.

The asymmetric information ensures that prices do not reflect marginal costs. Asymmetric information thus argues against a general equilibrium generated by full competition.

With the major economic crises at the beginning of the twentieth century, doubts about the effectiveness of the price mechanism in the self-regulating market are becoming increasingly common. A crisis calls for state intervention. Keynes (1936) lays the theoretical foundation for this. According to his concept, *it is not so much prices as flows*, such as household consumption and investment by entrepreneurs that play an important role.

2.7 Economic Crisis and Macroeconomic Stabilization by the Government (Keynes)

In economic crises, the economy is out of equilibrium. The price mechanism and thus the self-regulation of the market economy fail. The economic cycle falters. The demand for goods falls below the potentially achievable level in the economy. Entrepreneurs demand less labor than is offered. This under-demand can persist and over a longer period of time, workers do not find work and become unemployed. Unemployment becomes an individual and social problem.

This is where Keynes comes into play. He trusts market forces that still have a natural tendency to equilibrium. However, their movement toward it can take a long time—too long since the unemployment that goes with it is unacceptable. That is why the state should intervene in the economic cycle and ensure full employment. In the crisis, the state should expand its government demand in the short term, thereby compensating for and stimulating the under-demand in the private sector. Keynes assumes, as I said, that the economy is stable and only disturbed in the short term. Once the disruption is removed, the state can stop its intervention. The state should come to the rescue here for a short time and then leave further development to market forces.

In his novel concept, Keynes skillfully isolates the important economic areas necessary for his analysis and introduces *flows as the central economic variable*. For example, he disregards the accumulation of capital and the production function, which are important factors for economic growth. He instead focuses on the short-term economic situation. We will go into more detail about the isolating approach in the methodological part of Sect. 4.10 "Economic processes and their analysis".

His circular flow model looks at the economy at the macroeconomic level and deals with the equilibrium on the commodity and money market, a partial stationary equilibrium without a labor market and without a financial market. The key players are households and entrepreneurs. They are each grouped into a sector and act as both demanders and suppliers in its overall approach. The total supply of goods by enterprises is matched by the total demand by households for consumer goods and the total demand by enterprises for capital goods. The value of the goods produced by entrepreneurs is equivalent to the income of households. Their disposable income determines consumer demand. Goods not consumed are equal to savings. In the circular flow model, the revenues that are not used for consumption, i.e., the savings, flow to companies to finance their investments. Companies' investment decisions depend on the market interest rate. The amount of savings and the investment are determined simultaneously on the goods and money markets. In equilibrium, the savings are equal to the investment. The equilibrium income/production and the equilibrium interest rate balance household savings and business investment. The equilibrium interest rate is obtained on the money market, where the supply of money from the central bank meets the demand for money from households. Figure 2.8 "Circular flow scheme" explains the circular flow model.

So far, so good. Partially everything is fine. But not everywhere, and not on the labor market. There is an imbalance. That is where unemployment occurs, an individual and social evil that also threatens the social acceptance of the market economy. This evil must be eliminated in any case and, as I said, the state should intervene to do this.

What causes unemployment? As explained, there can be a partial equilibrium in the goods and money markets and an imbalance in the labor market. The supply of goods is below the level of the economy that could potentially be achieved if all

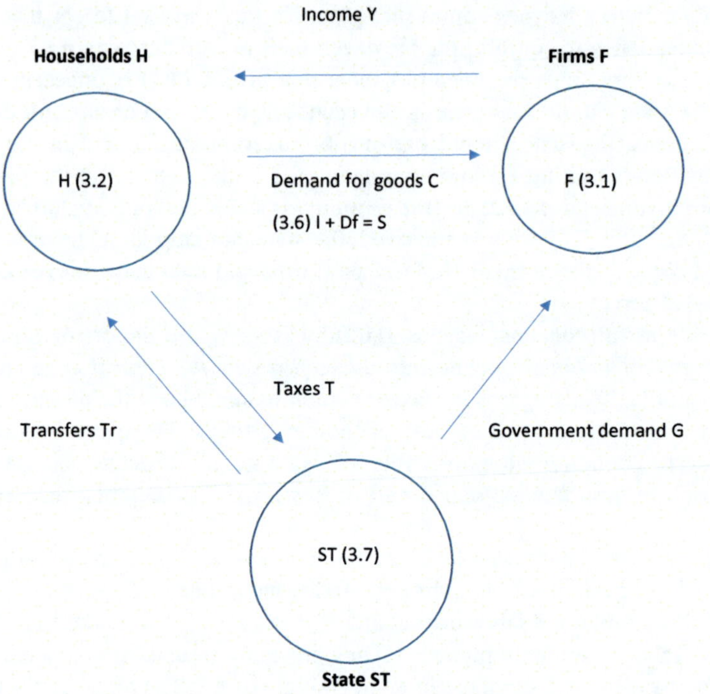

Fig. 2.8 Circular flow scheme for the goods market in equilibrium

labor were to be used in the production process. But this is not the case, resulting in involuntary unemployment. Entrepreneurs would be willing to demand more labor if the wage rate fell. But it is not flexible. The price mechanism is not fully operational. Keywords such as "sticky wages" and "rigid wages" stand for this.

The numbering refers to the formulae in Sect. 3.1 "Main principles of Keynesian macroeconomics". The direction of the arrow indicates the direction of money flow.

Budget equations for firms F, households H, and state St:

$$\mathrm{Y} = \mathrm{C} + \mathrm{G} + \mathrm{I}, \text{ national production } \mathrm{Y} = \text{ consumption } \mathrm{C} + \text{ government expenditure } \mathrm{G} + \text{ investment } \mathrm{I} \tag{3.1}$$

$$\mathrm{Yv} = \mathrm{Y} + \mathrm{Tr} - \mathrm{T}, \text{ disposable income } \mathrm{Yv} = \text{ income } \mathrm{Y} + \text{ transfers } \mathrm{Tr} - \text{ taxes } \mathrm{T} \tag{3.2}$$

$$\mathrm{Df} = \mathrm{G} + \mathrm{Tr} - \mathrm{T}, \text{ government deficit } \mathrm{Df} = \text{ government expenditure } \mathrm{G} + \text{ transfers } \mathrm{Tr} - \text{ taxes } \mathrm{T} \tag{3.7}$$

Partial equilibrium on the goods market:

$$\begin{aligned} \mathrm{I} + \mathrm{Df} &= \mathrm{S}, \text{ investment I} + \text{government deficit Df} \\ &= \text{savings S} \end{aligned} \tag{3.6}$$

Keynesian state intervention: With debt-financed additional state deficits Df, government consumption G and thus total national demand/production Y in (3.1) increase. In order to be able to meet the increased overall demand, entrepreneurs ask for more employees, which reduces the unemployment rate. The stabilization target has thus been reached.

As we know from Polanyi's explanations, work is not a good in itself. Its price determines the income and thus the livelihood of many people. And they will fight to ensure that the wage does not fall below a critical threshold that threatens their livelihood. The frictions between the market and politics become obvious.

According to Eq. (3.6), in the circular flow model, business investments I are financed from current household savings S that come from income Y. Companies therefore do not finance their investments through loans. Loans do not play a role. There are no commercial banks that could influence the formation of the interest rate in interaction with companies.

Keynes, in his circular flow approach, departs from the price mechanism that leads to the general equilibrium in classical and neoclassical economics. He puts the focus on flows and their interdependent relationships, which no longer need to lead to a general equilibrium, at least in the short term. And this short-term market failure is an intolerable social problem which the state can solve primarily through fiscal policy measures. Even if Say's law, according to which supply creates its own demand, may apply in the long term, the evil of unemployment calls for short-term state intervention.

The Keynesian approach, which in many cases still serves politicians today as an important theoretical model, is discussed in detail in Sect. 3.1 "Main principles of Keynesian macroeconomics".

2.8 Economic Evolution Through Innovation and Credit Creation (Schumpeter)

Schumpeter outlines the path of the economy into the modern age. His echo in economic literature would have been greater if his approach could have been better formulated mathematically.

He is interested in economic evolution in the capitalist market economy. He is interested in the dynamics in the economic processes that growth generates in the capitalist economy. These are based on innovation. Innovative entrepreneurs make sure that innovations prevail in the economy; with C. W. Field we have met an entrepreneur in the sense of Schumpeter. He took the first step with his cabling of the two continents America and Europe which, after many others, has led to the interconnectedness of the earth and fundamentally transformed the way business is done.

So far as we know, growth has been based on the accumulation of capital. It has increased production potential. Formally, we can imagine it as extending the production function further to the right, see Fig. 2.4. In the Schumpeterian approach, we must abandon the previous concept of a stable production function. This means that it can no longer play a major role in explaining growth, as we have seen in Fig. 2.4 "Production function F(K) and growth".

With the drastic change in production conditions, innovation overturns the law of diminishing marginal returns, which is fundamental to the Classical and especially to the Neoclassical Economics. The faster innovation progresses, the shorter the central economic law of diminishing marginal returns is valid and thus it loses much of its importance in explaining economic phenomena; as we know from Schumpeter (1939, p. 89), the old marginal cost curve is being destroyed in a process of innovative restructuring and replaced by new ones.

Innovations change the production and supply of goods. Entrepreneurs pave the way for the new supply of goods into the cycle of the previous economic cycle. In doing so, they transform the flows of goods and destroy the previous equilibrium. Schumpeter stresses that this process of change is "lopsided, discontinuous, and disharmonious", Schumpeter (1939, p. 102). Something new takes the place of the old.

So how does the new get into the existing economic cycle? Entrepreneurs are supported by the commercial banks. They provide the loans that entrepreneurs need to finance and market the production of their new goods, freely adapted from Schumpeter (1939, p. 111): "Credit creation is the complement of innovation". The credit transactions between innovative companies and commercial banks become the determining factor for the formation of market interest rates. And commercial banks are interested in expanding their lending business. For this is how they can increase their profits. Innovations change not only the flow of goods, but also the formation of the market interest rate on the financial market. Moreover, innovations generate substantial profits, which drastically change the income and wealth situation in society.

We want to take a closer look at credit creation. On the one hand, it shows that commercial banks have a method of generating enormous profits. On the other hand, as Schumpeter sees it, they assume the task of checking the creditworthiness of borrowers and constantly monitoring them, see Schumpeter (1939, p. 118): "… the banker's function is a critical, checking, admonitory one". However, if the commercial banks do not exercise their control function in the creation of credit, then, according to Schumpeter, the development of the capitalist system becomes crisis-prone. With responsible credit creation, the commercial banks are guardians of economic evolution.

Harari (2011, pp. 341–342) states the following on credit money creation:

"Economics is a notoriously complicated subject. To make things easier, let's imagine a simple example:

Samuel Greedy, a shrewd financier, founds a bank in El Dorado, California.

A.A. Stone, an up-and-coming contractor in El Dorado, finishes his first big job, receiving payments in cash to the tune of $1 million. He deposits this sum in Mr. Greedy's bank. The bank now has $1 million in capital.

In the meantime, Jane McDoughnut, an experienced but impecunious El Dorado chef, thinks she sees a business opportunity – there is no really good bakery in her part of town. But she does not have enough money of her own to buy a proper facility complete with industrial ovens, sinks, knives and pots. She goes to the bank, presents her business plan to Greedy, and persuades him that it's a worthwhile investment. He issues her a $1 million loan, by crediting her account in the bank with that sum.

McDoughnut now hires Stone, the contractor, to build and furnish her bakery. His price is $1,000,000.

When she pays him, with a cheque drawn on her account, Stone deposits it in his account in the Greedy bank.

So how much money does Stone have in his bank account? Right, $2 million.

How much money – cash – is actually located in the bank's safe? Yes, $1 million."

But that is not the end of the Harari story. Unforeseen events during the construction of the large bakery lead to additional costs of $1 million. McDoughnut receives the additional $1 million demanded by Stone from her bank and pays it to Stone, who puts the full amount in Greedy's bank. Now Stone has $3 million in his account and the bank still only has $1 million in cash.

The bank has a cash amount of $1 million and $2 million claims on Jane McDoughnut. This is offset by $3 million deposits from A. A. Stone. The interest rate for bank deposits is significantly lower than the interest rate on loans, so the bank's loans generate net interest income. The net interest income is the bank's profit. The bank aims to increase it. It is therefore interested in expanding its lending. And if everything goes well, the bank's credit creation is a secure source of profit. Running well here means that the wholesale bakery will indeed prove profitable in the future. Jane McDoughnut is making considerable profits from her project "Industrial Bakery" and can repay the bank the loans including interest on them.

Sometimes projects turn out not to be very profitable. As a result, the bank may not recover its loans or interest in full. It therefore bears a risk when financing a project. Samuel Greedy has not granted Jane McDoughnut the loan of $2 million because of her blue eyes. Therefore, before granting the loan, he carefully checks whether the project to be financed will be viable and profitable in the future. Mr. Greedy and Mrs. McDoughnut are closing the deal because both are convinced of the project and have confidence that it will be profitable for both in the future.

In general, the granting of loans is geared to the future and confidence in the future is the basis for the lending business. It counts on future earnings and, in general economic terms, it is based on expected growth. But if growth falls short of expectations, confidence in the future will dwindle, which is essential for economic activities.

Schumpeter emphasizes the importance of credit for the realization of innovations and at the same time underlines the importance of credit control for the functioning of the capitalist economy. Minsky points to the danger of growing debt financing due to an escalating credit supply. And we will see that commercial banks are innovative and can skillfully pass on the risks of the credit business to third parties and even earn money from it.

According to the laws of modern banking, the credit creation can be repeated as often as desired in Harari's example. Then A. A. Stone would have a multiple of the $1 million in the bank's account, but the bank would only have the original $1 million in the safe. The repetition is thus not quite possible. The central bank still comes into play. The interested reader can find out how this happens, for example, from Burda and Wyplosz (2009, pp. 268–272).

So what happens if, for whatever reason, borrowers lose confidence in the bank and withdraw their money. The bank goes bankrupt, generally the private banking system. But that must not happen. Otherwise, economic activity as a whole would collapse. It would lead to a devastating crisis like the one we experienced at the beginning of the twentieth century. Therefore, the deposits of private individuals and commercial banks in general must be secured. This calls on politicians to step in. Too much is at stake. Political intervention is called for. And the interaction between market and politics continues to this day and has rather intensified.

Schumpeter emphasizes not so much the profit motive as the central driving force for the implementation of innovations, but rather the profits as the result of the innovation process in the goods market. He sees profits as a "reward" for risky, labor-intensive, and capital-intensive companies; Schumpeter (1939, p. 105): "It—the profit—is the premium put upon successful innovation in capitalist society". The enforcement of innovations requires the active and controlling function of commercial banks. Schumpeter (1939) deals in detail with the role of commercial banks in the changing economic process with innovations in Section D. "The Role of Money and Banking in the Process of Evolution", pp. 109–123. He notes on p. 116: "… the banker should know, and be able to judge, what his credit is used for and that he should be an independent agent". And further on: "… the banker must not only know what the transaction is which he is asked to finance and how it is likely to turn out, but he must also know the customer, his business, and even his private habits, and get, by frequently "talking things over with him", a clear picture of his situation. But if banks, whether technically so-called or not, finance innovation, all this becomes immeasurably more important". And finally, he warns that without critical, verifying, and warning bank monitoring, the history of capitalist evolution can lead to a history of catastrophes, cf. Schumpeter (1939, p. 117).

Today, credit financing, the creation of money out of nothing, is sometimes viewed critically, for example by the supporters of the Swiss sovereign-money initiative (Vollgeld-Initiative). Interesting here are Schumpeter's positive remarks about John Law's credit financing, which plunged France into a long-standing economic crisis at the beginning of the eighteenth century: "The trouble with John

Law was not that he created means of payment in vacuo, but that he used them for purposes which have failed to succeed". For Schumpeter, the decisive factor is that the loans favor future economic evolution and are profitable and that the commercial banks ensure credit control.

Harari is also positive about credit creation: "It sounds like a giant Ponzi scheme, doesn't it? But if it's a fraud, then the entire modern economy is a fraud. The fact is, it's not a deception, but rather a tribute to the amazing abilities of the human imagination. What enables banks—and the entire economy—to survive and flourish is our trust in the future. This trust is the sole backing for most of the money in the world", Harari (2011, p. 343). Minsky points out, however, that quantity can turn into quality in the creation of credit. Debt financing can reach a level where it permanently burdens economic development and leads the economy into instability.

Moreover, and this may turn out to be serious, the current state-supported expansion of credit can significantly weaken the confidence of economic subjects in the future, if these loans are not matched by sufficient returns, by sufficient economic growth in the future. Then today's credit-financed expenditure may turn out to be a considerable burden on the economy tomorrow and endanger the intertemporal balance in the economy.

Credit creation is a privilege of the private banking system. It has been, as the Harari example of credit creation has shown us, the real basis for the banks to make a profit. However, the privilege is not free of charge originally: the price they have to pay is to take over the credit control and the risks if the lending leads to losses. Credit monitoring is expensive because banks have to hire experts who can evaluate the projects to be financed. If subsequently financed projects turn out to be unprofitable, the banks are threatened with losses and this can result in considerable loss of profits for banks. Private banks have recently become extremely innovative in this area. They are creating new financial products that enable them to get rid of their credit control and sell their risks to third parties. The products are complex. The supplier knows the product, whereas the buyer often has to rely on expert advice. The information is therefore asymmetric. But even experts sometimes fail to see through the full quality of the products, as the recent financial crisis has shown with the rating agencies. The question arises whether private banks have not opened Pandora's Box with their innovations and paved the way for an unleashed capitalism.

An ongoing process of innovation is ultimately the decisive factor for economic growth, for economic evolution. It determines the growth of the supply of goods in an economic process in which the old is constantly being replaced by the new. It is accompanied by credit flows, which flow in addition to the money flows in the economy. Schumpeter (1939, p. 114) explains the credit flows: "The loans to entrepreneurs need not—not entirely, at least—be repaid, but can be, and often are, renewed in such a way as to make the corresponding amount of means of payment permanently, or at all events indefinitely, part of circulating medium". Minsky takes up Schumpeter's ideas on credit flows and discusses how uncontrolled credit financing leads to economic instability. We discuss Schumpeter's and Minsky's ideas in the light of recent developments in Sects. 4.5 "Private banks: equity ratio, banking business, risks, and regulation" and 4.6 "Debt financing and risks: good times and bad times". In Sect. 2.13.4 "Central bank policy, market risks, and moral hazard", we look at Jack London's exposition of uncontrolled capitalism in his novel "Burning Daylight", which contrasts with Schumpeter's call for control of credit flows by banks.

2.9 Economic Instability due to Dominant Financial Market and Increasing Indebtedness (Minsky)

Schumpeter (1939) describes in his book "Business Cycles" how the capitalist market system drives economic evolution, in Chap. 3 "How the Economic System Generates Evolution", pp. 72–129. The decisive factor in this is innovation. In the capitalist market economy, it is the central driving force for change in economic processes. Innovation destroys, as we know, the old mode of production and gives rise to new ones. Innovation thus replaces old forms of production with new ones because, from the point of view of the companies, they have the advantage that they can reduce production costs considerably and increase profits drastically.

Schumpeter's exposition of innovation is closely linked to the commodity market. Minsky (1986) expands Schumpeter's ideas. He points to the enormous forces of innovation in the financial market, which have recently made it the dominant market in the capitalist system [financial economic revolution].

Commercial banks are weakening credit control. They market loans. New markets and new financial flows emerge. This increases the importance of the financial market and the commercial banks, which stimulate the expansion of credit and thus debt financing. Once loans have been granted, they are no longer repaid in full and new ones are added to the old ones, thus constantly increasing debt financing and risk.

Minsky has extended the Keynesian model. The extension is based on Schumpeter's approach to economic evolution and goes into detail on commercial banks. Sections 3.2 "Main features of Minsky's macroeconomics" describes Minsky's approach and 4.1 "Interest rate effect on Minsky's profit–investment dynamics, on inequality, and on monetary policy" extends Minsky's formal approach.

Minsky describes the expansion of debt as Ponzi financing and as particularly risky. As we will see in the future, the private bank system is innovative and is shaping finance in a variety of ways and creating markets for it. But one thing remains the same: credit demands and debt are growing. They are a burden on the circular flow economy. In addition to this, there is extensive trade in credit papers from stocks; a large part of the real estate, art, and share markets must be added to this stock economy.

In 1986, Minsky fundamentally questioned the longer-term stability of the market economy. In his approach, commercial banks play an essential role. They cross the line which, according to Schumpeter, can endanger the stability of the capitalist economy. For they drive the economy into instability with their uncontrolled, excessive credit policy. Debts are rising and with them the danger of insolvency in both the private and the public sector and thus the risks. Instability and the risk of crisis are growing. And right at the beginning of the twenty-first century, the real estate and financial crisis shook the world in 2007.

As early as 1986, Minsky described how the economy was becoming more unstable and more vulnerable to crises. What a contrast to the Nobel Prize winner R. Lucas, who in 2003, shortly before the crisis, in his presidential address to renowned economists praised his guild for now having the cyclical fluctuations under control, in the words of R. Lucas the "central problem of depression-prevention has been solved". We will discuss this in connection with the critical remarks of the Nobel Prize winner Romer in his essay (2016) "The trouble with macroeconomics" later in the methodological part in Sect. 4.10 "Economic processes and their analyses", where he strongly criticizes the New Keynesian Models, a synthesis of Keynesian and Neoclassical Ideas, cf. also The Economist (2016f): "The emperor's new paunch. No holds are barred in Paul Romer's latest assault on macroeconomics", and The Economist (2018a): "Economists still lack a proper understanding of business cycles".

It is remarkable that now, after the crisis, the magazine The Economist considers Minsky's remarks on instability to be one of the six big ideas in the recent economic literature alongside the Keynesian multiplier, cf. The Economist (2016c): "Financial stability, Minsky's moment".

2.10 Sluggish Growth and Social Inequality

Monitoring borrowers costs the private banks money. They are inventive. They create securitized bonds and create markets for them. They kill several birds with one stone. They save money on credit monitoring, earn money by trading new securities and get rid of risks. No wonder that the financial markets were booming at the end of the twentieth and the beginning of the twenty-first century. The City of London and Wall Street were experiencing an enormous boom. The financial sectors in England and the USA were growing faster than the other sectors of the economy, especially in England.

The money flows into investments with high returns, but which can also be achieved outside the economic cycle. Much of the money from savings and credit money creation no longer benefits productive investment in the goods market, and thus economic growth is lacking. This is because considerable sums of money flow into the estate and art and share market. Property prices and rents are rising, especially in metropolitan areas, and so are yields. The unproductive outflows of money have an impact on the economic cycle via higher rents. Rising rents restrict the purchasing power of tenants, especially those on low incomes. Affordable housing is becoming scarce for them. Landlords and property owners in general are the winners. And they usually already belong to the high-income stratum of the population. They can afford to buy real estate and benefit from their price increases and rent increases. The flow of money toward the property market thus weakens the productive forces in the goods market and exacerbates social inequality.

According to Gordon (2016), "The Rise and Fall of the American Growth", the weakness in growth that he identifies in his extensive and long historical study from 1750 to the present for the current period from 1970 to 2014 is due to the declining impact of innovation and technological progress on economic growth. The graph "Where's the tech?" in The Economist (2016a) is an eloquent testimony to the weakness of growth. It shows that in Japan, France, and Germany, for example, the annual growth rate of labor productivity fell from almost 3 to 1% in the period 1970–1996 to 2004–2014, see The Economist: "There are more explanations than solutions for the productivity slowdown (2016a)". We will discuss weak growth in more detail in Sect. 4.8 "Capital, growth, and sluggish growth".

Income and wealth grow through innovation. They are not only the driving force for economic change, but also the source of wealth accumulation: "It follows that the bulk of private fortunes is, in a capitalist society, directly or indirectly the result of the process of which innovation is the prime mover", Schumpeter (1939, p. 106). And further on, on page 106: "Saving, consistently carried on through generations, could not have been nearly so successful as it was if there had been surpluses, due to innovation, from which to save".

The 2015 Forbes list "The World's Billionaires" is evidence of the Schumpeterian hypothesis on wealth creation. Of the 25 richest people, 13 are "entrepreneurs", including Bill Gates (Microsoft), Larry Ellison (Oracle), Mark Zuckerberg (Facebook), and Larry Page (Google), who are innovators in the narrower sense. The others are heirs to great fortunes who created "entrepreneurs" in earlier years, such as the four siblings Walton (Wal-Mart) and Liliane Bettencourt (L'Oreal).

In theory, market forces of competition should ensure that a wider sharing of profits becomes possible and that profits eventually shrink and disappear. But there are sophisticated defensive strategies, as we learned from Schumpeter in Sect. 2.6.2 "Constitution elements of microeconomics and their critical evaluation".

High profits make great fortunes, as the Forbes lists confirm. However, the change in wealth does not only depend on the profits, but also on the increase in value of the asset portfolio, which can be enormous over a longer period of time. Savings from wage income are low. We neglect them. Because the use of the profits primarily determines how the assets develop, profits can be consumed or saved. Savings can be invested in either productive or unproductive assets. The distinction is irrelevant for the formation of wealth Σ. The growth rate of wealth $g_{\sum}$ is $g_{\sum} = p_{\sum} + s_{\pi} \cdot r$. Therein is $p_{\sum}$ the increase in the value of wealth, s_{π} the savings rate from profits, and r the return on investments. Piketty (2013) puts the growth rate of wealth $g_{\sum}$ in relation to the growth rate of national income g_Y in order to be able to make statements on the accumulation of wealth. According to Piketty, the relation $r > g_Y$ is of central importance in this context. Inequality is dealt with in detail in Sects. 4.2 "Inequality of income and wealth" and 4.3 "Piketty on inequality".

In addition to the dominance of the financial market, which leads to a financialization of the economy, increasing importance of stock trading can be observed, which, with its inflationary price development for stocks such as real estates, favors those who own them and thus also inequality.

The interaction between the stock economy and flow economy will become increasingly important for economic evolution. Although the central banks with their low-interest policy were able to prevent the current financial crisis after 2007 from sliding into a depression like the one at the beginning of the twentieth century, the economic crisis has not yet been overcome. But their low interest rate policy has led to a real estate boom with enormous price increases. Jorda et al. show that credit-financed property price increases in particular can be a threat to the financial market and also to the real economy, cf. Jorda et al. (2015).

2.11 Central Bank's Stabilization Policy in the Context of Weak Growth, Instability, and Inequality

Schumpeter's innovation, which originally related to production and the commodity market, is now bearing manifold fruits on the financial market. Private banks are the bearers of innovations. They are evolving from commercial banks to investment banks and carry out financial transactions on their own account. They are getting rid of the risk monitoring that Schumpeter still considered essential for economic evolution without crises and are making risk tradable without the central banks intervening to shape it. This creates a systemic risk in addition to the risk from debt financing, which can only be borne by society. The state must intervene more in the economic process in order to prevent crises from escalating. The interaction between the state and the market is increasing without the economic process being less susceptible to crises. On the contrary: instability is growing, and so is economic inequality.

Instability and weak growth tend to increase risks in the flow system. Central banks are primarily responsible for stabilization. They lower the central bank interest rate and buy securities on a massive scale. As a rule, these are government bonds which they purchase from private banks, major investors (pension funds), and also from private individuals. In this way, they increase the monetary base. The increase is intended to boost demand for goods, thus counteracting deflationary tendencies that paralyze economic growth and favoring inflation, which also helps to reduce debt. Inflation and deflation are dealt with in Sect. 4.7 "Inflation and deflation: good times and bad times".

In any case, central banks are increasingly taking risks out of the economic cycle in the short term. However, it remains to be seen whether this will also reduce risks in the economy in the long term. Rather the opposite will be the case because of moral hazard behavior. The consequence of this, however, is that central banks will not be able to end their stabilization policy so easily. A longer-term stabilization policy favors enormous outflows of money into unproductive investments, especially in the property market. They drive up inflation there, especially in conurbations. The rise in property prices and rents is increasing inequality in income and wealth. The unintended side effects of central bank stabilization are thus counterproductive and cannot be ignored. The central banks' stabilization policies will tend to increase risks and thus economic instability and will also deepen inequality. Similar to the Keynesian approach, the state also comes to the rescue, but now it is changing economic evolution as outlined by Schumpeter in a sustainable way in addition to market forces. In contrast to Keynesian, it is not clear when central banks will be able to end their intervention, especially not the ECB. For in the eurozone, the differences between the economies are likely to rule out an end soon. Central bank policy and especially ECB policy is dealt with in Sects. 4.11 "Stabilization policy in the post-Keynesian era" and 4.12 "Consequences of economic change and state stabilization: instability and inequality, distorted markets, and intertemporal imbalance".

Central banks are favoring the expansion of the credit market with their huge buy-up programs. This expansion corresponds to high yield expectations. A problem arises when these future expectations cannot be met because of weak growth. Then confidence in the financial system and in the economy as a whole is lost, a serious problem. This is dealt with in Sect. 4.11.3 "Profits and losses of central banks".

Risky undertakings are not fully calculable. They are open to results. They can fail, they can succeed. Great successes are matched by total failures. Central bank stabilization is also an open-ended process, but it must not fail precisely because of the possible loss of confidence.

2.12 People and the Economy

Man is cooperative, inventive, and eager to experiment. In modern times, his technical advances mark the steam engine, the assembly line (coordination of man and machine), the computer, and in general the IT economy as well as the upcoming networking of things. Man dares a lot. As a glance at the history of the economy shows us, he exploits his possibilities without being too concerned today about future effects. They will certainly set them new tasks in the future. But he trusts in his innovative power, which has accompanied him until today on his journey into the unknown.

The following points are benchmarks for understanding the modern economy:

- Capital accumulation, economic growth, and industrial revolution (Smith)
- Market economy, division of labor, productivity, profits, and international trade (Smith and Ricardo)

- Market economy and market society (Polanyi)
- Economic crises and government stabilization (Keynes)
- Economic evolution through innovation and credit creation (Schumpeter)
- Economic instability due to dominant financial market and increasing indebtedness (Minsky)
- Increasing social inequality (Piketty)
- Dominant role of central banks in economic processes
- Increasing trade in stocks such as real estate, shares, and securities
- ICT revolution, globalization, and international competitive struggle (Baldwin, Milanovic, Marx).

The last point is dealt with in the following.

But the economy cannot be seen in isolation from social development. The division of labor, as Adam Smith pointed out in the eighteenth century, is the cornerstone of the enormous economic achievements of the last three centuries. It is based on the willingness of people to cooperate. The division of labor has continued with trade in the international division of labor, which has led to a globalization of the economy. Adam Smith already pointed out the importance of market size. Because size promotes the division of labor and thus productivity and increases profits, we will see this in the example of the "iPad". And companies use the size of the market, whether for development, production, or sales, to make profits, especially innovative companies. And the statistics show that they can lead to considerable inequalities. On the one hand to immense wealth and on the other hand to unemployment with precarious living conditions. So, there are big winners and big losers in this development. The latter are dependent on state support.

The basis of the hitherto fruitful division of labor is the cooperation between people with very different talents and very different educational backgrounds. According to Tomasello (2010), as we know, the human tendency to cooperate is already evident in early childhood. In view of the dissatisfaction of the losers, however, the question arises whether cooperation is not overstretched in the globalization process. And the increasingly negative attitude toward the market and its results in the political sphere makes it clear that the social dichotomy between the market and politics, as highlighted by Polanyi, is highly topical.

The societal contradiction cannot be solved by the state coming to the rescue in case of market failures alone. At the time, the Keynesian concept was successful. The current central bank intervention lacks a coherent concept and may therefore fail. The Economist puts it similarly: "A compelling new paradigm seems a distant prospect", see The Economist (2018a). Politics must be as innovative as business, especially on a global level. It would have to come up with viable concepts to convince people and give them confidence. This is particularly necessary for the EU if it is to continue to grow together. But perhaps politics is too caught up in the national ideas that have given rise to large societies, nations, over centuries, in the words of Harari (2011, p. 115): "Myths, it transpired, *are* stronger than anyone could imagine. When the Agricultural Revolution opened opportunities for the creation of crowded cities and mighty empires, people invented stories about great gods, motherlands, and joint stock companies to provide the needed social links. While human evolution was crawling at its usual snail's pace, the human imagination was building an astounding network of mass cooperation, unlike any other ever seen on earth".

2.13 Recent Transformation in the Global Economy

2.13.1 ICT Revolution (Baldwin and Milanovic)

The division of labor has developed more and more in the course of history. Together with the markets, it has opened up enormous developments in Europe and the USA as well as Japan. The division of labor has taken on qualitatively different forms. In the beginning, there was self-sufficiency without market production. Then local markets emerged, where producers offered their goods and consumers demanded them, as outlined in Sect. 2.1 "The agricultural revolution". *Producers and consumers have emerged from self-sufficiency. The local markets become networked, and thus gradually a national market with a national production gradually emerges*, which is a central variable in macroeconomic growth theory in the form of the national production function, for example in Solow (1957). Industrial companies in Great Britain, France, Germany, and the USA, together with imperialism and colonialism, have been able to increase their productivity considerably in the course of the first and second industrialization and have thus provided their states with enormous growth. Together with colonialism, imperialism has led to an international division of labor. On the one hand, Europe and the USA with their rapid industrialization and on the other hand, countries that provide the raw materials for the industrialized countries: The North-South divide is forming. The advantage of the Northern Sphere is not only the richer supply of goods, but also the extensive technical expertise that can be gained there through innovation. This experience in production, together with science and technology, has enabled countries in the Northern Sphere to accumulate enormous innovative potential, to achieve world supremacy, and to leave their mark on the world with their rules and standards. The USA even protects its international interest through administrative and justice sanctions. The basis for this is the CAATSA law (Countering America's Adversaries through Sanctions) from 2017.

Baldwin (2016) has presented the shift in the world economy from industrialized countries to other countries in two figures, see Fig. 2.1: Globalization changed around 1990: the shocking share shift on page 2 and Fig. 23: Spot the phase transitions: World GDP shares, year 1000 to 2014, on page 81. Here, we summarize the essential information from these figures in Table 2.1.

We also summarize information from Fig. 2.2: The decline in rich nations'share of world manufacturing translated to gains by just six developing nations on page 3 in the following Table 2.2.

Table 2.1 Share of the G7 and China plus India (C + I) in world GDP

	1770	1820	1960	2014
G7	10%	12%	70%	46%
C + I	45%	49%	3%	16%

G7: USA, Germany, Japan, France, Britain, Canada, and Italy

Table 2.2 G7 and I6 share of world manufacturing

	1970	2000	2010
G7	70%	55%	47%
I6	3%	14%	24%

I6: China, Korea, India, Poland, Indonesia, and Thailand

A diagram in Milanovic (2019), see Fig. 1.2 Percentage share of global GDP for the United States versus China 1950–2016 on page 10, is also informative on the change in the global economy. Table 2.3a gives an extract of selected values:

A figure in Le Monde presents a similar result.

Table 2.1 shows that for a long time, from 1770 to 1820, production conditions remained the same throughout the world. *This is the time of self-subsistence.* At that time relatively few people lived above the subsistence level. From 1820 to 1960, during the first and second Industrial Revolution, the production of goods in the industrialized countries G7 increased enormously; their share in global GDP increased from 12 to 70%. China and India are unable to keep up with the pace of development and are falling considerably behind; their share shrinks from 49 to 3%. *This is the time of industrialization and the international division of labor between industrialized countries and raw material suppliers.* Industrialization further develops the division of labor. It leads to a division of labor in a highly hierarchical form, mostly in large factories. A representative example of this is the assembly line production that Ford has set up in car production. In this phase of industrialization, both highly and low-skilled workers find work, see Table 4.9 in Sect. 4.9 "Globalization: good aspects and bad aspects". It is only with the ICT revolution from 1970 onward that there is a significant shift in the employment structure in favor of white-collar workers and managers and professionals at the expense of blue-collar workers. In addition, the ICT revolution favored the splitting of the hitherto hierarchical division of labor within national factories into outsourced, internationally integrated production chains, in so-called global value chains.

The trend in favor of the industrialized countries changed considerably from 1960 onward, and the ICT revolution began to take effect. The "I" stands for "Information", the "C" for "Communication", and the "T" for "Technology". The ICT revolution has fundamentally changed the organization of production processes, see Baldwin (2016, p. 82). Baldwin considers all three adjectives "transformative, revolutionary, and disruptive" to be appropriate for the new ICT evolution stage.

The era of globalization is beginning. Domestic production is being subdivided into international production processes that can be coordinated efficiently and cost-effectively thanks to the ICT revolution, the third Industrial Revolution, and

national markets are networking to form a world market. Richard Baldwin explains this on page 109: "… The ICT revolution lowered the cost of coordinating complex processes across great distances. Once it was possible to separate manufacturing processes internationally, firms pursued the option with gusto. They started moving labor-intensive stages of production from high-wage nations to low-wage nations". Milanovic (2019) argues similarly in Sect. 4.2 "Capital: Global Value Chains, pp. 147–155", at the very beginning of which he states: "The global value chain, a way of organizing production such that different stages of production are located in different countries, is probably the most important organizational innovation in the era of globalization. Global value chains were made possible both by the technological ability to control production processes effectively from distant locations and by global respect for property rights". However, a large part of world production is still controlled by Western industrialized countries and Japan.

Baldwin speaks of a "second unbundling" of a "global value chain revolution" in the outsourcing of production processes from the national to the global level. He sees the "first unbundling" in the transition from self-subsistence to producers and consumers, which then leads to the emergence of national markets, which have then developed through international networking into a world market with international competition. Globalization has initiated a process of reversal, especially with the rise of China, which will lead to a rebalancing of worldwide living conditions.

2.13.2 Globalization and the Economic Change to the Disadvantage of the Old Industrial Nations

With globalization, the G7's share of world production is falling from 70 to 46%, and China and India's share is growing from 3 to 16%. The economic decline of the western industrialized nations is confirmed by Tables 2.2 and 2.3. Table 2.2 shows that the G7's share of the world manufacturing industry declined from 70 to 47% between 1970 and 2010. In this period, the share of the I6 increased from 3 to 24%. According to Table 2.3a, the US share of world GDP fell from 38 to 16% between 1950 and 2016 and China's share grew from 2 to 19%. The decline in trade was similarly dramatic. Here too, China's gain is considerable. This is illustrated by the chart "Tipping toward Beijing" in The Economist, Special Report: "China's Belt and Road", February 8th 2020d, p. 8. It provides information for selected countries on their share of trade with the US and China in the two years 2000 and 2018. We provide essential graphical information in Table 2.4.

These are dramatic changes in the economic structure of the world at the expense of Western industrialized countries and Japan. Globalization is stimulating growth worldwide, with China and other Asian countries benefiting to a greater extent from this, as the tables as a whole show. Here the example of the ICT revolution illustrates that technological change is the source of prosperity. But growth does not reach everyone in the same way. There are losers and these are the low-skilled workers in the old, industrialized nations who want to be protected.

Table 2.3 a Share of the USA and China in world GDP. b Share of USA, China, and Eurozone in world GDP

a

	1950	1990	2016
USA	38%	20%	16%
China	2%	4%	19%

b

	1980	2020
USA	21%	16%
China	2%	19%
Eurozone	22%	12%

Le Monde: "Quarante ans d'un lent déclin européen", 9 Décembre 2020, p. 20

Table 2.4 Share of trade in selected countries with the USA and China in %

	Japan		South Korea		Great Britain		Germany	
	USA	China	USA	China	USA	China	USA	China
2000	26	10	20	9	13	3	9	4
2018	14	22	15	23	11	8	8	9

But let us remain with the winners for a moment. They include the I6 countries, and in particular Asian countries. The income there is rising. The increase reduces global inequality, see Milanovic (2016): Who has gained from globalization, pp. 10–24. This is not surprising if labor-intensive production processes are outsourced from high-wage countries to low-wage countries. At first glance, however, it is surprising that China, for example, manages to become competitive in the world market for high-tech products. Here we need to only mention the 5G communications network market, which will launch the fourth industrial revolution; with 5G technology, the production process is further transformed and the Chinese technology group Huawei is one of the world's leaders in this technology. This new 5G technology enables networked production processes that run autonomously and, in agriculture, networked machines that also work by themselves.

Obviously, due to the international differentiation of production processes, emerging countries are not only able to join the productivity of the highly developed industrial nations, but thanks to their comparatively excellent education they can also become competitive in ICT innovation, a challenge for the traditionally leading industrial nations used to success. Globalization allows so many Asian countries to successfully participate in world production that no development aid could have provided them.

The losers are numerous, especially in the US, and can be found among the low-skilled workers in manufacturing, but not only among them. With the international outsourcing of production processes, Asian countries, above all China, are succeeding in becoming competitive in the international economy. As a result, the industrialized countries, which have been leading for many decades, lose their dominance in the world market, and the emerging countries become a challenge for them. The economic transformation is also a challenge for these states in their previous political dominance. Their dominance at the political level is under threat, and it is the conservative establishment that sees America's dominance in shaping international rules and treaties under threat. The conservative establishment, together with the low-skilled workers, is the pillar of American President Trump, who wants to save his country from decline with a protectionist policy and who is fighting against the globalization that international institutions such as the International Monetary Fund, the World Bank, and the WTO have supported; for rule-based multinational trade, see Rodrik (2011) Chap. 4, Bretton Woods, GATT, and the WTO: Trade in a politicized world, pp. 67–88.

2.13.3 Inequality, Blitzscaling, and New Monopoly Formation

Despite the change in the international economy in favor of underdeveloped countries, the wealth of the rich in the old industrialized countries is rising dramatically and, with it inequality, especially in the USA. This is pointed out by the studies in Piketty (2013), Saez and Zucman (2019), Milanovic (2016, 2019). Milanovic (2019) systematically discusses causes for the growing inequality, which he attributes to ICT evolution, among other things, see his comments in Sect. 2.2 "Systematic Inequalities", 23–42. According to Fig. 2.3, The top decile of capitalists in the top decile of workers (and vice versa), United States, 1980–2017 in Milanovic (2019), 35, the wealth of the 1% richest US-Americans doubled between 1980 and 2017. More precisely, the share income that the 10% households with the highest labor income have among the 10% households with the highest capital income has increased from just under 15% to nearly 30% in the above period. However, the figures on inequality in Piketty (2013) and Saez and Zucman (2019) are viewed critically by other studies, see The Economist: "Inequality Illusion", November 30th (2019h, pp. 11–12), and The Economist: "Measuring the 1%", (2019i, pp. 19–22).

According to Forbes lists, the super-rich are, on the one hand, heirs to great fortunes and, on the other, entrepreneurs who have driven ICT development and have rapidly accumulated great wealth by commercializing their products. When thinking of the companies here, one thinks above all of the US companies Microsoft—software products for computers, Google recently Alphabet—information platform, Facebook—communication platform, Apple—communication products,and Amazon—online trading platform. Facebook and Google earn their money mainly with advertising and are causing a radical change in the advertising industry at the expense of the traditional print media, among others. The production of Apple products is an eloquent testimony to the international outsourcing of production processes, the international value chain of IPad production is later discussed in more detail.

These companies, which are managed from the traditional industrial country of the USA, benefit from globalization: they grow rapidly and quickly make extremely high profits. This is known as "blitzscaling", and the name is a program for a risky entrepreneurial strategy, see Tim Sullivan, Blitzscaling (2016). The name "Blitzscaling" is derived from the German term "Blitzkrieg", which stands for the rapid advance of German combat tank units in World War II. They quickly made considerable gains in terrain, but at the expense of high risks. This is because, during their rapid advance, they have lost contact with supply units and have thus become vulnerable to adverse weather conditions, for example. The characteristic that "blitzkrieg" has in common with "blitzscaling" is not only its rapid success, but also its high risk.

The speed at which leading ICT companies are growing is illustrated by figures from Sullivan (2016), supplemented by data from two articles in The Economist magazine:

The five largest tech companies Microsoft, Amazon, Apple, Alphabet (Google), and Facebook are recording enormous growth in the following important areas of the US economy, according to the magazine The Economist: "Graphic Detail. Tech Titans", August 10th (2019c, p. 69) (Table 2.6).

The figures on advertising revenues clearly show a radical transformation, which we have already mentioned, a fundamental change in the advertising industry. The ICT companies are the big winners in this market. They are chasing substantial shares away from the traditional print media. They are increasingly lacking the money to hire qualified journalists; expensive investigative journalists who can research independently and thus provide well-founded reports.

The table values as a whole are eloquent evidence of the rapid growth of ICT companies, of blitzscaling. Revenue is growing much faster than the number of employees, visible by the ratio of revenue to employees. Let's take a closer look at the Google (Alphabet) figures in Table 2.5. From 2001, revenues grew 193% in 2007 and 1.570% in 2018. And this year, net profit accounts for 41% of the US$ 135 billion in revenues, reaching US$ 55 billion. With these figures, it is not surprising that ICT company founders are among the richest on the Forbes lists.

With big profits, rich people can dare a lot in contrast to poor people. Moreover, because of the low interest rate policy of the central banks, money is cheap. With enormous profits and cheap debt financing, rich investors can make risky financial investments on a large scale, which will yield high returns in the long run. The above-mentioned companies, for example, cleverly buy up start-up companies—new companies in the process of being formed with great profit prospects. This enables them to secure profits in their market segment for a longer period of time. They integrate potential competitors by making suitable start-up purchases and thus prevent significant competition in the early stages of their development, which could reduce their profits in the future. The narrative of the "invisible hand", which turns self-interest into the common welfare, has been severely damaged by this new risky corporate strategy. Its story is becoming less and less convincing and turns out to be a fairy tale. State antitrust institutions are not prepared for the dynamic growth process of blitzscaling to rapidly emerging monopolies and are more concerned with large

Table 2.5 Blitzscaling at Amazon, Alphabet, and Facebook

Amazon	1996	1999	2019[a]
Employees	151	7,600	
Revenue (US$)	5.1 m	1.64 bn	279 bn
Revenue/Employee	33,775	215,789	
Google (Alphabet)	2001	2007	2018[b]
Employees	284	16,805	
Revenue (US$)	86 m	16.6 bn	135 bn
Revenue/Employee	302,817	987,801	
Net profit			55 bn
Net profit/revenue			41%
Facebook	2006	2011	2019[a]
Employees	150	3,200	
Revenue (US$)	48 m	3.7 bn	70 bn
Revenue/Employee	320,000	1,156,250	

The share of the worldwide mobile operating system grew from 2% in 2009 to 77% in 2019 thanks to Android[b]

[a]The Economist: "Big Tech and Antitrust. How to Dismantle a Monopoly", October 26th (2019g), 57–59, 2019 revenue forecast

[b]The Economist: "Alphabet. Turning a Page and a Brin", December 7th (2019j), 61

Table 2.6 Selected shares of the five biggest ICT firms in four key economic variables in US in %

US stock market value		US non-financial corporate profits	
Mid-2005	Mid-2019	2010	2019
3%	13%	4%	12%
R&D spending among S&P 500 firms		US advertising revenue	
2005	2019	2010	2019
12%	31%	9%	41%

mergers of old structured companies. The blitzscaling companies, on the other hand, continue to secure their dominance unhindered by establishing new global standards for smart technology, as Alphabet, Apple, and Amazon are doing, see Google, Apple, and Amazon: Eine smarte Allianz (2019). In the longer term, dominance secures these companies considerable monopoly profits via high marks-ups.

Long-term high profits illustrate that the market mechanism with competition no longer functions properly. *There is a market failure. The "invisible hand" can no longer serve the common welfare to a sufficient extent.* The state can correct the market failure by taxing the big winners more heavily and using the additional tax revenue to improve equal opportunities, especially for children. In this case, taxation serves not only a fiscal but also a macroeconomic objective, the general interest, which the market endangers.

2.13.4 Central Bank Policy, Market Risks, and Moral Hazard

After the Keynesian fiscal policy has become ineffective, the central bank is the remaining state actor, which now tries to stimulate the growth of the national economies with limited resources alone. The central banks set their interest rate practically at zero and buy up market risks to a considerable extent by means of bonds, worldwide; The Economist: Special report. "The world economy. The end of inflation. Prices without borders", October 12th 2019f, 7–9, refers to this. In this way, they are accommodating companies. They are interested not only in stable high profits, but also in low risk. In addition, central banks in the important financial market are suspending the price mechanism that is central to the market economy. By takeover market risks, they favor "moral hazard" behavior in the economies. The takeover of risks and low interest rates increases the tendency of economic entities to incur risky debts, of the state, households, and traditional companies that depend on loans to finance their investments. This is the case, for example, in the automobile industry, which has to fundamentally realign its production for e-cars and invest heavily in this. The German Constitutional Court points to the damaging economic and social effects of the massive ECB interventions, which demands a deeper analysis of precisely these effects from the ECB and also more control, cf. Bundesverfassungsgericht, Beschlüsse der EZB zum Staatsanleiheaufkaufprogramm kompetenzwidrig, Pressemitteilung Nr. 32/2020, 5. Mai 2020, as well as the magazine The Economist: European law. Seeing red, May 9th 2020q, 16–17. The statement of the German Constitutional Court is discussed in more detail in Sect. 4.11.3 "Excursus: Federal Constitutional Court ruling of May 5th 2020 on ECB's government bond purchase programme [Public Sector Purchase Programme (PSPP)]".

After a brief decline in debt following the financial crisis in 2008, debt continues to rise again, see Le Monde, Alerte mondiale sur la dette des entreprises, 18 Octobre (2019, pp. 12–13). According to another article in Le Monde, Les entreprises face à un mur de dettes historique, 12 Juin 2020, pp. 16–17, even before the pandemic crisis, the indebtedness of non-financial companies in France in particular is increasing. Between 2004 and 2018, it rises considerably from 130.6% of the GDP to 195.46% and almost doubles the indebtedness of non-financial companies in Germany. There, the debt increases only from 98.6 to 100.03% in the above period.

In many cases, companies are no longer able to meet their interest payments despite low interest rates and have to make new loans to pay interest. *Ponzi financing* is rising again considerably, and according to Minsky—he pointed out the danger of financial crises due to over-indebtedness as early as 1986—this Ponzi financing endangers economic stability. Ponzi financing is typical for so-called *Zombie companies*, whose income is not even sufficient to cover current interest payments. Nevertheless, banks continue to grant loans to these structurally weak companies because they know they are protected by central banks. The ECB, in particular, favors debt and thus increases the instability of the economy. The Economist points out that these companies, artificially kept alive only with state aid, will go under in the next crisis, see The Economist: "Business and the next recession", February 22nd 2020j, 54: "A recession will come, eventually. When it does it will batter companies that have been sustained only by low interest rates". If The Economist is not mistaken, crises always call for further state aid.

In the economy, especially in the economies of the traditional industrialized countries, we can observe two extreme developments: On the one hand, ICT companies that are rapidly growing into profitable monopolies, and on the other hand, numerous traditional companies that can only survive with Ponzi finance. The ICT companies increase inequality, and the Ponzi companies increase instability. Both burden future economic activity and central banks increase inequality and instability. Inequality endangers social cohesion and confidence in the effectiveness of the "invisible hand" and instability increases the risk of insolvencies degenerating into economic crises. The justification of central banks to support the labor market is not convincing in the face of persistent and growing instability. Moreover, the CB banks weaken the self-cleaning process in the economy, which is necessary for Schumpeter's economic evolution. Schumpeter's process of creative destruction can no longer have its full effect on economic self-regulated evolution. The central banks also prevent low-income economic subjects from making provisions for their own future. In doing so, they undermine the socially important attitude of economic subjects to provide for themselves. The economic self-reliance of each individual is the basis for his or her autonomy and personal self-fulfillment and thus for his or her opportunities to cooperate with others as an equal partner.

Banerjee and Duflo highlight an interesting effect of the missing Schumpeter's process of creative destruction in the economic self-regulated evolution. *The so-called "evergreening", which favors existing unprofitable companies*, leads to rigid markets, which can intensify the negative effects of free trade on poverty. "Evergreening" supports companies even if they are already unprofitable and prevents them from disappearing in a process of creative destruction. They remain in existence, but their weakly secured existence at the edge of existence does not help the workers there in the long term and may aggravate their precarious situation under certain circumstances, cf. Banerjee and Duflo (2020), 82–95. In the recent pandemic crisis, the state is acting with "evergreening" according to The Economist: "Corporate Rescues, Great White Night, April 4th 2020m, 51".

What can be useful in the short term, for example to stabilize economic fluctuations, can prove harmful in the long term, for example by disturbing market mechanisms, leading to misallocations in the economy and weakening cohesion and the willingness to cooperate in society.

Just as Adam Smith was the fundamental economist for the market, division of labor, and productivity and David Ricardo for international trade, Joseph Schumpeter laid the foundations of economic evolution. In Schumpeter's narrative of economic progress, innovative entrepreneurs promote economic development. In a process of creative destruction, profitable innovations replace outdated, unprofitable productions. New is replacing the old. Commercial banks favor this process of renewal by credit creation and responsible bankers should monitor their loans.

In his novel "Burning Daylight", published in 1910, Jack London describes how tough the displacement struggle in the economic development process can be. His novel hero seeks to combat with the mighty nature in Alaska and makes a big fortune in the gold rush there. With this, he goes on hunting for money in civilization. He becomes a tough land and infrastructure speculator in San Francisco. Jack London portrays him as an unbridled money-greedy financial shark and gives us an insight into an uncontrolled capitalism with the story of his hero. Unlike Schumpeter, there is no responsible banker here to control the financial business. His role has recently become less and less important due to modern securities for risk hedging, see the comments in Sect. 4.5.3 "Risks and risk management". In view of the financial crises, however, the question arises as to whether a market with elaborate risk products can replace people with expertise and responsibility or whether these new markets are opening Pandora's Box.

2.13.5 The Narrative of the Self-regulating Market

Like Karl Marx, the Hungarian–Austrian economic historian Karl Polanyi (1886–1964) was critical of the capitalist market economy. He sees primarily its transformative effect on society, less so on the production sector. In this respect, he explains: "The innate weakness of nineteenth century society was not that it was an industrial society, but that it was a market society," cf. Polanyi (1944), 331.

The self-regulating market system is the core of the market economy and it has a transforming effect on society, see Polanyi (1944), 106. It turns the market economy into a market society where price determines value, see also the more recent remarks by Mark Carney in The Economist: "Putting values above valuations. In recent years the market economy has become the market society," April 18th 2020p, 51. On the self-regulating market, Polanyi explains: "Market economy means a self-regulating system of markets; more precisely, it is a form of an economy governed solely by market prices. Such a system, which is capable of regulating the entire economic life without external help or interference, can rightly be called self-regulating", cf. Polanyi (1944), 71. Economists are unlikely to object to Polanyi's characterization of the market economy. After all, they see the self-regulation of the market economy through the price mechanism as a central advantage: The price mechanism coordinates a multitude of plans of demanders and suppliers in different markets, and the competition there ensures that profits disappear. In this sense, as we know, according to Adam Smith and David Ricardo, the "invisible hand" of the market promotes the common welfare. The self-regulation of the market was at the heart of the Nobel Prize in 1963, when the French economist Gérard Debreu received this prestigious award for his mathematical formulation of the self-regulation of the market.

According to Polanyi, the self-regulating market forms a central autonomous unit in society, normally the economy is only one part of the whole social structure. Its market laws apply not only to goods but to all economic factors, i.e., also to labor, land, and money, fictitious goods according to Polanyi. Thus, the market expands and becomes the dominant factor in society and society becomes a market society, cf. Polanyi (1944), 6. The self-regulating market and fictitious goods: Labor, Land, and Money, 102–112.

Even though the Nobel Prize Committee celebrated the self-regulation of the market economy as a mathematical model as late as 1963 by awarding a prize to Gérard Debreu, the world economic crisis of 1929 already casts considerable doubt on the idea of self-regulation of the market. In the aftermath of the market failure of that time, which caused enormous social damage, the Keynesian narrative emerges when market self-regulation fails, the state—primarily its fiscal policy—can steer national economies for the common welfare; a new paradigm has emerged which has subsequently become the guiding principle of economic policy worldwide. This policy later results in an anti-austerity approach that is focused on growth, even if debts are incurred and no reserves are kept for crises.

With the financial crisis of 2008, a new government intervention has begun. Central banks take over market risks from companies, intervene in the price mechanism, and favor profits. They focus their attention on the mere functioning of the economy, even if their actions burden society with instability and inequality. In the forthcoming pandemic crisis, this fateful path is being pursued further. Despite enormous financial efforts, the government is no longer able to sustainably reinforce the economy and society. The state's effects on the economy have become weak. The economy has changed. Government policy must also change. It could find new strength by directly supporting society. We will go into this in more detail later.

2.13.6 Economic Concepts and Traditional Economic Policy

ICT development has a transformative, revolutionary, and disruptive effect on the organization of economic processes, according to Baldwin (2016). It changes profoundly how and where economic processes take place and what is produced. The new penetrates the old and next to it, the new emerges. The ICT transformation is bringing about a far-reaching reorganization of existing national production structures in the old, industrialized countries and an international breakdown of what was previously predominantly nationally oriented production into individual, well-coordinated production steps by means of "global supply chain management". This transition also has consequences for theoretical concepts. They lose their empirical validity and thus their relevance for state intervention in economic processes that pursue national macroeconomic goals. This is particularly evident in the production function, which is a supporting element in national macroeconomic economic governance.

The business cyclical policy has its origins in Keynes and here fiscal policy is of primary importance compared with central bank policy. It aims to eliminate national underemployment through additional debt-financed government spending. Because of underemployment, parts of the *national* production capacity lie idle and are to be reactivated via additional government spending, which leads to more employment. Keynesian fiscal policy generates higher national prosperity by increasing employment and the supply of goods in the economy concerned. This is where the state hand becomes visible, increasing the common welfare. *A new narrative is born, the Keynesian narrative, according to which the state—primarily fiscal policy—can manage national economies for the common interest: The market may fail in the short term, but the government can fix it and provide for the common welfare in national economies.*

The Keynesian narrative is implicitly based on an under-utilized *national* production potential, see the explanations in Sect. 2.2 "Capital accumulation, economic growth and the industrial revolution (Smith)" and in Fig. 2.4 "Production function F(K) and growth". Explicitly, the national production capacity appears formally as production function F(K, N, TF) in growth models. There it explains the development of the supply of goods Y of a national economy by the use of the production capital K and labor N as well as the effect of technical progress TF, Y = F(K, N, TF). Economists have also attributed the long constant distribution of income Y to the input factors capital K and labor N to properties of the production function F. In the case of constancy, one speaks of Bowley's law, Kaldor (1908–1986) of one of the few economic constants, of "stylized facts". Today there can be no more talk of constancy. Since the 1980s, the functional distribution of income has shifted in favor of capital income. In Sect. 2.2 "Systematic Inequalities, 2.2a Increasing Aggregate Share of Capital in National Income", 23–26, Milanovic (2019) attributes the shift, among other things, to the increasing degree of monopoly in the economy, especially in the rapidly growing IC sector.

The concept of the *national* production function has become fragile with recent economic developments. Even Schumpeter's explanation of economic evolution through innovation—the new takes the place of the old—has raised doubts about the construct of the production function. In the far-reaching reorganization of the economy created by the ICT revolution, the concept of the national production function no longer has any place and can therefore no longer be a relevant component in any modern economic policy. If it is to be effective, it must reorient itself. Nationally oriented employment policy will remain ineffective today, because its impact can spread far beyond national borders due to globalization. *The strict relationship between national government spending and national employment, which still prevailed at the time of Keynes, has been increasingly disintegrating with "global supply chain management".*

The ICT revolution also affects other macroeconomic variables such as inflation. The far-reaching reorganization of the economy through the use of enormously efficient and relatively cheap information and communication technology lowers the capital user cost and, as mentioned above, its increased use favors capital income. Moreover, the central banks' low-interest policy reduces the cost of borrowing, and the international breakdown of production processes exposes domestically low-skilled workers to foreign competitive pressure. Hayek's self-reinforcing effect of price level P and wage level W, the so-called wage–price spiral, which was previously observable, has weakened, compare Sect. 3.2.3 "The mark-up approach and price levels". Globalization has slowed down the price–wage dynamic, at least for the time being. Against this background, the rise in price levels targeted by central banks, which should lead to greater demand for goods and labor and to relative debt relief, can hardly be achieved; see the journal The Economist, "The world economy's strange new rules", October 12th (2019e), 13, and "Special Report: The end of inflation", (2019f), 1–12.

In this "Special Report" on economic concepts, The Economist magazine also addresses the disappearing relationship between inflation and unemployment. Under the heading "Flatting up", a graph shows monthly pairs of values of the unemployment rate and the inflation rate in the USA from 2000 to 2019. Two Phillips curves are plotted in the graph. The first is for data from 2000 to 2009 and the second for values from 2010 to 2019. The second flattens out so much compared to the first that the traditional negative correlation between inflation and unemployment is hardly discernible. Nor does the swarm of points itself reveal any significant link between the two key economic variables; the correlation is likely to be virtually zero.

In the face of low inflation and under-utilized national production capacities, which are linked to unemployment, especially in Europe and Japan, a new macroeconomic governance is being propagated, the so-called Modern Monetary Theory (MMT). This new approach, controversially discussed among economists, brings together monetary and fiscal policy, which in the Keynesian narrative of the "visible public policy for the common interest" still acted separately. Modern Monetary Policy might as well be called Modern Fiscal Theory (MFT). The government sets the priorities in spending policy and finances its expenditure by printing money or by obtaining the necessary money directly from its central bank. The central bank buys government bonds and thus provides the state with money directly. The detour via the private banking system is cut off. Money from nowhere leads to debt, but the state owes it to itself. This seems to be a magical solution to macroeconomic problems, see the comments in The Economist: "Magic or Logic. A New Macroeconomic Idea is Gaining in Popularity. Eminent Economist Think it's Nuts", March 16th (2019a), 70. The question arises whether the MMT will deliver the modern manna.

The approach is magical in that debtors and creditors form a governmental entity that can provide a seemingly free public good. However, the reservations are serious. One might object that the central banks have already de facto taken the path of financing government spending with their "quantitative easing QE", i.e., the purchase of risky government bonds—negative interest rates for government bonds in Germany, for example, bring the state additional revenue there. But there are also reservations about this central bank policy, as already mentioned under the headings of instability, inequality, and intertemporal imbalance. We will have to wait and see whether in the future a new narrative "common welfare from the public hand according to the MMT approach" can be written.

Now let us take a closer look at the MMT approach. Whether the government finances its expenditure with money printed specifically for this purpose or obtains the money it needs from its central bank, financing its expenditure increases the money supply outside the banking sector, as the government uses the money to pay, for example, salary increases for its employees, pension increases, or additional construction contracts. As the ISLM model shows, the increase in money supply causes interest rates to fall. This is discussed in detail in Sect. 3.1 "Main principles of Keynesian macroeconomics". The Economist: "Graphic detail 100-year bonds", September 14th (2019d), 81, shows the course of two interest rates from the USA and Great Britain over the long period from 1800 to 2019. A striking feature is a falling trend at the end of the period since the financial crisis of 2008. The historic low reached thereafter is further reinforced by the course of the interest rate of a ten-year bond from Austria, which reaches a low of almost zero in 2019. This development is not surprising. In fact, the QE policy of the central banks has the same effect on money supply and interest rates as the MMT approach. However, QE policy has little effect on employment, especially in EU countries. By directly linking monetary policy with fiscal policy, the MMT approach aims to remedy this weakness in central bank policy to date.

In contrast to the MMT approach, which is still in its infancy, there are empirical values for central bank policy after the financial crisis 2008. With its low interest rate policy and the risk-taking by its QE policy, it is just ensuring the functioning of the economy, guided by a short-term technocratic calculation. *In this approach, however, the public sector has lost the compass for the common welfare. For short-term functioning, central banks accept inequality and instability as well as distorted markets and intertemporal imbalance in the long run. These effects are damaging to the common interest.*

Both approaches, the MMT approach and the current central bank policy with "quantitative easing" and low central bank interest rates, have the disadvantage that the newly created money seeks *profitable investments worldwide, regardless of whether the financial investments are productive and provide for real economic growth or not.* Especially profitable are unproductive real estate investments, compare The Economist: "The horrible housing blunder", January 18th (2020a), 9, in its "Special Report: Housing. Shaking the foundations", January 18th (2020b), 1–14. The Economist points out that in 2019, worldwide residential property assets will be more than double the share capital—Graphic: Global values of asset classes —and that real estate prices worldwide, which remained virtually unchanged from 1870 to 1970, doubled from 1970 to 2012—Graphic: Global average house prices, real terms. In other words, a lot of money has recently been flowing into unproductive real estate, causing prices and thus also returns there to rise.

The money flowing out of the real economy is not only missing from productive investments, but also increases the instability of the entire economy through inflation in the real estate sector. Stagnating and falling property prices triggered the financial crisis in 2007/2008. And given the already high level of indebtedness in the economy, an MMT policy would further increase instability.

The MMT approach makes central bank policy a servant of fiscal policy, which likes to focus on popular short-term objectives. The central bank's previous strong focus on its core inflation target would be softened by its subordination to fiscal policy.

Another reorientation of the central bank did not weaken its autonomy, but reduced the power of the private banks, which are strongly profit-oriented in their actions and thereby promote instability through their risky financing, as Minsky (1986) has explained in detail, we discuss this in a more detailed manner in Sect. 3.2 "Main features of Minsky's macroeconomics". In its new orientation, the central bank opens itself *directly to private economic subjects, to society*.

In connection with e-banking, new perspectives are opening up for the central bank. The innovative Swedish Riksbank is experimenting with e-money. It intends to give private individuals direct access to it by allowing private individuals to open an account with it. Direct access by private individuals to the central bank would be revolutionary in several respects. It would pave the way for private individuals to enter e-banking. It would soften the privilege of private banks to channel money into the economic cycle: the central bank would compete with the private bank system. The money in the central bank account would be safe and would thus be a supplement to deposit insurance in private banking. Depending on its design, the state could use the central bank's private e-banking to stimulate demand in times of crises, a stimulus that fiscal policy is often denied due to the state's debt. In this respect, The Economist argues: "Central bankers could be more confident in the stimulative effect what Milton Friedman termed 'helicopter money': distributions to the public of newly minted dosh". And furthermore: "But used well, individual accounts could improve consumer welfare as well macroeconomic policy. It is a prospect that should interest", see The Economist: "All the people's money. Central banks should consider offering accounts for everyone", May 26th (2018b), 70.

The new approach of central bank policy could thus effectively complement the weakening fiscal policy, for example in the form of built-in stability. Furthermore, it could support fiscal policy in a new way in the area of social policy and also ensure more equal opportunities. In order to improve equal opportunities—intergenerational mobility—the state could set up an account for each child with a starting capital that can be used later in their education; to reduce poverty in old age, a corresponding account. To complement the support for the young and the protection of the elderly, the central bank could set up a sovereign wealth fund to better qualify the workforce for technological change. *The guiding principle of the new orientation of the central bank should be that prosperity should benefit everyone, i.e., serve the common interest.* The reorientation of the central bank is dealt with in Chap. 5 "Epilog: changing economic policies".

If cleverly designed, the central bank and fiscal policy could form two effective public hands that together can generate more public welfare, more jobs and growth, and less inequality. With this state innovation, we could speak of *a new narrative, according to which the state—primarily the central bank—could create public welfare by making society stronger.*

2.13.7 Globalization and the International Competitive Struggle (Marx)

Globalization has many aspects, as we have already seen. In recent times, the leading economic power, the USA, has seen itself threatened by global economic development. Although in the past it has played a decisive role in shaping international organizations such as the World Bank, the International Monetary Fund (IMF)—where it has by far the most voting rights—and the World Trade Organization (WTO), it is no longer satisfied with the results of world trade and the work of the supranational organizations. This is not surprising, given the upheaval in the world economy in favor of Asian states, especially China. It sees its previous global dominance threatened. The less powerful states such as Great Britain, France, and Germany are more willing to come to terms with the rising power of China. To a greater extent, this applies to states that China is trying to involve more closely in its sphere of influence through the "Belt and Road Initiative (BRI)". BRI is a key project with which China seeks to secure its influence worldwide, both by land and by sea. The chart "BRI in the eastern hemisphere" in The Economist, Special Report: "China's Belt and Road", February 8th (2020d), 4, shows how comprehensively and systematically China is expanding its trade routes in order to encompass much of the world in the form of a vast network. Here, China has learned from the earlier approach of Western industrialized countries, which have long expanded their markets through imperialist policies. At the expense of China at the time, now it is still a nightmare for this country, which can look back on centuries of highly developed culture.

The Marxist-communist central state leadership in China sees the opportunity to return to its old high culture, this time not isolated but connected to the world and influencing it.

China has learned lessons from the past. It has recognized that market size will be a decisive power base for future Chinese development—it has understood the teachings of Smith and Ricardo. The market favors the division of labor and specialization favors productivity. It opens up the basis for innovation where it can develop fully. The Chinese leadership wants to drive innovation forward. To this end, it is bundling all activities in one hand. The magazine The Economist speaks of "China's technological blitzkrieg". In connection with the Chinese dominance in 5G technology, it points to the bundling of innovative forces in the government apparatus, in companies, and in science to China's advantage in international competition, see The Economist: "The Qualcommunist manifesto. American state capitalism will not beat the Chinese at 5G", February 15th (2020h), 55.

The Chinese state plays a central role in this project. It wants to direct, shape, and control everything. It acts strategically and wants to exercise its power not only at home but also to establish its influence at an international level.

Interesting here are remarks by Karl Marx in "Die deutsche Ideologie" from the nineteenth century, on the one hand *on the international competitive struggle in world trade* and on the other hand *on the ruling class* leading this struggle. The connection of his second statement with the first one gives it a further meaning.

On the subject of the ruling class, he says: "The thoughts of the ruling class are the ruling thoughts in every epoch, that is, the class which is the ruling material power of society is at the same time its ruling spiritual power". We can replace ruling material power with ruling economic power. In China, the communist state apparatus pulls the strings. It brings together the political, business, and scientific potential to expand its economic power. And it is also anxious to keep the intellectual power of interpretation in its hands. *It alone should be allowed to tell narratives.*

The controversy in the totalitarian Soviet Union in the twentieth century between the biologists Lyssenko and Vavilov, which Stalin decided in favor of Lyssenko against scientific insight, is still known. The geneticist Vavilov, who looked around the globe for seeds and assembled one of the largest collections of seeds in the world, became interested in the genetic material. For him, it is the decisive factor in the diversity of phenomena in life. Lyssenko's thesis that the environment is the decisive factor fits better into the image of the communist idea. With a transformation of the environment, a new type of man can be created. This idea fits better into Stalin's communist worldview. With the decision for Lyssenko, the communist dictator has initiated a momentous misguided development in Soviet science, simply because Lyssenko's approach fitted better to the communist narrative, to Stalinist ideology. It is characteristic of the ideologically motivated decision that Stalin himself reformulated Lyssenko's speech manuscript for a scientific congress in the communist sense.

The power of the ruling class has recently been reduced by online platforms such as Facebook and Twitter, which provide a stage for a broad public to express its opinions. An exciting development is opening up here, even if extreme manifestations are shocking.

Karl Marx predicts international competition at a global level as follows: "In primitive history, every invention had to be made daily anew and, in each locality independently. …. Only when commerce has become world-commerce and has as its basis big industry, when all nations are drawn into the competitive struggle, is the permanence of acquired productive forces assured". Following the English version in Milanovic (2019), 129, we have replaced "Verkehr" with "commerce" and "Welt-Verkehr" with "world-commerce". According to Karl Marx, world trade —globalization—is an essential developmental step for humanity. Nothing is lost in productive forces; the wheel of innovation can now turn even faster. Marx assumes that globalization will lead to a competitive struggle between all nations, there is no question of this struggle being regulated by supranational organizations.

The competitive struggle of all nations mentioned by Karl Marx is increasingly evident in the newer phase of globalization. Here China is striving to win international know-how for itself. *It has learned from the industrial revolutions in the West that technical progress and large markets are the basis for economic and political power.*

For the international competitive struggle, too, the economy is the power base, which is also the basis for intellectual power worldwide, *for the possibility of creating and disseminating narratives that can provide global orientation in the interest of global acting powers.* This is about economic growth and growing influence worldwide.

Globalization, which has so far been based on international treaties and institutions, is currently leading to an international competitive struggle. This change may make international trade more difficult. The Nobel Laureate in Literature

William Golding highlights difficulties that can arise when rules are challenged. In his story "Lord of the Flies", Golding paints 1954 a picture of the adventurous life of an isolated group of adolescents on an island. This small society has to reinvent human coexistence. It becomes apparent that living with clear rules can be a challenge and that an attack on them can have fatal consequences.

2.13.8 China on the Path of Globalization to Become a Leading Economic Power

China is broadly positioned in innovation. This is demonstrated not only by IT companies like Huawei, Alibaba, and Tencent, but also by pharmaceutical companies. They are proving to be very competitive in the development of a new vaccine against the coronavirus. In the international vaccine race, Chinese companies are also in the lead.

The international race for an effective corona vaccine illustrates the emerging international competitive struggle. Some compare the vaccine race to the space race in the 1950s and 1960s. At that time, the democratically based USA competed with the communist-oriented Soviet Union; this time the whole world is at the starting line—more precisely the part that can keep up technologically.

According to the WHO, around 200 companies, universities, and institutes around the world are conducting research to develop a vaccine. Twelve research institutes are leading the field. As of July 31, 2020, they have already passed through or completed at least 2 test phases of the 3 phases internationally considered necessary for the reliable development of a vaccine. They come from the USA, China, India, South Korea, Great Britain, and Germany. Among them are companies that are cooperating. One cooperation consists of a group from Germany (BioNTech) and USA (Pfizer) and another from USA (Inovio Pharmaceuticale) and South Korea (International Vaccine Institute). Although Russia, the large successor state of the Soviet Union, has announced that it intends to use a vaccine as early as August 10, 2020, according to the WHO, the Russian vaccine was only in the first test phase of three phases internationally considered necessary for a reliable development of a vaccine. Among the five leading companies are the group of companies from Germany, USA, and China, two companies from China, one company from USA, and one from Great Britain, see www.zdf.de/nachrichten/wirtschaft/corona-impfstoff-108.htlm, 04.08.2020, 1–7.

As announced, Russia authorized a vaccine with the prestigious name Sputnik V on August 11, 2020. Russia took risk and simply shortened the usual development process for a vaccine, see www.zdf.de/nachrichten/politik/coronavirus-russland-putin-erster-impfstoff-100.html, 11.08.2020, 1–5.

National states are supporting the project with a lot of money. They support research and development. They are already trying to secure large quotas of production for their populations. The winners of the vaccine race can expect considerable profits. For example, the German company BioNTech is already worth billions of US dollars. According to a Forbes report, the physician Ugur Sahin is already a billionaire with his shares in this company.

In 5G development, China, with Huawei, has succeeded in taking a leading position in the struggle for global dominance in the ICT revolution. Possibly a result of the Thousand Talents Program that China launched in 2008 to attract leading international experts in science, innovation, and business management. Despite warnings from the U.S., the Chinese technology group is gaining international success because of its powerful technology. In early 2020, for example, Huawei management announced that it had signed 91 contracts with mobile phone providers worldwide to build 5G mobile networks, 47 of which were with European mobile phone providers, see www.zdf.de/nachrichten/heute/bei-47-europaeischen-providern-huawei-gewinnt-5g-vertraege, February 21, 2020. Huawei was the frontrunner in 2019 when it filed a patent application with the European Patent Office, followed by the Korean electronics groups Samsung and LG, see www.zdf.de/nachrichten/heute/spitzenreiter-in-europa-huawei-groesster-patentanmelder, March 12, 2020. 5G technology will give a further boost to ICT development by revolutionizing the transmission and processing of data. It will replace the current technology in telecommunications and will be the new basis for networks that will form the backbone of activities in industry, trade, agriculture, and the media. After all, 5G technology will accelerate the flow of information everywhere. This is where the US warns that China could disrupt the flow and siphon off information. In view of the unsuccessful US strategy of stopping Huawei's success, The Economist magazine advocates a new technology approach based on open systems with secure standards, see The Economist: "America v China. Huawei and 5Geopolitics", April 11th (2020n), 10, and The Economist: "Telecommunications. 5Geopolitics", April 11th (2020o), 47–49.

A leading science expert accused by the American government of involvement in the Thousand Talents Program is the American Harvard professor Charles Lieber. He is in the middle of the China–US controversy in 2020. His case is significant for China's development strategy to become a world power and the US reaction to it. Charles Lieber holds a chair of chemistry and chemical biology at Harvard University, where he is one of the few senior professors. He is even considered a Nobel Prize candidate. He has helped Wuhan Technical University (WuT) to international reputation. For his work on WuT, Professor Lieber received $50,000 a month and an additional $150,000 for living expenses. China has also provided him with $1.5 million for the establishment of a research laboratory. Now he has been arrested on the Harvard campus and is on trial for participating in the Thousand Talents Program. A shock wave has hit the American scientific community, see www.nytimes.com, 2020, and The Economist: "The arrest of Charles Lieber. No small matter", February 1st (2020c), 67.

A German university magazine Forschung & Lehre reported on the departure of a German brain researcher in February 2020, after which the world-renowned brain researcher Nikos Logothetis will move from the Max Planck Institute for Biological Cybernetics in Tübingen to Shanghai. China is setting up a new research campus there especially for him. Professor Logothetis will be accompanied by many of his colleagues and their families.

In addition to Huawei's leading position in 5G technology and the two examples from the scientific sector, which are characteristic of how China is exploiting international know-how for its own benefit, another example from the field of entrepreneurship training should be mentioned. Sino-European cooperation led to the founding of the "China Europe International Business School (CEIBS)" in Shanghai in 1994. When the Financial Times published its annual ranking of the 100 best Master of Business Administration Schools (MBAs) in 1999, no Asian school was included. In its publication in 2020, 17 Asian schools are now included in the list, 9 of them from China, and CEIBS is now ranked 5th. The CEIBS claims to have the broadest and most prestigious network in China, with over 22,000 graduates. Among them are 3,000 CEOs alone, see The Economist: "Business education. MBAs with Chinese characteristics", February 15th (2020g), 53–54.

The examples from ICT innovation (Huawei), science (Charles Lieber and Nikos Logothetis), and modern business management (CEIBS) are eloquent examples that China is systematically preparing itself for international competitive struggle.

China emphasizes the national idea, and the communist state machine there knows about the power of a national mass movement. The Economist magazine, for example, states: "Mass mobilization has a dark history in China. Majoritarianism is a temptation in a big and quarrelsome country because of its power to unite people against a suspect minority", see The Economist: "A people's war. China's communist rulers see a chance to mobilize the masses behind the party", February 8th (2020e), 46. A mass movement has a tendency not to let marginalized groups, often minorities, and their views come to the fore and even to suppress them in the border. The national-communist state does not promote diversity in society, neither in the way of life nor in the way of thinking. Unlike in an open society, minorities find it difficult to maintain and preserve their independence. The Turkic-speaking ethnic group of the Uighurs is an eloquent example of how minorities are systematically restricted in their autonomy, see The Economist: "Uighurs. From slammer to serfdom", March 7th (2020l), 51. The same applies to individual expressions that do not fit into the image that the national-communist state apparatus wishes to give both internally and externally. This is why it persecutes dissenters like the Swedish Chinese bookseller Gui Minhai. This Hong Kong bookseller has distributed politically sensitive books about China and disappeared under mysterious circumstances on holiday in Thailand in 2015. Now he has been sentenced to ten years in prison in China in 2020, see www.tagesschau.de/ausland/gui-minhai-buchhaendler-china-urteil, February 25, 2020.

The ophthalmologist Dr. Li Wenliang got off lightly. He has already pointed out cases of illness in the Central Wuhan Hospital from December 20, 2019, which reminded him of the SARS epidemic. That is why he immediately sounded the alarm. On January 1, 2020, the police approached him and on January 3, the state television CCTV called his alarm a spreading of false rumors. Li Wenliang had to sign a protocol with the police that he had endangered public order by reporting the SARS-like disease. The police intimidated him and muzzled him. On January 20,

2020, one of the country's medical capacities, Zhong Nanshan, confirmed Li's suspicions. He himself was infected with the coronavirus and died on February 7, 2020. Before his death, Doctor Li Wenliang told Chinese media: "I think that in a healthy society there should be more than one voice", see The Economist: "Death of an everyman. A virus-related tragedy lays bare the costs and trade-offs of life in a Communist-led dictatorship", February 15th (2020f), 45, and The Economist: "The man who knew Dr. Li Wenliang, one of the first to raise the alarm about a new coronavirus, died of it on February 7th, aged 33", February 15th (2020i), 74; see also www.lemonde.fr/international/article/2020/02/06/emotion-a-l-annonce-de-la-mort-du-docteur-li-wenliang.

The examples of the oppression of minorities, the punishment of a bookseller who promotes the dissemination of ideas, and the reprimanding of a doctor who points out the danger to society from an infectious disease show that China is not an open society that gives individuals room for autonomous development. Rather, they highlight the gap that exists between China and Western industrialized countries with their open societies, functioning separation of powers, and freedom of expression. Not only the gap, but also the danger that has arisen with globalization, global supply chain management: the dependence in the production of essential products—for example in pharmaceuticals—on China with a nationally oriented authoritarian state leadership that is determined to make its country the world leader. This is referred to in The Economist magazine. According to The Economist, production will no longer be outsourced worldwide solely on the basis of efficiency considerations. Nevertheless, China will be the future market for promising industries such as the production of autonomous vehicles, robots, and the Internet of Things and also pharmaceutical products, see The Economist: "Globalization under quarantine. The COVID-19 virus is teaching the world hard lessons about China-only supply chains", February 29th (2020k), 48.

In competition with the Soviet Union, the USA emerged victorious at the end of the twentieth century, and with it the democratically constituted West with its capitalist market system. At the beginning of the twenty-first century, a new competitor with different qualities appears in the form of China. It can count on a great potential for innovation and a huge market that is globally networked. Thus, it becomes a global power in the international competitive struggle. China, for example, has a share of over 30% of the global technology market in 2020 in many sectors. China's activities cannot be contained so easily, even if various measures of the US government are aimed at doing so. Although direct investment from China to the US has been declining in recent years, conversely it will remain more or less constant from the US to China from 2012 to 2019. For information on direct investment and the global technology market, see The Economist: "Sino-American commercial relations. Endgame", August 15th (2020s), 52.

According to The Economist, instead of an isolation strategy, the Western industrial nations should find a stable way of cooperating with China. In doing so, they can count on the strength of their civil society in international competitive struggle. The Economist assesses this new challenge from China as follows: "China hopes that its new techno-centric form of central planning can sustain innovation, but history suggests that diffuse decision-making, open borders, and free speech are the magic ingredients", see The Economist: "Xi's new economy", August 15th (2020r), 9. Here, The Economist argues for Western civil society, its traditional strength. As is argued in Sect. 1.7.2 "Reorientation of economic policy in democratically constituted states", the state should further develop a powerful knowledge-based civil society. State support of an autonomous society makes the difference to the Chinese approach, which is too one-sided and narrow to allow future technical possibilities to develop to their full potential.

2.14 Realignment of Government Economic and Social Policy

2.14.1 Democracy, Capitalism, and Prosperity (Iversen and Soskice)

Two leading Western industrial nations, historically first Great Britain and then the USA, are constitutional democratic states with a pronounced capitalist market economy, which can look back on a long period of economic prosperity. The same is true of other Western industrialized countries. The historical development from the industrial revolution to the current ICT revolution suggests that democracy and prosperity go together. Iversen and Soskice (2019) intensify this connection in the thesis that in progressive economies, democracy and capitalism support each other, see Torben Iversen and David Soskice, Democracy and Prosperity: Reinventing Capitalism through a Turbulent Century, Princeton 2019, and The Economist: "Votes of confidence. Just how compatible are democracy and capitalism?", June 15th (2019b), 66.

Soskice and Iversen see three central factors that promote prosperity in democracies with capitalist market economies. The first is a *strong state that ensures competition in the markets*. This is because capitalist companies strive for protected markets with low risk, which provide them with permanently high profits. However, competition in open markets is a precondition for profits to disappear and for innovation to be able to prevail. Large profit flows lead to unjustified distortion, on the one hand through excessively high prices at the expense of consumers and on the other hand through inequality of income. Both limit the effect of the second factor, which is of a social nature. *The majority in democracy must be convinced that it can share in the success of the economy.*

In a knowledge-based society, economic players can participate in economic prosperity through education and training and contribute to it together with innovative enterprises. The third factor comes into play here: *cooperation between skilled workers and leading companies takes place at* the *national level*. Even in globalization, where production is outsourced worldwide, the leading management in the local centers is firmly connected with the local network of highly qualified employees, for example in the centers of Paris, Berlin, London, New York, and Silicon Valley. These centers are experimental platforms for innovations with a high quality of life. These national centers are attractive for scientists, entrepreneurs, and graduates of all disciplines and also for their families. The two authors discuss the third factor. "A central aspect of our book is the extent to which advanced capitalist companies are tied geographically into national systems", see Iversen and Soskice (2019), 2.

They see nations in competition with each other, they emphasize, as David Ricardo does in international trade, the comparative advantages that invite cooperation between states. According to them, more advanced states win in globalization, see Iversen and Soskice (2019), 8. In this context, specialization at the global level, as we know it from the individual level, leads to symbiotic effects in advanced states. These states complement each other and gain in cooperation: "... advanced nations gain from globalization with other advanced nations, at least in advanced sectors. This then is a game of strategic complementarities. In our broad model the greater the specialization, the greater the value the community of advanced governments gain from each individual advanced economy: hence the symbiosis between the advanced nation-state and the extent of advanced globalization", see Iversen and Soskice (2019), 8.

In theory, complementarity speaks in favor of cooperation. Karl Marx's statement on international competitive struggle only seems to contradict this. Extreme situations often make cooperation take a back seat. The pandemic caused by the coronavirus 19 in 2020, for example, makes it clear that national interests may then dominate. A significant example is the production of a vaccine against the new virus. The rights to a German company that is working at high pressure on a corona vaccine are said to have been exclusively secured by the USA, with a lot of money, see www.tagesschau.de/inland/corona-impfstoff-deutschland-usa-101 and www.zdf.de/nachrichten/politik/coronavirus-impfstoff-konflikt-usa-deutschland-100.

In times of the ICT revolution, individual countries are less concerned with seeing their comparative advantages in a *static* comparison, as shown by Ricardo, than with securing future advantages in the international competitive struggle in a *dynamic process. Advantages in specialization create a better basis for cooperative negotiations on the international stage. Here, the modern state will be challenged to be a central actor in this struggle if it wants to successfully represent its national societal interests in upcoming strategic negotiations at the global level.*

A comparison of democratically constituted societies such as the USA with the communist-led in China reveals hardly any differences with regard to the three factors highlighted by Iversen and Soskice. These three factors are, in brief:

- A strong state to ensure competition in the markets: no market distortion through profit and corruption, and open markets for entrepreneurs who innovate and bear their own market and business risks
- A majority of the population that can participate in the success of the economy
- A cooperation between qualified employees and leading companies in the societal and national interest.

The difference must lie elsewhere. But where?

2.14.2 State, Economy, Democracy, Society, and Ecology

In answering the question "What makes the difference?" we are guided by Iversen and Soskice. In the context of their outlook on the future of advanced capitalist democracies, they address future developments in their technology debate that may reshape the role of the state, the economy, and society. They are cautious in their view of the future, see Iversen and Soskice (2019), The great technology debate, 260–261. Nothing is more uncertain than what lies ahead. Historically, we may be at the beginning of a major global transformation driven by new technology and innovation. Especially when it comes to innovation, it is impossible to make a prediction. Even a trend is difficult to discern. As far as the economy is concerned, Iversen and Soskice refer to Gordon's pessimistic remarks on technological progress and Piketty's on inequality in national economies, which can endanger society's approval of the capitalist market economy, see Gordon (2016) and Piketty (2013). Worldwide, globalization with the ICT revolution has led to considerable upheavals, as we mentioned at the beginning. Asian countries have caught up with the prosperity of Western industrial nations. Worldwide, as Milanovic points out, inequality has decreased, see Milanovic (2016).

Where the dynamic process of innovation will continue must remain open. But what we can say following Karl Marx's remarks on international competitive struggle is that nothing is now lost in innovation and that, driven by global competition, the wheel of innovation will continue to turn at an accelerated pace worldwide. The Israeli–American economic historian Joel Mokyr sees the future economic development in a similar way. Quoted on here by Banerjee and Duflo: "Mokyr, on the other hand, sees a bright future for economic growth, spurred by nations competing to be the leader in science and technology, and the resulting rapid spread of innovation worldwide. He sees the potential for progress in laser technology, medical science, genetic engineering, and 3D printing." And in medical science, we can add the innovation potential of computational biology, see The Economist: "Computational biology. The shapes of things to come" (2020t). On Gordon's claim that nothing much changed in fundamental ways in how we produced in the last few decades, he counters: "The tools we have today make anything that we had even in 1950 look like clumsy toys by comparison", see Banerjee and Duflo, "Good economics for hard times" (2019, p. 151).

The state, the economy, and society are, as Iversen and Soskice point out, key players on the world stage, where the future development of humanity takes place. The world stage itself, the environment, is however increasingly under threat. As we know from Polanyi's remarks, the exploitative capitalist market economy is putting more and more pressure on the environment and ultimately on people themselves. Today, the environmental pollution caused by the Asian economy is also growing. The environment is not a freely available resource that the capitalist economy or the centrally administered economy of China can exploit at will for profit; rather, it is a basis for the quality of life for all people that must be protected.

The function of the state is developing steadily, in crises by leaps and bounds. The state originally provided, for internal and external security, its traditional task.

Added to this is social stability, and in concrete terms, the fact that the majority of society can participate in economic development, which could not develop without the broad masses. With Keynes, the state became visible, which can manage the economy for the benefit of the general public; it can boost the economy for the benefit of all in the short term, increase the supply in general, and bring the unemployed back into employment. However, Keynesian business cycle policy is becoming less and less helpful in overcoming the crisis in the longer term. Nonetheless, states still have recourse to Keynesian spending policies. This, however, increases debt and thus economic instability in Minsk's sense. Recently, the less effective central banks have been acting alone. They are increasingly taking on market and business risks that should actually be borne by entrepreneurs and are severely interfering with the mechanisms of the market economy.

In the network of state, economy, and society, it is the economy that benefits more than society. The economy strives to restrict competition in the markets, secure profits in the long term, and pass on risks: an endeavor that burdens society. By assuming risk, central banks are acting in the interests of the economy, which also wants to eliminate competition in its favor. Blitzscaling is an eloquent testimony to this. Continued government support for the economy is harmful to societal development.

The close connection between the state and the economy must be broken and the bond between the state and society strengthened. The first step in this direction could be a reorientation of central bank policy. It can provide direct support to society without having to resort to the private banking system, by giving citizens direct access to it. In this way, it can, as already roughly outlined, increase equal opportunities for young people, alleviate poverty in old age, and establish a new economic crisis policy. The crisis policy to date makes society more vulnerable to crises instead of enabling it to be armed against them. The opening of the central bank to private economic subjects could be a turning point that will make citizens more responsible and stronger and promote their own responsibility.

In addition to the strength of the state in the economy, where it has to enforce competition in the market against the resistance of companies for the benefit of the general public, as recently demanded by Iversen and Soskice, the strength of the state is also needed in society, where it has to secure the general rules in social life. Gandhi's idea that decentralized units could in themselves be the basis of the common good is contradicted by his opponent Ambedkar, who helped to shape India's constitution: "For him, the law, the state as its enforcer, and the constitution from which it derived its force were the best guarantors of the rights of the underprivileged *against* the tyranny of the locally powerful against the community", cf. Banerjee and Duflo (2019, p. 106, 2020, p. 147). The question arises, however, whether these centralist efforts to solve social problems are still workable.

However, the measures introduced in the most recent crisis—the corona pandemic—do not indicate any change in state crisis management. As explained in Sect. 5.2 "On the path from crises with old methods to state directed economies", the state, primarily the central bank, intervenes in the economic process. The continued low interest rate policy and the ongoing takeover of market and business risks of companies, mainly unprofitable ones, seriously disturb the market mechanism and lead to misallocations in the economy. Moreover, as discussed in Sect. 5.2 mentioned above, these exacerbate economic instability and social inequality. Ultimately, without a convincing long-term concept, government intervention undermines economic sustainability and jeopardizes social consensus. It tends to make society even more vulnerable to crises.

The recent pandemic crisis continues to cause states to intervene massively in the economy. Many projects are strengthening the "evergreening", for example the support programs for airlines. The subsidization of unprofitable airlines by over-indebted states contributes little to sustainable restructuring. The extent to which investments designed to improve a country's competitiveness in international competitive struggle will be successful remains to be seen, see the statements on the 750 bn euro reconstruction fund of the EU in Sect. 5.2. "On the path from crises with old methods to state directed economies".

The international competitive struggle gives the state another new function: to be the promoter of international trade. The basis for this is a knowledge-based society, which must be built up consistently. In addition to professional training for everyone, science must be promoted. Analogous to the autonomy of American elite universities, the financial independence of national research institutions must be expanded. The autonomy of science can best guarantee the diversity on which social development can flourish. Above all, it is this autonomy that can create a great national potential for the new international cooperation that is emerging for the future, as outlined in Iversen and Soskice (2019).

The market is the center for exchange, trade, and cooperation. According to Adam Smith, the market enables specialization and the development of talent through the division of labor. Recently, it has increasingly become a platform for innovation. It can only fully fulfill its fruitful function if it is subject to competition. Then it can remain open for innovations, for example. Companies play a dominant role here. They are interested in restricting competition. Closing off the market against competition ensures long-established companies more lasting profits and lower market risks. This keeps their returns high. A strong state ensures that competition can function and eliminates undesirable outcomes at the earliest stages of development, as we discussed in connection with blitzscaling. A functioning market is a basis for economic growth that can benefit everyone.

It is necessary, as already mentioned, *to loosen the bond between state and economy and to tie the bond between state and society more firmly, to strengthen society and, in the spirit of Polanyi, to protect and care for the environment as a finite resource for the quality of life of mankind*. This involves the following areas:

- Strengthening the market mechanism with competition
- Separation of powers with effective rules of law and free press
- Strengthening the knowledge-based society and science
- Facilitating the cooperation between the knowledge-based society and innovative companies from the local level
- Participation of society in political decisions to strengthen society at a local level

- Protection of minorities to promote diversity
- Protection of the environment and promotion of local quality of life in communities.

Here the state can initiate a development from a market society to a civil society. Of particular importance will be the local level, where local social life can develop and where cooperation between qualified employees and innovative entrepreneurs can unfold to the benefit of the economy as a whole, see R. Rajan, The Third Pillar. How Markets and the State Leave the Community Behind, New York 2019.

In a strong, self-reliant society with great power of initiative, the difference is to be sought. The old western democracies can strengthen this pillar. Centrally administered communist China cannot go down this promising path with its ideology and cannot allow an autonomous and self-responsible civil society to develop from the bottom up.

2.15 Summary

The economy is constantly transforming: from the agricultural to the industrial revolution, from land use to capital accumulation, and from exchange economy to market economy with credit money creation. Today, the financial sector, with its ever-expanding debt financing, dominates the economy and makes it unstable. Innovations increasingly support the process of economic evolution, creating enormous wealth for innovative entrepreneurs in a short period of time and increasing social inequality. The ICT revolution unbundles national production processes and, with globalization, further drives economic change. Globalization has recently led to an international competitive struggle. Here, China's centralized economy is challenging the democratically constituted states. A new perspective in their intervention policy is opening up for them. They can turn their attention more toward society: A strong knowledge-based society, together with innovative local companies, can bring new prosperity to the national economy from the bottom up.

State stabilization leads not only to distorted markets but also to an intertemporal imbalance, thus endangering the foundations of the modern economy with "Much credit", "High growth", and "High trust in the future". One more reason for a reorientation of state intervention policy.

References

Akerlof, G.A.: The Market for "Lemons": Quality Uncertainty and the Market Mechanism, The Quaterly Journal of Economics, 84, (1970), 488–500

Baldwin, R.: The Great Convergence, Information Technology and the New Globalization, London (2016)

Banerjee, A.V. and Duflo, E.: Good Economics for Hard Times, New York (2019)

Banerjee, A.V. and Duflo, E.: Économie utile pour des temps difficiles, Paris (2020)
Bundesverfassungsgericht, Beschlüsse der EZB zum Staatsanleiheaufkaufprogramm kompetenzwidrig, Pressemitteilung Nr. 32/2020, 5. Mai 2020, 1–2
Burda, M. C., Wyplosz Ch.: Makroökonomie. Eine europäische Perspektive, München (2009)
Forschung & Lehre: Von Deutschland nach China – Hirnforscher fühlt sich von der MPG allein gelassen, 2/2020, 101
Friedman, M.: The Social Responsibility of Business is to Increase its Profits, New York Times Magazine September 13 (1970), 211–214
Google, Apple und Amazon: Eine smarte Allianz, htttps://www.tagesschau.de/wirtschaft/technik-apple-amazon-google-101.html 2019
Gordon, R. J.: The Rise and Fall of American Growth, Princeton (2016)
Harari, Y. N.: Sapiens. A brief history of Humankind, London (2011)
Iversen, T. and Soskice, D.: Democracy and Prosperity: Reinventing Capitalism through a Turbulent Century, Princeton (2019)
Jordà, O, Schularick, M., Taylor, A.M.: Leveraged Bubbles, National Bureau of Economic Research June 2015, 1–38
Keynes, J. M.: The General Theory of Employment, Interest, and Money, New York (1936)
Le Monde, Alerte mondiale sur la dette des entreprises, 18. Octobre 2019, 12–13
Le Monde, Les entreprises face à un mur de dettes historique, 12 Juin 2020, 16–17
Le Monde: "Quarante ans d'un lent déclin européen, 9 Décembre 2020, 20
Milanovic, B.: Global Inequality. A New Approach for the Age of Globalization, London (2016)
Milanovic, B.: Capitalism, Alone. The Future of the System that Rules the World, London (2019)
Minsky, H.P.: Stabilizing an Unstable Economy, Yale (1986)
Piketty, T.: Le capital au XXIe siècle, Paris (2013)
Polanyi, K.: The Great Transformation (1944), Deutsche Fassung Wien (1978)
Rajan, R.: The Third Pillar. How Markets and the State Leave the Community Behind, New York (2019)
Rodrik, D. The globalization paradox. Democracy and the future of the world economy, New York (2011)
Romer, P.: The Trouble with Macroeconomics, New York University 2016, 1–26
Rousseau, J.-J.: Discours sur l'origine et les fondements de l'inégalité parmi les hommes, Paris (1992)
Saez, E., Zucman, G.: The Triumph of Injustice. How the Rich Dodge Taxes and How to Make them Pay, London (2019)
Scheidel, W.: The Great Leveler. Violence and the History of Inequality from the Stone Age to the Twenty-First Century, Princeton (2017)
Schumpeter, J. A.: Business Cycles. A Theoretical, Historical, and Statistical Analysis of the Capitalist Process, New York (1939)
Scott, J. S.: Against the Grain, Yale (2017)
Smith, A.: The Wealth of Nations (1776), in A. Skinner (editor), Harmondsworth (1970)
Solow R. M.: Technical Change And the Aggregate Production Function, The Review of Economics and Statistics, Vol. 39 (1957), 312–320
Sullivan, T.: Blitzscaling, https://hbr.org/2016/04/blitzscaling
The Economist: Special Report: The Third Industrial Revolution, April 21st 2012, 3–18
The Economist: There are More Explanations than Solutions for the Productivity Slowdown, June 4th 2016a, 68
The Economist: Information Asymmetry. Secrets and Agents, July 23rd 2016b, 52–53
The Economist: Financial Stability. Minsky's Moment, July 30th 2016c, 52–53
The Economist: Tariffs and Wages. An Inconvenient Iota of Truth, August 6th 2016d, 52–53
The Economist: Special Reports: Companies. The Rise of the Superstars, September 17th 2016e, 1–16
The Economist: The Emperor's New Paunch. No Holds are barred in Paul Romer's Latest Assault on Macroeconomics, September 24th 2016f, 68

The Economist: Economists still Lack a Proper Understanding of Business Cycles, April 21st 2018a, 66
The Economist: All the People's Money. Central Banks Should Consider Offering Accounts for Everyone, May 26th 2018b, 70
The Economist: Toast before Tillage, July 21st 2018c, 65
The Economist: Rousseau, Marx and Nietzsche. The Prophets of Illiberal Progress, September 8th 2018d, 55–56
The Economist: Magic or Logic. A New Macroeconomic Idea is Gaining in Popularity. Eminent Economist Think it's Nuts, March 16th 2019a, 70
The Economist: Votes of Confidence. Just how Compatible are Democracy and Capitalism?, June 15th 2019b, 66
The Economist: Graphic Detail. Tech Titans, August 10th 2019c, 69
The Economist: Graphic Detail 100-year Bonds, September 14th 2019d, 81
The Economist: The World Economy's Strange New Rules, October 12th 2019e, 13
The Economist: Special Report: The World Economy. The End of Inflation. Prices without Borders, October 12th 2019f, 1–12
The Economist: Big Tech and Antitrust. How to Dismantle a Monopoly, October 26th 2019g, 57–59
The Economist: Inequality Illusion, November 30th 2019h, 11–12
The Economist: Measuring the 1%, November 30th 2019i, 19–22
The Economist: Alphabet. Turning a Page and a Brin, December 7th 2019j, 61
The Economist: The Horrible Housing Blunder, January 18th 2020a, 9
The Economist: Special Report: Housing. Shaking the Foundations, January 18th 2020b, 1–14
The Economist: The Arrest of Charles Lieber. No Small Matter, February 1st 2020c, 67
The Economist: Special Report: China's Belt and Road, February 8th 2020d, 1–12
The Economist: A people's War. China's Communist Rulers See a Chance to Mobilize the Masses behind the Party, February 8th 2020e, 46
The Economist: Death of an Everyman. A Virus-related Tragedy Lays Bare the Costs and Trade-offs of Life in a Communist Led Dictatorship, February 15th 2020f, 45
The Economist: Business Education. MBAs with Chinese Characteristics, February 15th 2020 g, 53–54
The Economist: The Qualcommunist Manifesto. American State Capitalism will not Beat the Chinese at 5G, February 15th 2020 h, 55
The Economist: The Man who Knew. Dr Li Wenliang, one of the First to Raise the Alarm about a new Coronavirus, Died of it on February 7th, aged 33, February 15th 2020i, 74
The Economist: Business and the Next Recession, Downturn, Disrupted, February 22nd 2020j, 51–54
The Economist: Globalisation under Quarantine. The Covid-19 Virus is teaching the World Hard Lessons about China-only Supply Chains, February 29th 2020 k, 48
The Economist: Uighurs. From Slammer to Serfdom, March 7th 2020 l, 51
The Economist: Corporate Rescues. Great White Night, April 4th 2020m, 51
The Economist: America v China. Huawei and 5Geopolitics, April 11th 2020n, 10
The Economist: Telecommunications. 5Geopolitics, April 11th 2020o, 47–49
The Economist: Putting Values above Valuations. In Recent Years the Market Economy has become the Market Society, April 18th 2020p, 51
The Economist: European Law. Seeing Red, May 9th 2020q, 16–17
The Economist: Xi's New Economy, August 15th 2020r, 9
The Economist: Sino-American Commercial Relations. Endgame, August 15th 2020s, 51–52
The Economist: Computational Biology. The Shapes of Things to Come, December 5th 2020t, 68–69
Tomasello, M.: Warum wir kooperieren, Berlin (2010)
www.nytimes.com/2020/01/28/us/charles-lieber-harvard. 28.01.2020

www.lemonde.fr/international/article/2020/02/06/emotion-a-l-annonce-de-la-mort-du-docteur-li-wenliang-lanceur-d-alerte-du-coranavirus.

www.zdf.de/nachrichten/heute/bei-47-europaeischen-providern-huawei-gewinnt-5 g-vertraege. 21.02.2020

www.tagesschau.de/ausland/gui-minhai-buchhaendler-china-urteil. 25.02.2020

www.zdf.de/nachrichten/heute/spitzenreiter-in-europa-huawei-groesster-patentanmelder. 12.03.2020

www.tagesschau.de/inland/corona-impfstoff-deutschland-usa-101. 15.03.2020

www.zdf.de/nachrichten/politik/coronavirus-impfstoff-konflikt-usa-deutschland-100. 15.03.2020

www.zdf.de/nachrichten/wirtschaft/corona-impfstoff-108.htlm, 04.08.2020, 1–7

www.zdf.de/nachrichten/politik/coronavirus-russland-putin-erster-impfstoff-100.html. 11.08.2020, 1–5

Zweig, St.: Sternstunden der Menschheit, Frankfurt am Main (1964)

Keynes' and Minsky's Macroeconomics

3

Abstract

In Minsky's novel economic paradigm, unlike the Keynesian-influenced ISLM model, profits, private banks and debt financing play a central role. Minsky replaces the Keynesian relationship between investment and saving with the future-oriented interdependence between investment and profit. Profit is ultimately the focus of economic activity in the capitalist market economy. In good times, debt financing increases the chances of profit drastically through its leverage effect, but in bad times the risk of loss is even more drastic. Private banks, together with central banks, favor economic risks and make the economic process inherently unstable.

3.1 Main Principles of Keynesian Macroeconomics

3.1.1 Basic Concept

Macroeconomics equally simplifies and expands. Simplifications help to advance to the core of economic processes on an aggregated level and expansions help to analyze it more comprehensively. Macroeconomic theory detaches itself from the multitude of goods markets and theoretically combines all goods and services into a single commodity that is traded on a single market. It assumes that supply and demand functions exist for the commodity and that the price mechanism of excess supply and excess demand also functions. Thus, it constructs a market at the macro level, as micro-theory has derived it from the utility and profit-motivated rationale. In the same way, it generates the labor, financial, and money markets and considers in these markets how economic variables such as household consumption, production, and investment of entrepreneurs influence each other. In addition to households and companies, the state, the central bank, and foreign countries also act

R. Pauly, *Economic Instability and Stabilization Policy*,
https://doi.org/10.1007/978-3-658-33626-4_3

as players. The companies include private banks, which, like IT companies, offer their goods and services. They offer new products such as bonds, shares, and derivatives as well as services such as asset management for rich bank customers. Private banks are major players in the financial market. But they rarely appear in macroeconomic approaches as separate economic units as important players.

The state intervenes in market activities. It taxes income and sales. It uses tax revenues to finance transfer payments to households in precarious living conditions —part of its social policy—and subsidies to companies in difficult situations of radical change or with promising innovative strength—all part of its economic policy. Other expenditures are, roughly speaking, for education and internal and external security. EU member states also finance the EU budget. Tax revenues are usually not sufficient to cover all government spending. Therefore, it borrows additional money on the financial market. It gets into debt. It justifies its debt policy with its investments, which benefit future generations, and more recently mainly with the positive effects that its "deficit spending policy" has had on employment and growth. This spending policy is often denoted by the name of Keynes. We will discuss this in more detail in the following neoclassical ISLM model and in Minsky's economic concept in Sect. 3.2 "Main features of Minsky's macroeconomics".

The central bank channels money into the economy via the private banking system which forms the transmission channel through which central bank money flows into the economy. The central bank grants money to private banks against certain securities at the central bank interest rate, which varies according to macroeconomic objectives. It also adapts the security requirements to its macroeconomic goals. Central bank money is passed on by private banks to companies as loans to finance investments and is also profitably invested in financial investments, whether they use it to buy government or corporate bonds, to grant consumer loans or real estate loans to private households, or to buy shares or credit hedging instruments such as credit default swaps. The private banks benefit from their *privilege* of being able to channel central bank money into the economy. They earn money with every euro, every dollar, and every yen that they can channel into the economic system.

The central bank does not directly control the circulation of money in the economy. It can only indirectly control the flow of money from it to the economy through the private banks. To control the demand for money from the banks, it changes its central bank interest rates and also its security requirements. In times of crises, as in the recent recession, it buys real estate securities and government bonds, lends money at low central bank rates, and reduces the required security deposits. Its primary concern is to assume risks that weigh on the economy and to stimulate real investment. In most cases, the central bank is independent, at least formally, and is committed to macroeconomic goals. The US Federal Reserve, for example, is responsible for price stability, growth, and the functioning of the American banking system. Less comprehensive is the objective of the European Central Bank ECB, whose primary objective is to ensure price stability in the euro zone. But it wants to ensure the functioning of the financial market and also to defend the euro. To achieve these objectives, it too buys government bonds on the financial market. It is intended to relieve the financial pressure from states with high levels of debt financing and give them time to restructure their economies.

Similar to microeconomics, classical macroeconomics also postulates equilibrium in the markets. In view of the global economic crisis at the beginning of the previous century, with high unemployment and galloping inflation in Germany and deflation in the United States, the equilibrium postulate has lost much of its credibility. Keynes (1936) points out that underemployment can last longer. Keynes' remarks have provided the impetus for the neoclassical Hicks–Hansen ISLM model; John Richard Hicks (1904–1989) a British economist and Alvin Harvey Hansen (1887–1975) an American economist.

After that, the economy can remain in an underemployment equilibrium, and internal market forces—price mechanism and competition—are not sufficient to bring it back into a general equilibrium sufficiently quickly. The necessary impetus must come from outside. This is the foundation of Keynesian state interventionism, which, however, as a result of a permanent "deficit spending policy", leads to a national debt crisis and increases the instability of the financial market.

To gain an introduction to the ISLM model, we follow Keynes' view of his macroeconomic cycle approach. According to his "General Theory of Employment, Interest, and Money", entrepreneurs with N workers produce Y goods. Of these, households demand consumer goods C. If the entrepreneurs know the consumer demand C, they can produce just enough investment goods I that the total demand C + I equals their production Y. The plans of entrepreneurs and households are thus balanced on the goods market. And the part that households do not consume is equal to the investment I of the firms, i.e., I = S, the savings of households S.

To the traded goods Y, the flow of goods corresponds a monetary income Y for households, a flow of money. They save the money that they do not spent to buy goods. Their savings S households can invest in financial securities. They are faced with the decision to invest their money profitably in the long term or to keep it in liquid form and thus be prepared for unforeseen events at any time. Formally, Keynes captures this fact in the form of the liquidity function $L_2(i)$, which represents the speculative motives in the money demand of households. The higher the market interest rate i for financial securities, the more households demand them and the less money they hold in liquid form as a precaution. In addition, households ask for money to make their purchases. The higher their income Y is, the more money they ask for to buy goods. According to Keynes, this demand is captured by the transaction function $L_1(Y)$ depending on income Y. The function $L_1(Y)$ reflects the transactions motive for money demand of households. Together with the speculation function $L_2(i)$ depending on interest rate i, it forms the total household demand for money $L(Y, i)$, which is matched by the money supply M of the central bank. The private banks are *not* included.

If production Y falls below the full employment level Y_v, unemployment arises in the labor market. The state can then intervene to bring production Y back to the full employment level Y_v and thereby eliminate unemployment.

Now let us take a closer look at the ISLM model. It describes the goods market and the money market, illustrates how both markets work, and shows how they interact and how state intervention works. Let us start with the goods market and the so-called IS curve, which shows the equilibrium in this market. For the time being, let us exclude foreign countries; we look at a so-called closed economy, with state activity.

3.1.2 Commodity Market and Equilibrium Curve IS in the ISLM Model

Households demand goods for consumption, consumer goods C, companies demand investment goods I, and the state demands goods, for example, to ensure internal and external security, government consumption G. In equilibrium, total economic demand is equal to the production of goods by companies, the supply of goods Y

$$Y = C + I + G \quad \text{[Equilibrium on the commodity market]} \tag{3.1}$$

Equation (3.1) thus contains the equilibrium on the commodity market. Expenditures on goods also represent income, in this case, macroeconomic income Y. This results in the disposable income of households Yv after payment of income tax T(Y) and after receipt of the state transfer payment Tr

$$Yv = Y - T(Y) + Tr \quad \text{[Definition]} \tag{3.2}$$

The disposable income Yv determines consumption and the market interest rate i determines investment

$$C = C(Y - T(Y) + Tr) = C(Yv) \quad \text{[Consumer behavior]} \tag{3.3}$$

and

$$I = I(i) \quad \text{[Investment behavior]} \tag{3.4}$$

The consumption function C = C(Y) captures the propensity to consume of households. Of additional income, one part is spent, and the other is saved. Accordingly, the propensity to consume lies between 0 and 1. The same applies to the propensity to save. An example for a consumption function is the linear function $C = b + cY$, where c is the propensity to consume, $0 < c < 1$.

At interest rate *i*, firms can borrow on the financial market to finance their investments I. The interest rate i is an essential cost component in the external financing of the investments. With falling interest rate *i*, more and more investment projects become profitable, i.e., with falling market interest rate *i*, investments I increase. Firms invest when the expected profitability of investment projects is greater than the market interest rate, or more precisely, greater than the market interest rate plus risk premium, which is priced in because of future uncertainty.

According to Keynes, the *constellation between return, market interest rate, and risk premium* has a decisive influence on economic dynamics. The static ISLM approach does not consider this constellation, which can change significantly over time and, for simplicity, focuses only on the market interest rate *i*.

Disposable income Yv is used by households to buy goods C and the remaining income is saved. Thus, savings S and consumption C are also equal to income Yv

$$\mathrm{Yv} = \mathrm{C} + \mathrm{S} \tag{3.5}$$

If we replace Yv in Eq. (3.5) according to Eq. (3.2) by Y – T(Y) + Tr, we obtain a central macroeconomic relationship after transformation, namely

$$\mathrm{I}(i) + \mathrm{Df} = \mathrm{S}(\mathrm{Y}) \quad \text{[Equilibrium on the commodity market]} \tag{3.6}$$

where

$$\mathrm{Df} = \mathrm{G} + \mathrm{Tr} - \mathrm{T}(\mathrm{Y}) \tag{3.7}$$

is the state deficit. If, for the sake of simplicity, we do not consider the state deficit Df, Eq. (3.6) states that in the equilibrium of the goods market, the investment I of firms is equal to the savings S of households, which are the result of their consumption plans. This equilibrium statement is astonishing since consumption is directed to the present, whereas investment is directed to the future.

If one regards Eq. (3.6) in isolation, then one could come to the conclusion that intensified saving leads to higher investments. In the demand driven interdependent ISLM model, however, as we will see in the derivation of the IS curve, the opposite is true. Krugman (2012) points to this "paradox of thrift" and likes to stress that "your spending is my income, and my spending is your income" (2012, p. 28). Indeed, saving does not help in the case of underemployment, because increased saving reduces consumption C, and according to Eq. (3.1), reduces total demand and thus total income Y, and because of declining production, also the demand for labor N. According to Keynes, the actual driving forces for investing are the expected future profit flows, which depend very much on the abovementioned constellation of profitability, market interest rate, and risk premium. We will go into this in more detail later.

Let us take a closer look at the income Y (=supply of goods) and the interest rates *i* for which we have the equality I(i) = S(Y), and thus derive the equilibrium curve IS on the goods market in an (*i*, Y) diagram.

Households plan higher savings S with higher income Y. Companies plan to invest more at lower interest rates i. The lower the cost of debt financing, here covered by the market interest rate *i*, the more investment projects become profitable and the larger the companies' investment plans I. Thus, with higher income Y and low interest rate *i*, and with lower income Y and high interest rate *i*, the plans of households and companies coincide. Accordingly, the equilibrium curve IS in the

(i, Y) diagram has a negative slope. In Fig. 3.2, two IS curves are shown, which are derived from Fig. 3.1 in the excursus "Derivation of the equilibrium curve IS".

The dashed IS curve in Fig. 3.2 has a greater negative slope than the solid IS curve. The steeper gradient is due to a situation where investments I(i) react less to changes in interest rates i. This weak interest rate responsiveness of investments is due to circumstances where the profitability of investment projects is low and the risk of profit is high, such as in the recent economic crisis. If the responsiveness is close to zero, then the IS curve falls steeper and steeper and becomes vertical at the boundary.

With this extreme constellation, the economy is caught in the so-called *investment trap. In the event of unemployment, central bank policy aimed at lowering the market interest rate i no longer bears fruit.* It can then no longer work by lowering the market interest rate i to stimulate investment I(i) and thus production Y and the demand for labor N. In this situation, the market economy typically slides into crisis, monetary policy becomes ineffective.

An increase in the propensity to save in the savings function S(Y) has a similar effect to a decrease in interest rate responsiveness. This would also lead to a steeper drop in the IS curve. An economic crisis would be further aggravated by a greater propensity to save.

Excursus: Derivation of the Equilibrium Curve IS

In order to derive the IS curve, we specify three different interest rates in a comparative static analysis. In the (S,Y) diagram of Fig. 3.1, the savings function S(Y), which depends on income Y via consumption C(Y), is plotted with a positive slope—

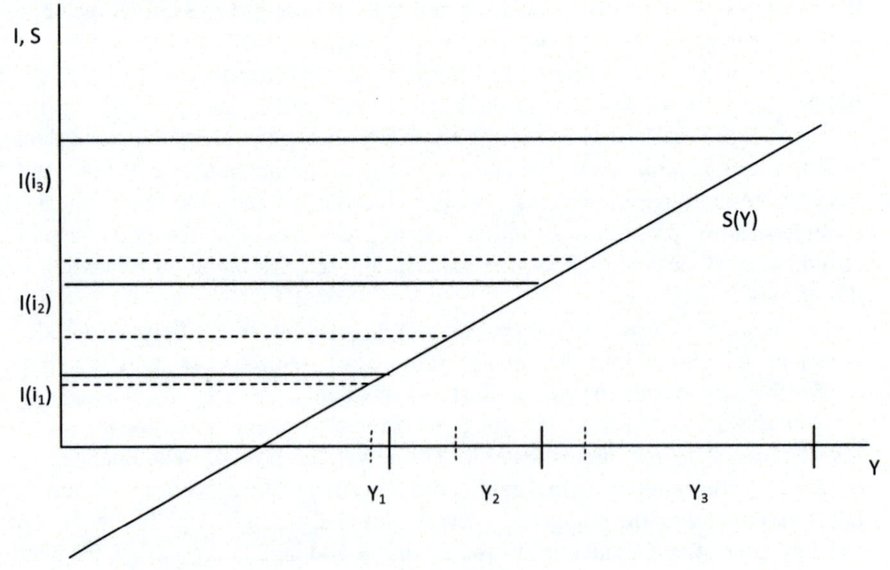

Fig. 3.1 Savings S(Y) and investments I(i) at alternative interest rates i

according to the linear consumption function $C = b + cY$, the savings function $S = -b + (1 - c)Y$, where $1 - c$ is the propensity to save, $0 < 1 - c < 1$; it is plotted very high for better representation in Fig. 3.1. In many industrialized countries it is close to 0.1 and in the consumer-driven US economy, it is significantly lower. Accordingly, the savings function in many real economies is significantly flatter than shown here. In addition, the three interest rates $i_1 > i_2 > i_3$ are marked with the investment function I (i) in the form of solid lines. They run parallel to the Y-axis, because here, according to the assumption, the investments are independent of the income Y. They depend on the conditions of external financing, which are covered by the market interest rate i. The cheaper the debt financing, the more investment projects are profitable. This is expressed in Fig. 3.1 by the fact that the parallel with the highest interest rate i_1 is closest to the Y-axis. Its intersection with the savings curve results in the low supply of goods Y_1. If the interest rate falls from i_1 to i_2, additional investment projects become profitable and the supply of goods increases to Y_2. Accordingly, the highest supply Y_3 results in the lowest interest rate i_3. The three points of intersection are shown in Fig. 3.2 and their connection produces the sought-after equilibrium curve IS in the (i, Y)-diagram.

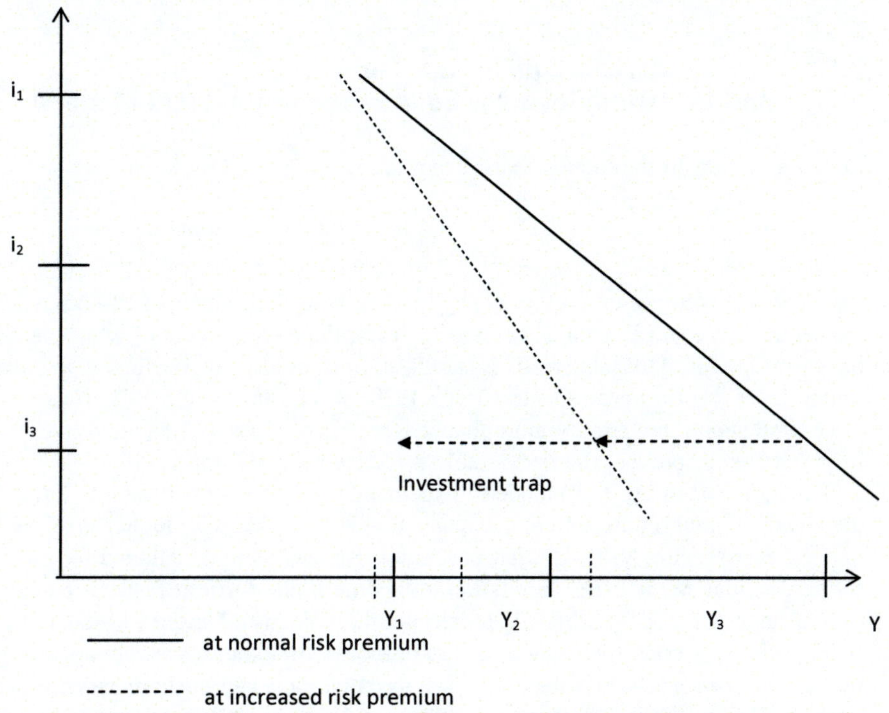

Fig. 3.2 IS curve [Equilibrium on the commodity market in (i,Y) constellations]

The distance between the parallels in Fig. 3.1 expresses the interest effect on the investment. The larger the distance, the more the investment reacts to a change in interest. If future profit prospects become cloudy, either because the profitability expectations decrease or because the uncertainty increases, which can only be compensated by additional hedging costs—i.e., the financing costs increase—then the parallel distance is reduced and thus the position of the equilibrium curve IS changes.

If interest rate sensitivity decreases due to lower future profitability or greater uncertainty in the future, the investment parallels shift downwards with decreasing distance; in Fig. 3.1 the dotted parallels show the decreasing interest rate sensitivity. In Fig. 3.2, the shift downwards causes the equilibrium curve IS to slip to the left and fall steeper. As a result, the equilibrium income Y decreases. Lower returns on investment thus cause the equilibrium income Y (=production of goods) to shrink. To counteract the decline in the production of goods, and thus the demand for labor, the central bank can increase its money supply and reduce the refinancing interest rate for commercial banks. However, this central bank intervention has little effect when interest rates are low. If the sensitivity is close to zero—the distance between the three investment parallels is further reduced in Fig. 3.1 and as a consequence, the IS curve in Fig. 3.2 falls steeper and steeper and becomes vertical at the boundary—*then the central bank policy is ineffective.*

3.1.3 Money Market, Equilibrium Curve LM, and Underemployment Equilibrium in the ISLM Model

Let us now turn to the money market and the LM curve. Here is

$$M/P = L_1(Y) + L_2(i) = L(Y, i) \quad \text{[Equilibrium on the money market]} \tag{3.8}$$

the equilibrium condition on the money market. M is the money supply offered by the central bank and P is the general price level, the development of which central banks are supposed to stabilize. This stabilization is, as already mentioned, the main objective of the European Central Bank ECB. According to the ECB treaty, the price level should not rise by more than 2% per year, otherwise it should intervene in the market to prevent the undesirable price increase, inflation.

The right side in Eq. (3.8) models the demand for money of households. $L_1(Y)$ is the so-called transaction function. It states that households with higher incomes Y demand more money to make their purchases. Keynes puts the demand for money for transactions $M_1 = L_1(Y)$ in relation to income in the form of Fisher's equation of exchange $M_1 = Y/V$, where V represents the velocity of money circulation. It will be relatively constant because the use of money for expenses should not change much, see Keynes (1936), Chap. 15, "The psychological and business incentives to liquidity". With the use of e-money, however, there is no longer any reason for supposing that V is a constant.

The situation is different for the liquidity or speculation function $L_2(i)$. The double name indicates the double face of the function $L_2(i)$. The name "liquidity" refers to the demand for money, and thus to the money market. The other name "speculation" refers to the demand for financial securities, and thus to the financial market. Households are faced with the choice of either keeping their money in reserve for short-term unforeseen expenses in bad times or investing their money profitably in financial securities in the longer term in order to build up assets that will provide them with an additional source of income. Households thus weigh up liquidity for precautionary purposes against speculation for future financial returns. When interest rates are higher, households invest more money in financial securities, thereby reducing their liquidity and their provision for future eventualities. Accordingly, when interest rates rise i, the liquidity function $L_2(i)$ falls.

In Minsky's approach, which emphasizes the role of the financial market, the speculative aspect plays a central role. And indeed, households are increasingly inclined to borrow, which is clearly reflected in the financing of property purchases—according to a graph from The Economist, the recent crisis is slowing down the increase in household debt in the USA. However, the slight decline since 2007 will lead to an increase again in 2013, see the "Re-leveraging" chart in The Economist (2014c, p. 56). Similar to the situation at private banks, where the capital buffer is shrinking, households' liquidity reserves for precautionary purposes are also likely to shrink. As a consequence of this trend, the liquidity function will also change over time.

As for the goods market, we want to determine the equilibrium curve LM for the money market. The higher the costs i for money are, the less money households demand. Therefore, the money demand function $L(Y, i)$ in the (i, M) diagram has a negative slope. If the costs i are close to zero, then the demand for money rises dramatically. Thus, the money demand function $L(Y, i)$ runs out flat when the interest rate i is low. With the same interest rate i, households demand more money for their transactions $L_1(Y)$ as their income Y grows. An increase in income Y thus shifts the money demand function $L(Y, i)$ to the right in the (i, M) diagram, as shown in Fig. 3.4 in the Excursus "Derivation of the equilibrium curve LM and underemployment equilibrium'. This means that as income Y increases, higher interest rates i are needed to match a fixed central bank money supply M_0 with household money demand plans $L(Y, i)$—higher interest rates i reduce household money demand $L_2(i)$ for liquidity in favor of Y-increased money demand $L_1(Y)$ for transactions, so that total money demand $L(Y, i)$ can remain at the level of money supply M_0. The equilibrium curve LM_0 belonging to M_0 thus has a positive slope in the (i, Y) diagram.

The equilibrium curve LM_0 is shown in Fig. 3.4, and the equilibrium curve LM_1, which belongs to the higher money supply M_1, $M_1 > M_0$, is shown dashed. The central bank lowers the equilibrium interest rates i in the equilibrium curve LM_1 by its higher money supply M_1; for each Y, the equilibrium interest rates i of LM_0 are greater than those of LM_1. In Fig. 3.4, the effect of central bank policy is expressed by the downward shift of the LM curve. Monetary policy thus lowers the interest rate i by increasing the money supply M via the money demand $L(Y, i)$ of

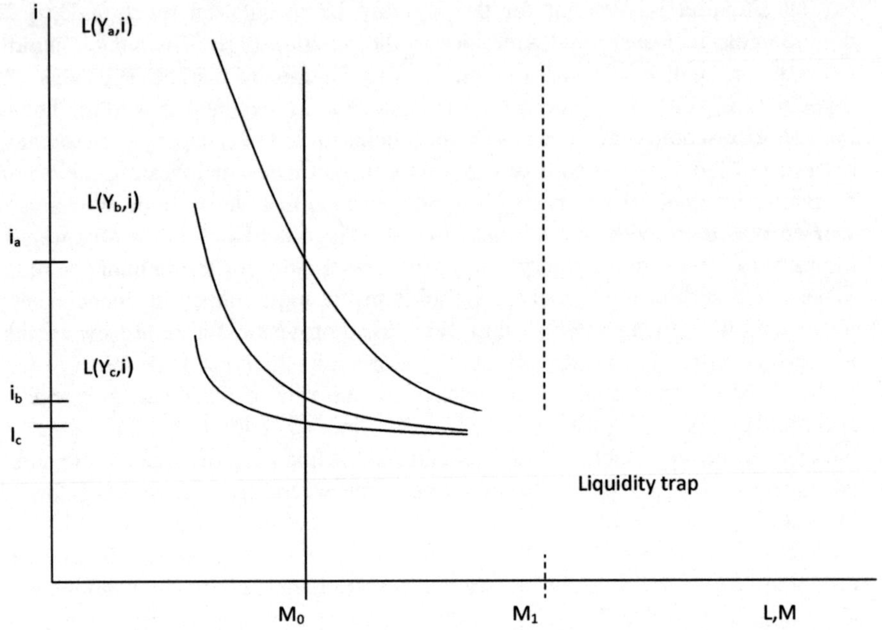

Fig. 3.3 Money supply M and money demand L(Y, *i*) for alternative income Y, $Y_a > Y_b > Y_c$

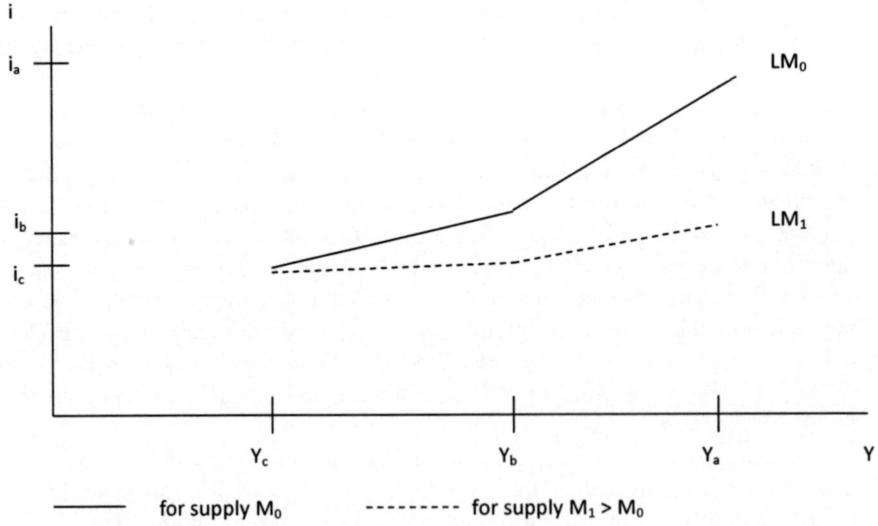

Fig. 3.4 LM curve [equilibrium on the money market]

households, and thus stimulates the investment demand I(*i*) of firms and thereby the total demand Y, which will be illustrated further in the following graphical analyses.

However, before we do so, we will enlarge upon the so-called *liquidity trap*, which sets limits to money supply policy. It consists in the fact that at high money supply M a further increase has no further effect on the position of the equilibrium curve LM, it then remains practically unchanged despite a drastic expansion of money supply—this is the case for money supply $M > M_1$ in Fig. 3.4. *This means that monetary policy no longer has any significant effect on production Y and on the demand for labor N.* The economy is then caught in the *liquidity trap*. And monetary policy can then have no significant effect on reducing unemployment.

Excursus: Derivation of the Equilibrium Curve LM and Underemployment Equilibrium

As with the goods market, we also want to graphically depict the supply and demand structure for the money market. Figure 3.3 illustrates in a (*i*, M) diagram the demand for money L(Y, *i*) for three income units $Y_a > Y_b > Y_c$. The central bank money supply M_0 is exogenous. It is, therefore, independent of the interest rate *i* and represents the perpendicular to M_0 in Fig. 3.3. Its intersection with the three money demand curves provides three points of equilibrium in the money market and their connection gives the equilibrium curve LM in Fig. 3.4. An increase in the money supply from M_0 to M_1 shifts the curve LM downwards, indicated by the dotted lines in Figs. 3.3 and 3.4, i.e., the equilibrium interest rate falls. The increase in the money supply from M_0 to M_1 still causes a significant shift in the equilibrium curve LM. This is different in the area above M_1. There the distance between the three money demand functions L(Y, *i*) shrinks when the money supply M is high, so that an increase in money supply beyond M_1 has no significant effect on the equilibrium curve LM. In this constellation, the economy is caught in the *liquidity trap*: a change in the money supply by the central bank fizzles out and no longer has any effect on the interest rate. Additionally, it cannot stimulate investment I and thus cannot stimulate economic growth.

Figure 3.5 presents an equilibrium curve IS together with the equilibrium curve LM_0. Their point of intersection is the equilibrium in the goods and money market. According to Fig. 3.5, this simultaneous equilibrium of the two markets is at a supply of goods Y_u, which is below full employment production Y_v. In the case of Y_u, one can speak of an *involuntary unemployment as an equilibrium* in so far as the goods and money market are in equilibrium, but not the labor market. A wage reduction could increase the demand for labor there. However, wages W are not very flexible downwards. Workers will defend themselves against wage cuts with their trade unions out of self-interest. Especially since they can point out that wage cuts may also result in a loss of income and consequently a contraction of total demand Krugman (2012) refers to this fact in his "*paradox of flexibility*".

An example of recent wage rigidity is France. Despite the economic crisis, real wages there have continued to rise since 2007, see The Economist (2014d, p. 65). The Conseil d'analyse economique (CAE) explains the increase by the fact that

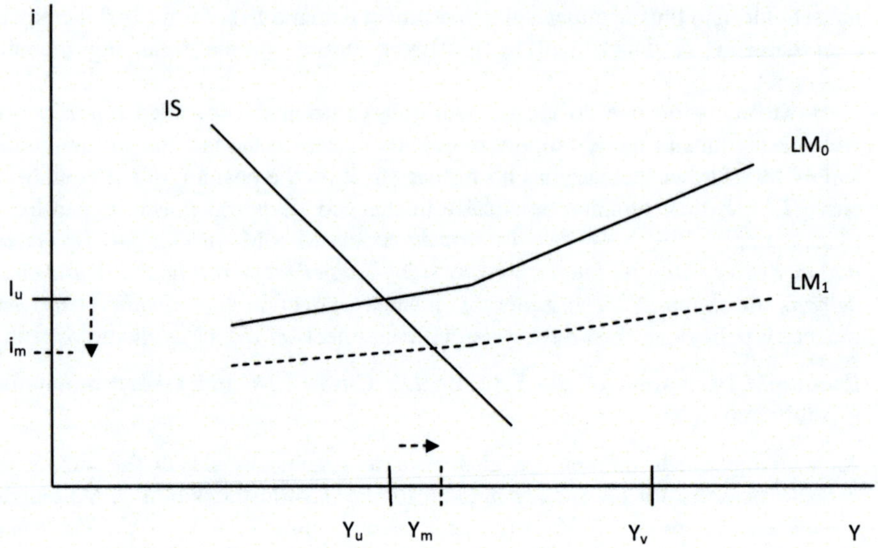

Fig. 3.5 Equilibrium on commodity and money market in case of underemployment Y_u Increasing money supply from M_0 to M_1 does not ensure the full employment equilibrium Y_v

companies in France prefer to reduce employment rather than wages to safeguard productivity: "Pour préserver la motivation des travailleurs et le climat social, deux déterminants essentiels de la productivité, les entreprises préfèrent reduire l'emploi que les salaires", observe le CAE, cf. Le Monde (2014).

The supply of goods Y_u in Fig. 3.5 corresponds to underemployment on the labor market—the link is the macroeconomic production function F(N, K, TF), in which employment—the number of workers N—together with the production capital K and technical progress TF determines the production of goods Y and its growth $g = \Delta Y/Y$, as explained in Sect. 4.8 "Capital, growth and sluggish growth". Underemployment means underutilization of production capacity. In other words, there is an excess supply on the labor market. According to the price mechanism, which we know from microeconomics, the excess supply would have to reduce wages and thus provide an increase in employment, which would ultimately lead the production of goods to increase to full employment production Y_V. However, the effect will not be sufficiently rapid or strong enough due to the low downward flexibility of wages W. The *low downward flexibility of wages (stickiness of wages, wage trap)* is one of the main reasons for a persistent underemployment equilibrium. The market mechanism no longer leads the economy toward full employment equilibrium, the general equilibrium. It persists in this socially fatal imbalance with unemployment. Only impulses from outside, from the state, can help overcome the crisis.

Keynes has pointed out that this underemployment equilibrium may last longer. According to Keynes, because of the "liquidity trap", it is not so much monetary policy as government spending policy, above all, that can cure the market failure. In view of the high level of unemployment in the global economic crisis after the First World War, the Keynesian thesis of a longer-lasting underemployment equilibrium has been very popular and has opened the door widely to macroeconomic state interventionism, which has ultimately led to the public debt crisis in market-economy industrialized countries through the permanent deficit spending policy. A deficit spending policy can stabilize employment in the short term, but in the long term, it increases instability on the financial market through debt—the external financing of expenditure.

3.1.4 Government Intervention to Stabilize the Commodity and the Labor Market: Fiscal and Monetary Policy

As already indicated, the effectiveness of public intervention to achieve full employment and thus free society from the scourge of unemployment depends on economic constellations which are more or less favorable to state intervention. Unfavorable is a *low interest rate sensitivity of investment*, which may include an *investment trap* at the edge, and unfavorable is also *a low interest rate sensitivity of the LM equilibrium curve to an increase in the money supply*. According to Figs. 3.3 and 3.4, this is the case when the change in money supply takes place in the area of the *liquidity trap*.

An increase in the central bank money supply from M_0 to M_1 has an indirect effect on aggregate demand Y. In a long chain of effects via household behavior in the money market, it causes a reduction in interest rates, which, in turn, increases investment I by firms, thereby ultimately stimulating aggregate demand of goods Y and demand for labor N. Figure 3.5 illustrates the effect of the money supply increase. The point of intersection of the LM_1 curve with the IS curve shifts to the lower right. As a result, the interest rate falls from i_u to i_m, and consequently, the investment activity of entrepreneurs increases, thereby raising production from Y_u to Y_m. However, this positive effect of the money supply increase will not materialize if investment demand is less sensitive to interest rates. This is because, as noted in Fig. 3.2 under "investment trap", the IS curve falls sharply, so that there is practically no interest rate reduction effect. Especially in economic crisis, interest rate responsiveness is likely to be low, because then uncertainty increases and profitability expectations thus fall. On the other hand, the risk premium increases, so that investment projects remain less and less profitable.

According to Fig. 3.5, the increase in the money supply on M_1 is too small to achieve full employment production Y_v by lowering interest rates, Y_m is significantly below Y_v. However, a further increase in the money supply beyond M_1 into the area of the liquidity trap remains *ineffective*. This is because the equilibrium curve LM_1 is not shifted significantly downwards any further, so that the further increase in the money supply has practically no interest rate effect and thus no employment effect.

Overall, *monetary policy does not appear to be particularly effective on its own.* For in times of crises, the confidence of entrepreneurs in future profits darkens. Declining yield expectations reduce the interest rate responsiveness of investments, and because of the low level of responsiveness, money supply increases have a little stimulating effect on investment. And these are crucial in the capitalist economy if full employment and economic growth are to be achieved in the longer term.

In the ISLM model, besides the money supply M, government expenditure G and the income tax rate T(•) are instrument variables. More effective than the money supply M is the instrument "government expenditure" G, at least in the *short term.* It can *directly* close the demand gap and ensure full employment in a targeted manner. Figure 3.6 makes this clear. According to Eq. (3.6), I + Df = S, an increase in deficit-financed government spending G produces via Df, in Fig. 3.1, an upward shift in the three investment parallels, and thus a rightward shift in the equilibrium curve IS. The new IS curve with higher income is shown as a dashed line in Fig. 3.6. It intersects the LM_0 curve at the point (i_d, Y_v). The increase in expenditure ensures full employment and thus a general equilibrium. It is important that the additional government expenditure—as the name deficit suggests—is debt financed. This is because tax-financed expenditure reduces consumption and thus increases savings; tax-financed expenditure turns the savings function in the upper left-hand corner in Fig. 3.1, and this effect in itself, as we know, would reduce output.

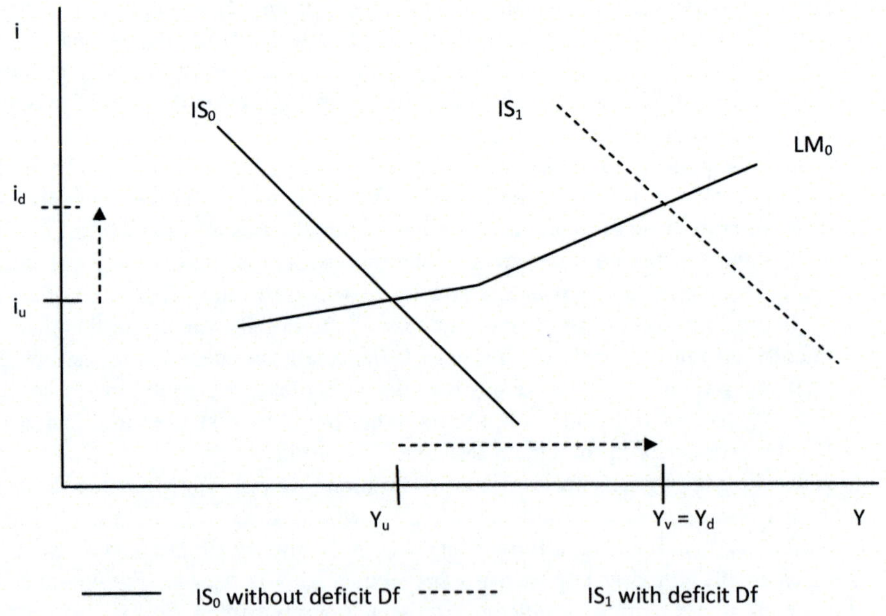

Fig. 3.6 Equilibrium on commodity and money market in case of underemployment Y_u Increasing government expenditure G with a deficit Df ensures a general equilibrium Y_v

In practice, this deficit spending policy has proved to be effective over a long period of time in a number of countries to close macroeconomic demand gaps. Initially, Keynes advocated deficit spending as a temporary stimulus to overcome the scourge of unemployment in times of cyclical underutilization of production capacity. In the meantime, politicians are permanently applying this policy and using it to generate growth as well.

In Fig. 3.6, it is also noteworthy that government deficit policies lead to a higher interest rate $i_d > i_u$. The increased government demand thus crowds out investment I(i) and weakens the growth momentum of the economy in the longer term. The interest rate increase can be avoided by combining government expenditure policy with monetary policy. The result of a joint intervention is shown in Fig. 3.7: Full employment is achieved at the lower interest rate $i_{md} < i_u$. Private investment is not crowded out.

To sum up in a first conclusion: *The market can fail, the state can fix it, not so much through its monetary policy as through its fiscal policy, for the sake of public welfare. That is the Keynesian narrative of the regulating state.*

A nice result, but its brilliance is clouded by the extreme constellations of "investment and liquidity trap". Following Minsky's concept, we will ask ourselves what price society has to pay for permanent state intervention and then draw another conclusion.

Before we critically assess the ISLM approach, we would like to discuss a modification that is linked to the term "wealth effect" or "real balance effect". Monetary policy has shown that an increase in money supply from M_0 to M_1 can in

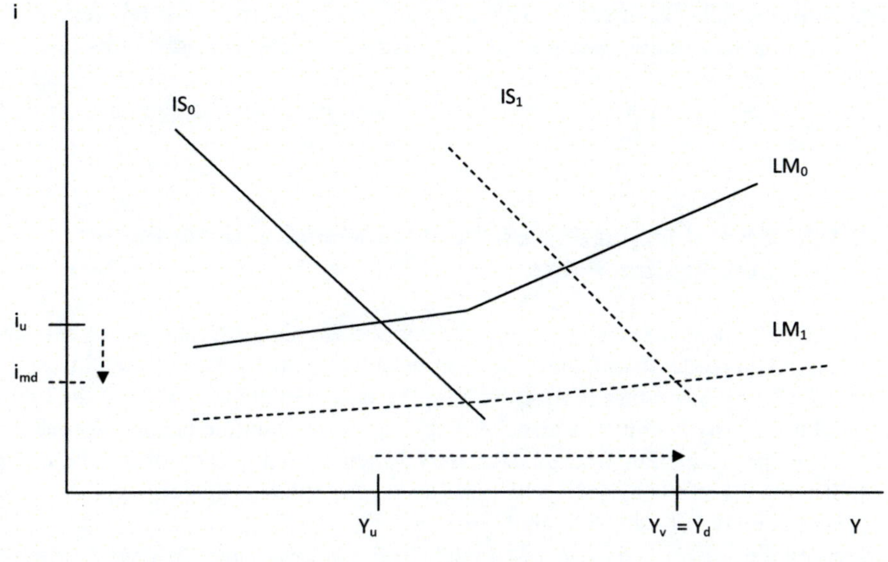

Fig. 3.7 Equilibrium on commodity and money market in case of underemployment Y_u Money and fiscal policy together ensure a general equilibrium Y_v

principle contribute to stabilizing the economy. A larger money supply pushes underemployment production Y_u upwards toward full employment production Y_v. A falling price level P, deflation, has a corresponding effect. This is because it increases the real money supply M/P in Eq. (3.8), and thus analogous to M_1, shifts the money supply in Fig. 3.3 to the right and the equilibrium curve LM in Fig. 3.4 to the bottom. As we know from the graphical analysis, this leads to an expansion of production from Y_u toward Y_v. This effect is reinforced by the so-called "wealth effect". It acts via the consumption function Eq. (3.9), if this is extended by the "real assets" M/P to

$$C = C(Yv, M/P) \tag{3.9}$$

In this expansion, which is linked to the name of the Israeli American economist Don Patinkin (1922–1995), a falling price level, deflation, generates higher consumption C via the "wealth increase" M/P; this shifts the savings function in Fig. 3.1 and also the IS curve in Fig. 3.5 to the right, which ultimately increases the supply of goods Y even further toward full employment production. This wealth effect is mainly of theoretical interest, since it shows that within the extended neoclassical ISLM model, market forces can bring about a full employment equilibrium.

This expansion is interesting in that it highlights wealth as another important determinant that positively influences consumption. The US Federal Reserve also considers wealth to be an important influencing factor. It regards bond and share values rather than the money supply as a suitable approximation variable for wealth. In crises, such as the recent ones, prices of bonds and shares and thus the propensity to consume fall, which can lead to a worsening of the crises. For this reason, the Fed's monetary policy measures are also aimed at stabilizing securities prices in order to prevent a collapse in consumption in the USA. Even though the ownership of securities in the USA is comparatively broad, price stabilization tends to favor the rich.

3.1.5 Critical Evaluation of the ISLM Model and the Public Stabilization Policy

The ISLM model is a static interdependent model for the goods and money markets. In the ISLM model, fiscal policy has a direct effect on the goods market through its deficits Df by increasing production Y in the equilibrium curve IS, and the higher equilibrium production Y is associated with an increase in the demand for labor N through the production function. Monetary policy, with its supply of money M, acts indirectly via the behavior of households on the money market. An increase in money supply, via the household money demand function L(Y, *i*), causes the equilibrium interest rate *i* in LM to fall, and the lower interest rates *i* stimulate business investment I(*i*), and via this, total demand for goods Y and for labor N. As we shall see, economic transformation is changing the mechanisms of economic processes and the sequence of effects of state intervention. *In line with Minsky, the growing importance of the financial market is particularly noteworthy. As we shall see, it is not so much households as private banks that play the central role here.*

The ISLM model is a *formal* framework in which the relationships between key macroeconomic *flow variables* such as investment I, production Y, and consumption C are structured. The model describes how household and business decisions interact. Household consumption determines the production of firms, and firms determine household income, which, in turn, is the basis for their consumption decisions. The interest rate determines the investments made by firms and, remarkably, it depends on the liquidity preference of households. These *interactions* are typical of economic processes; economists speak of *interdependence.*

In the ISLM model, the flow variables consumption C, income Y of investment I, and government expenditure G are at the center of the economic analysis, and money supply M is a *stock variable*. We will see later in Minsky's treatment on economic instability that, as debt financing continues, another stock variable, debt D, will play a significant role in economic activity.

In addition to the interest rate *i*, the labor market comes into indirect play with downwardly inflexible wages W. The inflexibility leads to longer-lasting underemployment, to longer unemployment. And this evil cannot be tolerated inactively by society. The *market failure calls for state intervention* to free society from the burden of unemployment.

The ISLM model represents a simple, coherent, and closed concept. It brings order to the interaction of macroeconomic variables and allows fundamental questions to be discussed at the macroeconomic level: is there a general equilibrium, under what conditions can an economy remain in an underemployment equilibrium for a longer period of time, by what means can and should the state intervene in the economic cycle in the event of market failures? The discussion is based on *comparative-static analyses.* We consider alternative economic constellations, which are reflected in graphical analyses in the form of the equilibrium curves IS and LM and their shifts. Generations of students of economics worldwide learn about a central core of the economic mechanism at the macro level using the *ISLM model. It forms the foundation for government market interventions, the basis for fiscal and monetary policy.*

The state intervenes in the interdependent economic process in order to correct any disturbances that occur. Disturbances are considered to be when unemployment and inflation are too high, which leads to excessive monetary devaluation and a substantial loss of wealth. The state thus acts in a specific context, its actions are, therefore, *context-dependent and not independent*. In this light, the state is also part of the interdependent economic cycle and its actions will, in turn, involve other players such as companies, and in particular, private banks.

Although the central bank is formally independent, it is not bound by instructions. But its actions are geared to economic activity and are, therefore, increasingly dependent on it. While Keynesian economic stabilization is based on deficit policy, in particular, the stabilization of the economy has recently been based to a greater extent on monetary policy in view of the high debt levels. Keynesian deficit policy has shot its bolt. The national debt has turned it into a blunt weapon. Nowadays, no state can do without cheap money from the central bank. The stabilization of the goods and labor market must increasingly be handled by monetary policy alone, although, as the ISLM model shows, it is less effective than fiscal policy. The focus has shifted over time. It is now less focused on stabilizing the economy than on stabilizing the financial system to ensure the functioning of the economy as a whole.

Although Hayek is strongly committed to entrepreneurial freedom in the market economy, he does not deny that stabilizing the economy is a state task. He states in his paper "The Constitution of Liberty" (Hayek 1960, p. 230): "Nobody will deny that economic stability and the prevention of major depressions depends in part on government action". However, Hayek also sees monetary policy as dependent on trade union wage demands. Like Keynes, he points out that wages are sticky, even in the case of underemployment. According to him, the trade unions are fighting for higher nominal wages W despite unemployment, so that the central bank is forced to raise the price level P through an expansive money supply policy in order to boost employment and the economy by reducing real wages W/P. According to him, this creates a dangerous wage-price spiral. Hayek argues here in view of the situation in England at the time.

Today the framework conditions are of a different kind. Today, central bank policy is under pressure from the threat of deflation, high government debt, and under pressure from the threat of falling wealth, and at the ECB, under the pressure of the break-up of the euro zone.

The Keynesian narrative has increasingly distanced itself from its theoretical basis with the transformation of the economy and state intervention.

3.1.6 The ISLM Model and the Power of Simplification

The ISLM model captures the interactions between the goods and money markets in a closed approach. The interdependence shows that primarily positive effects of state intervention can be counteracted by negative secondary effects. To simplify matters, let us consider the goods market in isolation and thus cut the relationship with the money market. In this simplified partial analysis, a deficit-financed increase in government expenditure ΔG leads to an increase in output ΔY of $1/(1 - c)$. We can easily understand this result, because with (3.1) $Y = C + I + G$ and with the consumption function $C = b + c(Y - T)$ we obtain after transformation

$$Y = [1/(1 - c)](b - cT + I + G) \tag{3.10}$$

and thus

$$\Delta Y = [1/(1 - c)]\Delta G.$$

An increase in expenditure ΔG thus increases total output Y by a factor of 1/(1 − c). If the propensity to consume c = 0.9, the factor is equal to 10, which is called a multiplier because of the strong effect. According to the so-called Haavelmo theorem, if the increase in expenditure is financed by taxes, the multiplier is 1. This can easily be seen from the above relationship for Y if we take into account that the increase in expenditure is financed by an equivalent increase in taxes, i.e., ΔG = ΔT, formally

$$\Delta Y = [1/(1-c)]\Delta G - [c/(1-c)]\Delta T = 1\,\Delta G.$$

The multiplier is a simple and fascinating result, which at first glance clearly speaks in favor of increased state intervention. At second glance, however, one becomes suspicious. Can a constantly continuing deficit policy really become an inexhaustible source of growth? It is too good to be true, common sense will tell you, that a continuous expansion of government spending will keep increasing national income; the state cannot so easily make society happy.

And indeed, the multiplier result is based on inadmissible simplifications, but the power of simplification makes deficit-financed public expenditure policy in particular attractive.

The inadmissible simplification consists of the fact that the *partial analysis* is separated from the *interdependent economic events* and that the *comparative-static analysis* result is seen to be detached from the *economic dynamics.*

If we return to the extended ISLM model, we know about the crowding-out effect of a government spending increase. According to Fig. 3.6, deficit spending policy leads to an increase in interest rate i and this knock-on effect causes investments I to decline. However, as we will see in Minsky's profit-investment dynamics, they are a very central variable in the capitalist development process. This is endangered by rising interest rates *i*. The multiplier analysis in the partial model omits this danger. Like the ISLM model, it also excludes the longer-term consequences of a permanent deficit policy in the form of rising debt.

Multipliers from the comparative static analysis have a qualitative but not a quantitative economic policy relevance. The actual quantitative and numerical effects of an increase in government spending over time can only be analyzed in a "correctly specified" global and dynamic model. Econometric models have been designed for a statistically reliable numerical estimate. We will look at their performance from the Keynesian perspective later in Sect. 4.10 "Economic processes and their analysis".

The ISLM approach, as explained above, provides a formal framework that enables economic constellations to be discussed in a *comparative static form. It is neither a quantitative nor a dynamic model*. It is, therefore, not possible to use this approach to estimate how strong and how quickly state intervention will have an effect. This is the kind of information that the public wants to know, and it is often provided, but usually without any foundation. We will also discuss this in Sect. 4.10.

With their ISLM model, Hicks and Hansen have *closed the open* Keynesian approach by assuming, in a simplistic way, that the investment depends *solely* on the market interest rate *i*. Although the interest rate is an important indicator variable, it cannot adequately capture the causal complex of investment activity. With this simplifying investment assumption, the ISLM model closes itself off from investment processes at the microeconomic level, which decisively influences macro-relations and their changes over time: essential elements of the economic process are thus excluded from the formal ISLM model.

3.1.7 Microeconomic Dynamics, Debt Financing, Profits, and Expectations

In his central work "The General Theory of Employment, Interest, and Money" Keynes emphasizes the dynamics of economic processes. Keynes' approach is *open* to a variety of dynamic processes that interlock below the macro level at the microeconomic level. This is particularly true for investment processes. Entrepreneurs make investment decisions today in order to make profits in the future. To this end, they develop new products and new production processes. Development takes time. Not all products are, as expected, successful on the market. A number of them turn out to be profitable innovations, others are flops. Opportunities and risks are close together. Development work and marketing on international markets strengthens companies' know-how and thus their long-term competitiveness.

It is pointless to argue about why certain new products attract lively demand and others do not. In any case, buyers welcome innovation, and so progress continues. The market economy offers entrepreneurs the freedom for development which is the basis for economic dynamism and growth and social prosperity. If the state restricts this freedom too much, it weakens entrepreneurial drive and thus growth. Hayek (1960) often refers to this.

Whether newly developed goods will be as profitable as expected is uncertain and will only become apparent after some time through future sales revenues and also future financing conditions. Profits are the driving force for investment. And entrepreneurs can increase returns by using debt capital in addition to their own resources. With debt financing, the market interest rate comes into play. It is variable and can change abruptly in times of crises, as can the risk, which can abruptly put pressure on expectations of profitability.

The return on equity depends on the constellation between project return, market interest rate, and risk premium. This constellation is unstable and highly responsive to fluctuations in sales on the goods market and to uncertainties on the financial market: return, market interest rate, and risk together determine investment activity and not just the market interest rate. The constellation between the three determinants changes over the course of the business cycle, and this change has a strong impact on the investment decisions of entrepreneurs.

With increasing debt financing, the opportunities but also the risks of investments increase. According to Minsky, it endangers the stability of the capitalist economic system, of which Keynes was still convinced. He regarded underemployment as a cyclical rather than a structural problem. According to Keynes, the state should temporarily intervene in economic activity. However, through its deficit policy it intervenes permanently and thus systematically increases debt financing in the economy, which leads to enormous debt levels, and thus permanently burdens economic development. Debt financing permeates the entire economy, and this permeation is expressed by the new term "financialization of the economy".

Debt financing, as mentioned above, not only increases the opportunities, but also the risks of an investment, whether in tangible assets or in financial securities. The same applies to the externally financed purchase of real estate or a work of art. The increase results from the so-called *leverage effect*. We will go into this effect in more detail later and illustrate it in detail with examples in Sect. 4.6 "Debt financing and risks: good times and bad times".

A formula based on the leverage ratio v shows the extent to which debt financing affects opportunities and risks. Here, the leverage ratio v puts the debt capital DC in relation to the equity capital EC, v = DC/EC. According to Eq. (3.11), the leverage ratio v, the market interest rate i and the risk premium rz determine the return on equity r_e from the project return r_p as follows:

$$r_e = r_p + v(r_p - i \cdot rz). \tag{3.11}$$

The development of the return on equity r_e determines the future profits Π which the current investments I should generate.

Without a high level of debt, a high leverage ratio v, Deutsche Bank would not be able to target a return on equity of 25%, as it did under its CEO Ackermann. For banks, however, the difference between project return r_p and market interest rate i is less important than the difference between market interest rate i and the central bank interest rate.

A small example shows us how the leverage of debt financing works. Here the project yield r_p is 0.08 and exceeds the market interest rate $i = 0.06$ by only 0.02. Nevertheless, the leverage ratio v = 8 causes the return on equity r_e to rise to 0.24, thus increasing the project yield by a factor of 3 from 8 to 24%

$$r_e = 0.08 + 8(0.08 - 0.06) = 0.24$$

The example contains no risk premium, rz = 1.

The leverage ratio v is variable and reflects changing expectations in economic conditions. The same applies to the risk premium rz. In boom periods, bright prospects make ratio v grow and in recession periods, lower expectations make ratio v shrink. And so, it reinforces the upswing and downturn. Thus, the constellation between project returns, market interest rates, and risk premiums changes over the course of the economic cycle. Companies are aware of the financing conditions, at least in the short term. By contrast, the calculation of project returns is based on expected future revenue flows. The expectations are revised according to actual market developments. For example, stock corporations report on their sales situation quarterly, also publishing their outlook for future market revenues.

The upturn with its higher revenues leads to an upward revision of project returns, and the improved market opportunities provide an impetus for increased debt financing. And the rise in the *leverage ratio* v suggests an increased return on equity. In the downturn, in the economic crisis, with shrinking revenues, companies revise their project returns downwards. They cannot easily get out of the currently costly debt financing. They can now only replace expiring loans with new ones at poorer conditions because lenders hedge the increased risk with a risk premium.

To make profits in the future, entrepreneurs invest today. And the interdependence between profit Π and investment I over time carries the capitalist dynamic, Minsky emphasizes. Innovations are the driving force behind this, they ensure competitiveness, and debt financing increases the prospects of profit. Like Keynes, he gives time a central place in the dynamic economic processes. Investment is at the heart of it. It is through investment that entrepreneurs look to the future. They invest when they can expect their current investments to pay off in the future. Profitability depends not only on future sales proceeds, but also on future financing conditions. This is because a large proportion of today's investment projects are debt financed at variable conditions and are therefore subject to future financial market conditions. And times change; good times quickly turn into bad times.

Investment decisions are, therefore, based on expectations. In contrast to models of rational expectation—they go back to the American economists J. F. Muth (1930–2005) and R. E. Lucas (1937), the latter received the Nobel Prize for his work on rational expectation (1995)—these cannot be expectations in the mathematical sense. What do we already know in detail about what may happen tomorrow, and how should we be able to reliably assign probabilities to individual events? Keynes (1937) argues in a similar way and even speaks of "*pseudo realistic notions*" on p. 13. Expectations enter our future calculations differently. According to Keynes, economic entities base their expectations on the economic trend, knowing full well that these expectations are subject to constant change. They are, therefore, prepared to react to changes in trends as soon as a change in the economy becomes apparent. Optimistic attitudes of economic players toward economic development replace pessimistic ones. Prior to these different attitudes, Keynes (1937) also analyses the consequences of a shrinking population on the demand for goods and labor.

The expectations of economic entities on future profits and losses are unstable (myopic expectations on future profits and losses). They adapt quickly to real economic fluctuations, and especially in times of upheaval, overstate the real situation. Optimism quickly turns into pessimism, and through the activities it triggers, has a knock-on effect on the real economy. The propensity of households to consume declines and so does the propensity of firms to invest. External debt intensifies this reaction. Particularly due to the high level of debt, these days the state lacks the scope for counteracting it with a deficit policy.

Companies arm themselves against unforeseeable events by taking precautions. They do this in many different ways. Export-oriented companies use contracts on the financial market to protect themselves against currency fluctuations, while airlines also protect themselves against volatility on the oil market. As we will see, the financial market offers a number of innovations for hedging financial risks. Adequate equity ratios can contribute to security. The international Basel rules apply to private banks to ensure sufficient equity ratios. Households make provisions for future imponderables by means of their liquidity fund. States do not need to do this as a matter of principle. Their central bank can provide them with liquidity. The case of the euro countries is different. The ECB is prohibited from providing state financing. These states would have to have a buffer and be financially flexible, especially in economic downturns, because raising money through tax increases or cuts in social benefits exacerbates the crisis and causes social tensions.

In his comments on dynamics, Keynes goes into detail about the risk in economic development and also about how economic entities form their expectations about future uncertain developments. They form the basis of the Keynes-Minsky momentum, which captures how an economic turnaround can lead to a crisis. The turnaround leads to the disappointment of previous expectations, and according to Hayek, the change in expectations is accompanied by a learning process: "Man learns by the disappointment of expectations" (Hayek 1960, p. 28). And sometimes only bitter real losses force a rethink.

Economic developments take place on two levels, in the world of real decisions (real world), which manifest themselves in the variables: consumption C, investment I, and return on equity r_e, and in the world of expectations (world of expectations), which influence what happens in the real world, and vice versa. The Keynes-Minsky momentum describes interactions between both worlds.

3.1.8 Keynes-Minsky Momentum

According to Keynes, *two types of risk* affect the volume of investment: The first is the *entrepreneur's or borrower's risk and the second is the lender's risk*, see Keynes (1936), section IV in Chap. 11 "The marginal efficiency of capital". The future return on current investment projects depends on the expected revenue streams. They may be lower than expected and may reduce the return to such an extent that it falls below the market interest rate. In retrospect, the projects prove to be unprofitable. It would have been more advantageous for the entrepreneur to put his money into a financial investment at the market interest rate. Keynes refers to this as entrepreneurial risk. If today's investments are also financed by debt, as usual, the lender is subject to the risk that the borrower, the entrepreneur, will no longer be able to meet his payment obligations under the loan agreement because of the lower revenue streams.

Now any investment can be seen as a risky business, as a venture. From an entrepreneurial point of view, the expected return should therefore be higher than the market interest rate plus a sufficient risk premium. Accordingly, lenders want to protect themselves against the risk of a loan default and demand a risk premium on top of the market interest rate. Keynes sees this double risk premium as an amplifier of economic fluctuations. This is because it can amplify both the boom phase—the upswing—and the recession phase—the downturn. This is due to the asymmetrical perception of risk. In an upswing, risk is ignored and opportunities are seen.

Boom periods open up new possibilities and new opportunities that many households and businesses do not want to miss. There is a situation of "over confidence, error of optimism". Households buy real estate and shares, and in doing so they are betting on increases in value. They increase their purchasing power through debt financing. Companies see new sales opportunities and thus new sources of profit and start additional investment projects that now seem worthwhile. And they increase their return on equity through increased debt financing. Banks promote debt financing through a higher financing leverage because this is the business that brings them profits.

At the end of the boom the outlook darkens, value increases fail to materialize, business prospects cloud over, and sales expectations have to be revised downwards. Prosperity leads to a recession. Banks become more cautious in their lending. The risk is reflected in the rise in financing costs, an increase in the risk premium. The continuation of so-called Ponzi financing becomes more difficult, refinancing debt, rescheduling, becomes more expensive, parts of the revenue streams have to be redirected into current financing, investments are cut back, and consumer spending is delayed. Deflation threatens. The profit-investment dynamic is slowed down. To avert insolvency, securities have to be sold and their market prices fall. As assets fall, the propensity to consume continues to decline, and despite the sale of assets, falling prices threaten to increase real debt, as we know from Fisher (1933) and Krugman (2012).

In a downturn, when the risk becomes visible in the form of imminent insolvency, it is perceived as overly large. The state of confidence changes abruptly into a state of fear (over fear, error of pessimism) when the economy turns into a recession. The expectation of continued prosperity disappears and the latent fears that one's own and the general situation could deteriorate become clearly visible. The change—well-founded in real terms and exaggerated in perception—causes risk premiums to rise abruptly, with the consequence that investments with low liquidity must be liquidated prematurely and quickly. The downturn thus leads to a crisis. The turnaround is the core of the Keynes-Minsky momentum, which makes the economic process unstable. Much trust is lost in the turnaround to recession, especially between creditors and debtors, and it takes a long time to rebuild trust. The Keynes-Minsky momentum will be discussed more often.

This momentum is often associated with the name Minsky. It describes the shift from stable to unstable situations in the recently highly leveraged economy. Keynes aims at reversals in the goods and labor market. The mechanism hardly differs, so we call it *Keynes-Minsky momentum*. The Economist points to more recent behavioral studies that show fluctuations in risk propensity over time, see The Economist (2014a).

The central banks, in particular the Fed, want to counteract this turnaround. The turnaround is forcing economic entities to sell their financial assets in order to become liquid again. A massive sale of bonds and shares causes prices to tumble. This downward spiral has two effects. On the one hand, the sales are generating less and less revenue. More must be sold than expected. And on the other hand, assets are dwindling. According to the "wealth effect", declining wealth reduces the propensity to consume. In order to avoid this spill-over effect from the financial market to the goods market, the Fed makes substantial purchases of government bonds and mortgage-backed securities. This purchase keeps interest rates low for the government, thus easing the burden on government spending and creating favorable financing and refinancing conditions for the real estate market. The ECB, the Bank of England, and the Bank of Japan are acting in a similar way.

It is the increasing tendency to borrow from outside sources that is leading to a highly debt financed economy that is increasingly vulnerable to crises. Households' liquidity preference, and thus their precautionary needs, is declining more and more, and the increasing debt financing of real estate purchases and financial investments is seen as a rise in their risk propensity. Banks' equity ratios are shrinking and increased debt financing increases profitability in boom periods. It allows share prices to rise, and thanks to the high market capitalization, also protects against the danger of hostile takeovers. Politicians shy away from the resistance of citizens to tax increases to finance growing expenditure, especially for social tasks, and prefer to borrow the necessary money on the financial market. They do not have to go down the idle path of persuading citizens to pay extra taxes on certain public projects. They are getting rid of this current task and shifting the problems associated with debt financing into the future. With the ever-increasing amount of debt financing, credit demands are growing enormously, and in times of crisis they reinforce the Keynes-Minsky momentum: quantity turns to quality in debt financing by increasing the instability of the economy through the accumulation of debt, which has grown sharply over time. This is one of Minsky's core theses.

Another core thesis is that private banks are key players in the economy. They decide where central bank money M flows into the economy on the basis of return and risk considerations. They create new financial products and new markets for them in order to increase their profit prospects and hedge their risks, thereby increasing the dynamism and instability of the economic process. Private banks are not included in ISLM's "script". Minsky turns away from the simplistic money market model of the ISLM approach and turns to the financial market. In doing so, he dispenses with formal design and verbally describes the manifold processes in this market. In doing so, he places leverage financing, i.e., debt financing with its leverage effect, at the center of his considerations. He sees it as the main cause of the growing instability of economic processes. He gives the goods market a different formal shape, in which profit is a central variable for investment and the price mark-up is a different approach to the development of inflation.

3.2 Main Features of Minsky's Macroeconomics

3.2.1 Basic Elements

Schumpeter emphasizes in his remarks on economic evolution:

- The innovations
- The profits
- The risk-bearing entrepreneurs
- The creation of credit by private banks and
- The credit monitoring of private banks

All these aspects are missing from the Keynesian perspective, which focuses on a short period of time when the economy is temporarily out of equilibrium.

Minsky expands the stationary Keynesian concept to a dynamic approach influenced by Schumpeter. In his expansion, he includes profits and the private banks, whose uncontrolled expansion of credit makes the economy unstable.

Minsky (1986) creates a *new paradigm*. In it, profits Π play a central role. He directs investments toward the profits Π. According to Minsky, investments I are the decisive determinant for the development of the capitalist economy. They essentially determine its growth path (core element 1: investments). Investment decisions are geared to the future. Today's investments must prove profitable in the future, they must generate profits (core element 2: profits). Profits are achieved by a mark-up on the technologically determined variable production costs. Profits include the general costs of the large number of highly trained specialists such as product developers and marketing experts, as well as the revenues and bonuses of the company's management. The mark-up approach also determines the price level P on the goods market and thus determines inflation (core element 3: mark-up pricing). Increasingly global competition threatens profits and increases the pressure to innovate. Products and services with new quality and new cost-effective product processes improve the competitive position in the struggle for market share and profits (core element 4: innovation). Innovations continually reshape the supply of goods and services, thereby promoting the dynamism of economic development, the growth rate g of total economic production Y (core element 5: dynamism).

The leverage effect of debt financing in the private sector increases the volatility on the financial market and, with the increased risks, the danger of insolvency in crises. Government debt financing increases the currency risk, and in the case of euro states, also the government insolvency risk (core element 6: debt financing).

To finance investments, companies borrow by offering bonds on the financial market. This is done through private banks. They are the key players in the financial market. Without them, nothing works. They channel central bank money to companies, governments, households, and abroad. They do not do this as public service providers. They are also companies that seek the highest possible profits and returns. They are well informed about the profitability prospects of entrepreneurs in the goods market and they know where in the world they can invest their money most profitably. Bankers are constantly trying to find new ways to lend money, attract new customers, acquire profitable parts of businesses, create new financial products, and thus create new markets, such as asset-backed securities, like ABS, and credit insurance securities, like CDS. They are aware of their business risk. Uncertainty is, therefore, a major determining factor in their business calculations, alongside profitability. They are also aware of the power they have as a result of their interconnectedness and their central importance for the functioning of the economy as a whole. Bankers are the central players in the capitalist economic system and are, therefore, indispensable in the economic game.

The banking business has three facets:

- To strengthen the customers' desire for debt financing
- To constantly create new financial products for financing, investment, and risk hedging
- Monitor the creditworthiness of debtors.

However, banks are increasingly getting rid of the tiresome and costly task of local creditworthiness monitoring (credit monitoring) by creating securities for risk hedging and thus selling the risk. They can also earn money from their worldwide sales (core element 7: private banks).

States are also key players. They are increasingly intervening in the economy to combat underemployment in the labor market and also to stimulate growth. Under the popular deficit spending policy, government activity has expanded considerably and has now developed into a sovereign debt crisis, particularly in Europe. This is increasingly restricting the scope for action of states, as they have increasing difficulties as debtors in meeting their payment obligations. Other solvent states, particularly in the euro area, feel increasingly obliged to provide assistance (core element 8: "big government").

Because of the high level of debt, governments' hands are tied in the crisis. They can no longer manage without the cheap money from the central banks. The central banks have become *lenders of last resort*. Their role is more that of lenders of last resort, but because of the weakness of fiscal policy, they are increasingly finding themselves obliged to intervene in the economy to stimulate it, for example, by providing the banking system with a lot of money at low interest rates in times of crisis. In doing so, they favor *credit expansion*. Central banks act in crises primarily to ensure the functioning of the financial system, they seek to reduce the risks of bank and state insolvencies—the latter applies primarily to the ECB—and thus contribute to the stabilization of an unstable economic process (core element 9: central banks as lenders of last resort).

The stability of economic processes is increasingly at risk. One cause is to be seen in innovation, which is constantly reshaping the macroeconomic system. Another lies in the expansion of debt financing. Investment in new products is usually capital-intensive, and their development takes a long time to market. Moreover, revenues flow over several periods after their launch. During this period, the market environment that determines the success of the investment can change significantly. Competitors bring a comparable product to the market at a lower cost or in a better quality, for example, in the car, telecommunications or solar energy markets. As a result, the sales of individual companies may collapse before the break-even point. Global competitive pressure can even cause a crisis in a sector of the economy. Real estate crises—households are no longer meeting their payment obligations, as is the case in the USA and Spain, for example, and national debt crises, states have overstretched their deficit spending policies and can no longer bear their own interest debts—can cause a banking crisis which, because of the interconnectedness of private banks, can rapidly spread to other sectors of the economy and affect the functioning of the economy as a whole.

Mild recessions can quickly turn into crises. We have explained the development in this respect under the heading Keynes-Minsky momentum. The change in expectations plays a central role here. The less provisions market participants have made for future crises, the more severe the impact of a turnaround will be on them. And provision is shrinking. This is because debt financing is expanding more and more at the expense of provisions for future uncertainties. This circumstance is expressed in the dual aspect of the $L_2(i)$ function, which Keynes described as a liquidity function on the one hand and a speculative function on the other. Households' demand for liquidity to provide for future uncertainties is decreasing in favor of speculative demand on the financial market.

In general, the alliance of private banks with households, companies, and governments is leading to an increase in credit financing, increasingly favored by central banks. With borrowed money, households can fulfil their long-awaited desire to own their own home, entrepreneurs can increase their return on equity, and consequently, their profits, market value, and dividends, and politicians can distribute benefits to citizens without burdening them with additional taxes. And the private banks earn a lot of money from each of these types of debt financing. This debt financing increases risk, and the increase in the volume of credit increases the instability of the market economy (core element 10: instability).

3.2.2 Interdependence Between Profit and Investment

Minsky moves away from the formal comparative static equilibrium analyses common in micro- and macroeconomics, from the formal quantitative analysis. He also largely avoids postulating behavioral equations. He limits himself to a few economic relations. They form an *open frame* of reference in which he discusses the dynamics and instability of the goods market, including not only *price-profit interdependence*, but also, and in particular, the *interdependence between profits and investment*. Both form a structure that allows a qualitative discussion of the interaction of central economic variables. Formally, Minsky's approach corresponds to that of Fisher (1933), who also uses in his equation of exchange the relationship between central economic variables to discuss their mode of action. In

Minsky's view, the interdependence of the goods market with the financial market takes place via the banks. They finance the investments and ultimately state deficits.

The profit equation emphasizes the interdependence dynamics of profits and investment. Thus, investment is linked to profits by its actual driving force. This creates a *new perspective* on macroeconomic processes compared to the ISLM model. It also uses profits to draw attention to economic inequality. According to Minsky, entrepreneurs secure their profits with a profit mark-up and thus he moves away from monetary inflation theory. Because of these new perspectives on the interaction of economic variables, we will devote a great deal of attention to the relationship between profit and investment as well as the mark-up approach and the determinants of price levels and thus inflation.

Minsky replaces the IS relationship from the ISLM model with the future-oriented profit-investment interdependence. In interdependence, the revenue from the goods and services sold, after deduction of variable wage costs, gives the profit, which includes the general costs for the highly skilled professionals in the development and marketing of the goods. Thus, the profit Π_c in the consumer goods industry is the difference between market revenue P_cQ_c and variable costs W_cN_c for less qualified workers

$$\Pi_c = P_cQ_c - W_cN_c, \tag{3.12}$$

with

$P_c =$ price level of consumer goods,
$Q_c =$ quantity of consumer goods,
$W_c =$ wage rate in the production of consumer goods,
$N_c =$ number of workers in consumer goods production.

The same applies to investment goods, goods for government consumption, and export goods, which we will leave out of consideration in a first step. The supply P_cQ_c on the goods market is equal to its demand. It results from the wage and profit sum and the state transfer payments. The wage total Ws is—the index I points to the investment goods sector and the index g to the government sector:

$$Ws = W_cN_c + W_IN_I + W_gN_g \tag{3.13}$$

and after deduction of the wage tax $T_w(Ws)$ the net wage total is

$$W^* = Ws - T_w(Ws). \tag{3.14}$$

From the profit sum

$$\Pi s = \Pi_c + \Pi_I + \Pi_g = \Pi \tag{3.15}$$

results after deduction of income taxes $T_\pi(\Pi)$ the net profit

$$\Pi^* = \Pi - T_\pi(\Pi). \tag{3.16}$$

The disposable income Yv from Eq. (3.2) in the ISLM model is here

$$Yv = W^* + \Pi^* + Tr. \tag{3.17}$$

With the consumption propensities c_w from wage income W* and c_π from profit Π*, the equilibrium relationship on the goods market results

$$P_cQ_c = c_wW^* + c_\pi\Pi^* + Tr. \tag{3.18}$$

The right side in Eq. (3.18) corresponds to the right side in the consumption equation Eq. (3.3) in the ISLM model, except that here a distinction is made between wages and profits and that all transfer payments are used for consumption.

As in Eq. (3.7) in the ISLM model, the government deficit Df is the difference between government expenditure and tax revenues

$$Df = P_gQ_g + Tr - T_w(W) - T_\pi(\Pi). \tag{3.19}$$

Some transformations, which the reader can skip, give the central profit-investment relationship.

Excursus: Transformations for Profit-Investment Interdependence

With $P_gQ_g = W_gN_g + \Pi_g$ we obtain from Eq. (3.19)

$$Df = W_gN_g + \Pi_g + Tr - T_w - T_\pi \tag{3.20}$$

and from this the transfer payments Tr in the form of

$$Tr = Df - W_gN_g - \Pi_g + T_w + T_\pi. \tag{3.21}$$

Inserting Tr from Eq. (3.21) into Eq. (3.18) gives

$$P_cQ_c = c_wW^* + c_\pi\Pi^* + Df - W_gN_g - \Pi_g + T_w + T_\pi. \tag{3.22}$$

With $c_wW^* = (1 - s_w)(Ws - T_w) = Ws - T_w - s_wW^*$ we write the Eq. (3.22) to

$$P_cQ_c = Ws - s_wW^* + c_\pi\Pi^* + Df - W_gN_g - \Pi_g + T_\pi. \tag{3.23}$$

If we replace in Eq. (3.23) the wage total Ws according to Eq. (3.13) by its components, we obtain

$$P_cQ_c - W_cN_c = W_IN_I - s_wW^* + c_\pi\Pi^* + Df - \Pi_g + T_\pi. \tag{3.24}$$

With $P_cQ_c - W_cN_c = \Pi_c$ und $W_IN_I = I - \Pi_I$ the result of Eq. (3.24) is

$$\Pi_c = I - \Pi_I - \Pi_g + T_\pi + c_\pi \Pi + Df - s_w W^* \tag{3.25}$$

and from Eq. (3.25) it follows

$$(1 - c_\pi)\Pi^* = I + Df - s_w W^*$$

and thus, the profit-investment relationship

$$\Pi^* = (I + Df - s_w W^*)/(1 - c_\pi). \tag{3.26}$$

The *central* relationship between profits Π and investments I is according to the above transformation

$$\Pi^* = (I + Df - s_w W^*)/(1 - c_\pi). \tag{3.26}$$

It contains the IS equilibrium condition (3.6) on the goods market known to us from the ISLM model in the form

$$I + Df = (1 - c_\pi)\Pi^* + s_w W^* = S. \tag{3.27}$$

Minsky is less concerned with the relationship of investment I to savings S in Eq. (3.27), which is familiar to us than with the relationship of investment I to profit Π in Eq. (3.26). Taking into account foreign trade relations, it extends to

$$\begin{aligned}\Pi^* &= (I + Df + Exü - s_w W^*)/(1 - c_\pi)\\ &= (I + Df + Exü + (c_w - 1)W^*)/(1 - c_\pi)\end{aligned} \tag{3.28}$$

including the export surplus

$$Exü = P_x Q_x - P_m Q_m \tag{3.29}$$

Therein is

P_m = import price level,
Q_m = import volume,
P_x = export price level,
Q_x = export volume.

It should be noted that the inclusion of foreign countries not only adds the export surplus in Eq. (3.29), but that Π^* also includes profits Π_x from the production of export goods and W* wages W_x from this very production of export goods.

Equation (3.26) puts three core variables from Minsky's basic concept into context with Π^*, I, and Df. In contrast to the classical equilibrium relationship (Eq. 3.27), which emphasizes the equality between investment I and savings S, in Eq. (3.26), it emphasizes *the future-oriented interdependence between investment I and profit Π^**, which is the core of the dynamics in the capitalist economic process, the core of the capitalist interdependence dynamics. And it is precisely this interdependence dynamic, the future interaction of investment and profit, that Minsky is concerned with. He is interested in showing how the interaction of profit and investment works together and which main factors influence this interdependence mechanism.

The profits Π on the left side of Eq. (3.26) result on a *microeconomic* level from the interaction of project return r_p, market interest rate i, and risk premium rz, as well as the debt financing ratio v, the leverage ratio, cf. Eq. (3.11). High project returns are the result of the development of new competitive products and their successful marketing. The interest rate is determined on the financial market and the risk premium depends on the assessment of the economic situation.

Favorable for the profit Π^* is the demand of the state, foreign countries, and especially the demand of households, but also the investment demand of entrepreneurs. On the right-hand side of Eq. (3.28), all demanders appear, the enterprises with their investments I, the state with its budget deficit Df, the foreign countries via the export surplus Exü, and the households with their propensity to consume c_w and c_π.

Investment I is the source of future revenue streams and the future flow of profits, in turn, restores confidence in future profitable investments. Profits Π and Investment I complement each other in the interdependence dynamic and are naturally good partners in the capitalist dynamic. Investment I is the manifestation of future profit expectations.

According to Eq. (3.28), government deficits Df and export surpluses Exü also promote the flow of profits and thus economic growth, the growth rate g of total economic production Y. Continued deficit financing of government expenditure, however, is increasingly expanding government debt. Moreover, as we shall see later, the associated interest payment obligations increasingly restrict a government's room for maneuver in key areas such as education and social policy and may even jeopardize its payment obligations. And the risk premiums on government bonds and on the credit insurance CDSs taken out on them skyrocket precisely when there is a threat of insolvency, thereby further increasing the risk of state insolvency. This is the case in some euro countries, for example, and in a similar form in Argentina.

Initially, private banks also benefit from the growing national debt. They are able to make a substantial profit from the associated expansion of credit. However, the threat of state insolvencies, later on, reduces the expected profit streams of banks, reduces their profitability, and, in the absence of state protection, endangers their own solvency. A prolonged deficit spending policy, therefore, has undesirable effects that increase the instability of the economic process. An alliance between politicians and bankers can therefore develop, which can endanger not only economic, but also political stability, for example in the EU.

One example of this alliance is Greece. After the introduction of the euro, Greek politicians profited from the initial low interest rates and the supposed protection of the euro countries, and with the support of the international financial system, forced their deficit spending policy without keeping to EU contractual ties. However, they cannot bear the consequential costs on their own, and also because of the systemic risk, other euro states are forced to support them despite the "no bail-out" clause in the Maastricht Treaty, an example of *how the power of facts can prevail over contractual rights*, which in the long run can undermine confidence in contracts; we will return to this later in connection with ECB policy.

Similarly disastrous as the politician-banker alliance in deficit spending policy can be the alliance between banks and households in the real estate market. Low mortgage interest rates with low security requirements and expected increases in property prices can trigger a boom in demand. And this, through the expansion of mortgage lending, will increase the profit flow of banks. But it can dry up when market conditions change, and households are no longer able to meet their long-term payment obligations, and the boom bursts. Evidence of this instability emanating from the housing market is provided by the housing crises in the US and Spain and Ireland.

According to Eq. (3.28), private households influence profits Π via their consumption behavior. In prosperous economic times, their consumption increases. In Eq. (3.28), this is expressed in the rising propensity to consume c_w and c_π or in the falling propensity to save s_w and s_π. If the future prospects are promising, they are prepared to spend more and even go into debt for larger purchases. In a prosperous phase, rising share prices and high dividend payments also stimulate consumption, especially from profit income. Good economic prospects and then rising prosperity—the "wealth effect"—thus increase the propensity to consume c, and according to Eq. (3.28), profits Π.

The trend is tilting after the economic turnaround and consumer behavior is accelerating the downturn. Because then sinking consumer spending slows down the Π-I dynamics and increases economic instability. It is, therefore, not surprising that the US Federal Reserve has recently started to focus its stabilization efforts not only on inflation and growth, but also on bond and equity prices. In the current economic crises, the Fed's monetary policy measures—*huge purchases of badly rated securities*—are also aimed at ensuring that US securities prices do not plummet too sharply because of their wealth creation effect on consumption. It assumes that the "wealth effect" that we have come to know in connection with the ISLM model in the form of the real money supply M/P is now acting in the American economy via securities prices.

These days, central banks have greatly reduced the abovementioned interest rate risk. However, society has to pay a high price for this. By buying up high-risk securities, central banks *encourage "evergreening"*—the existence of unprofitable firms—and *credit expansion* in the economy. *Central banks are creating a dilemma with serious consequences for their national economies.* On the one hand, they stimulate credit expansion—they expand current spending possibilities—on the other hand, they support unprofitable firms—they shrink tomorrow's revenues. *They are about to jeopardize the intertemporal balance between today's expenditure and tomorrow's earnings, and thus society's vital trust in the future.* We will return to this issue later in Sect. 4.12 "Consequences of economic change and state stabilization: instability and inequality, distorted markets, and intertemporal imbalance".

3.2.3 The Mark-Up Approach and Price Levels

Besides profits and investment, the development of price levels plays a central role in the capitalist economic system. It can have devastating consequences for economic, as well as social development, both as deflation—as in the world economic crisis after the First World War in the USA and also in the more recent economic crisis in Japan—and as inflation—as in the economic crisis after the First World War in Europe.

According to Krugman, the enormous money supply growth in the recent crisis—one has to think of the expansive money supply policy in the USA, Japan, Great Britain, and the euro zone—will not pose a threat of inflation as long as the economies do not come out of recession. And indeed, that is likely to be the case. Minsky provides an important argument for this. He explains the development of the price level P with his mark-up approach.

We develop Minsky's price mark-up approach by following his Eq. (3.12) $\Pi = PQ - WN$, or rather by assuming the distribution of market revenues PQ between variable labor costs WN and profits Π, $PQ = WN + \Pi$. According to Minsky, as we know, this relationship applies not only to consumer goods, but also to capital goods, government consumption, and export goods. We do not make this subdivision. This has advantages: The reader is spared a series of algebraic transformations; the resulting mark-up is simpler and easier to interpret. Moreover, the profit Π appearing in it combines the price level P with the profit-investment interdependence (Eq. 3.28).

The equation

$$PQ = NW + \Pi \tag{3.30}$$

can be transformed into

$$P = (NW/Q)(1 + \Pi/NW), \tag{3.31}$$

or to the price mark-up equation

$$P = (W/A_p)(1 + m), \tag{3.32}$$

with labor productivity

$$A_p = Q/N \tag{3.33}$$

and the profit mark-up

$$m = \Pi/NW. \tag{3.34}$$

According to Eqs. (3.32), (3.33), and (3.34), the price level P has three determinants: wages W, labor productivity A_p, and the profit mark-up m. The relationship between the price level P and wages W corresponds to Hayek's P–W spiral. The spiral effect has been weakened by globalization, see The Economist: "The world economy's strange new rules", October 12th 2019, 12.

As we know from the profit–investment interdependence (Eq. 3.28), a high demand on the goods market is favorable for the enforcement of the profit mark-up m = Π/NW, which promotes profits Π. The profits, in the form of

$$\Pi = T_\pi + (I + Df + Ex\ddot{u} - s_w W^*)/(1 - c_\pi) \qquad (3.35)$$

also make it clear that entrepreneurs are striving to pass on the profit tax T_π to the demanders via the price mark-up m = Π/NW.

The profit–investment interdependence (Eq. 3.28), like the price level equation (Eq. 3.32), relates key macroeconomic variables. Equation (3.32) uses W/A_p to relate the price level P to elements of consumer goods production and m = Π/WN to elements of demand, which are listed in the profit equation (Eq. 3.28). And this closes the circle from the price level equation (Eq. 3.32) to profit–investment interdependence (Eq. 3.28).

Unlike in Fisher's equation of exchange or Friedman's monetary approach, there is no money supply M in Minsky's approach. His price mark-up approach (Eq. 3.32) has other determinants of inflation with the profit mark-up m, labor productivity A_p and wages W. At the same time, he turns away from the Keynesian money market equation (Eq. 3.8). For central bank, money does not enter the economy directly as supply quantity M. Rather, it is the private banks that channel it into the economic cycle. Central banks offer private banks favorable conditions for central bank borrowing by lowering their interest rates and weakening collateral requirements—in times of crises, such as the current ones, they offer extremely favorable conditions. Private banks respond to the conditions and extend their credit lines with the central bank when they are offered additional profitable investments, but in crises, profit opportunities are less likely to be found in the real economy with *flow variables* and more likely in *stock trading*, thus reducing the effects of central bank policy on labor demand N, output Y and its growth rate g, as well as on price level P, on inflation.

3.2.4 Evaluation of the Formal Minsky Approach

Minsky opens up a new view of economic processes. He has initiated a paradigm shift. He reinterprets the IS relationship of the goods market by orienting the economic process on the goods market toward the future by means of profit–investment interdependence, he breaks away from the money market relationship LM by making private banks central players on the financial market in his open approach. They promote debt financing and thus increase economic instability. He presents an alternative explanation of price levels, i.e., inflation and deflation. Finally, with the profits Π, Minsky opens his approach to discussions of economic inequalities.

The Π-I interdependence (Eq. 3.28)

$$\Pi^* = (I + Df + Ex\ddot{u} - s_w W^*)/(1 - c_\pi)$$

changes the previous view of what is happening on the goods market. It replaces the traditional equilibrium relationship

$$I + Df + Ex\ddot{u} = S$$

between the forward-looking investment I of firms and the non-consumption S of households, their savings, resulting from current consumption decisions.

In Eq. (3.28), Minsky links Investment I with the profits Π, and with this Π−I dynamic, brings a central relationship of the capitalist economic process to the fore. It represents the core of *the capitalist dynamics* on the commodity market, *it is oriented toward profits Π and the accumulation of wealth Σ.*

Profits Π Minsky introduces by splitting the market revenues PQ between labor costs WN and profits Π according to Eq. (3.30). In doing so, he separates the *variable labor costs* WN of the less qualified workers N, which fluctuates with the demand for goods, from the *general costs* for higher qualified workers, which bind companies for the development and marketing of goods in the longer term. Minsky attributes the fixed costs for higher-paid skilled workers to profits Π. We will return to Minsky's allocation later when we come to talk about *economic inequality*. This distinction between low and high skilled work opens up a view of economic inequality that arises from the payment for different work services; Rajan (2010), who sees education as one of the causes of inequality, also refers to this, see Sect. 1.1 "Financial crisis at the beginning of the twenty-first century".

Minsky uses his division of PQ revenues into variable labor costs WN and profits Π to postulate his price mark-up hypothesis (Eq. 3.32)

$$P = \left(W/A_p\right)(1 - m) \text{ with } m = \Pi/NW$$

According to Eq. (3.32), the price level P—and thus inflation and deflation—depends on the labor costs W, the labor productivity A_p, and the actual price mark-up m, which is determined by the profit Π and thus by the Π−I interaction (Eq. 3.28).

The Π−I interdependence (Eq. 3.28) interacts with the price mark-up (Eq. 3.32). If the Π−I dynamic is triggered by the demand components on the right-hand side in Eq. (3.28), companies can more easily implement price increases in accordance with the profit mark-up m = Π/NW. Higher profit margins m mean higher prices P and higher prices P mean higher profits Π. Thus, we can also speak of an interdependence relationship in the price mark-up (Eq. 3.32), of price–profit interdependence. Both interdependencies—Π−I and P−Π interdependence—reinforce each other, both in upturns and downturns, and are the dynamics of economic evolution.

If future prospects become gloomy, the $\Pi - I$ dynamic loses momentum, profits Π shrink, and companies grant price discounts when demand falls, causing the price mark-up m to fall and thus the price P. An economic downward spiral threatens the goods and labor market and on top of that deflation, which further intensifies the downward spiral on both markets. The same applies to the upswing.

Future profits Π depend on current investments I. And these are largely financed by borrowing. Through *debt financing*, the *private banks* play a significant role in the interdependence dynamics. Minsky sees the increasing debt financing, the so-called financialization of the economy, as the cause of the *growing instability* of the economy. And the private banks promote debt financing because that is what they earn money from. The financial market is becoming increasingly important. This is where the action is, where debt financing sets the course for development in the real economy. It opens up opportunities that the market participants there are only too keen to exploit: Households to buy a property, entrepreneurs to increase their return on equity, and politicians to provide benefits without having to ask citizens to pay.

3.2.5 Finance Market: Private Banks, Debt Financing, and Instability

We have identified the interaction between profit Π and investment I, the $\Pi - I$ interdependence in Eq. (3.28) as the core of the interdependence dynamics of the capitalist economic process. In it, investment I is the supporting element in economic growth g.

Investing is a time-consuming process for entrepreneurs. They need time to plan and implement their investment projects. This is the technical side. And from an economic point of view, time is also an essential factor. Whether or not an Investment I proves to be profitable will only be revealed in the future, sometimes after a longer period of time. Profitability depends, on the one hand, on future profit flows Π, and on the other, on outstanding payment obligations that companies incur when financing their investment decisions for the future.

By financing investments, banks become key players in the profit-investment interdependence (Eq. 3.28). The private banks set the lending conditions according to profitability considerations. They change their conditions over time and, especially in times of crises with high risk, they raise their requirements, thus reducing the already declining profit flows. Thus, the profit–investment interaction is exposed to the risks that increasingly emanate from the financial market.

But the role of private banks is not limited to financing real investment I. They finance purchases of real estate, works of art and company takeovers, grant household loans for consumption and also for the purchase of bonds and shares, and grant loans to companies and governments, for example, by subscribing to their bonds.

Debt financing of both real and financial investments increases economic instability, as the Keynes-Minsky momentum illustrates. Minsky shows differences in debt financing by means of classification. For this purpose, he compares income with expenditure resulting from payment obligations arising from loans. All players can be at fault: households, companies, banks, and states, as well as foreign countries. For details see Minsky (1986), Chap. 9 "Financial commitments and instability".

Minsky distinguishes three types of financing:

1. hedge finance
2. speculative finance
3. Ponzi finance

With hedge financing, current revenues are sufficient to meet all payment obligations over a longer period of time. Current interest is paid, and outstanding debts are repaid. In the case of speculative and Ponzi scheme financing, current income is not sufficient to meet all payment obligations over a longer period of time. In the case of speculative financing, the old debts repaid are replaced by the taking on of new debts without increasing the indebtedness. In the form of refinancing, old debt is replaced by new debt.

In the case of Ponzi financing, the debt level is increasing. Here one speculates on increases in the value of the debt-financed investments, for example, on a rise in the price of real estate or a rise in the price of financial securities. Both debtors and creditors—mainly private banks—are dependent on the development of the financial market in the case of speculative and especially Ponzi financing. The volatility on the financial market and also non-occurring but expected increases in value can endanger solvency and thus increase instability. The risk of insolvency and instability arises in particular from Ponzi financing. It causes debt levels to rise, it increases debt financing, which, with its leverage effect, increases volatility and thus instability.

Growing debt financing with high levels of debt reinforces the Keynes-Minsky momentum, with a double effect on the turnaround: On the one hand, the usual expansion of borrowing, the Ponzi scheme, is made more difficult and in many cases even prevented, and on the other hand, follow-up financing of the repayments then due becomes considerably more expensive.

Even though private banks are indebted too, mainly to the central bank and to each other, they should be seen as those who are constantly trying to expand their business by selling credit to households, to companies, to governments, and to foreign countries. They encourage the indebtedness of other players and favor speculative and Ponzi scheme financing. They themselves are also prepared to increase their leverage ratio v and reduce their equity ratio (EQ) in order to maximize profitability and increase their market value and market power. Banks are the "*Master of the Universe*". They direct the destiny of the real economy through financing.

Central banks have recently assumed a key role in the economy. According to The Economist, they are not only "lenders of last resort", but now also "*market-makers of last resort*", as we know from 1 Introduction.

Let us return once again to Minsky's classification of financing and take a closer look at the financing situation of individual players. Let us start with the budgets. Minsky's economic approach distinguishes households with predominantly wage income WN and transfer income Tr from households with predominantly profit income Π. Both can be overburdened in terms of financing and get carried away with Ponzi scheme financing. They finance the acquisition of larger durable goods such as buying a car through consumer credit and buying a house through mortgage credit. The increase in value on the real estate market, for example, tempts them to finance Ponzi schemes, i.e., to increase their debt, as they see their debts covered by the increase in value. Unemployment and loss of value of their real estate holdings thwart their plans and drive them into private insolvency. Recent examples of this can be found in the USA, Spain, and Greece, as well as in Ireland.

For some time now, states have been using their permanent deficit policies to finance their expenditure through the Ponzi scheme. As a result, their debt levels are growing steadily. The continuous deficit-spending policy has intensified the profit–investment interaction over a longer period of time, not only in Western countries, and thus provided increased impulses for employment and growth. It has thus been able to stabilize economic development over a longer period. Here, too, the flip side, the price society has to pay for it, only becomes apparent later, with some delay. The Ponzi financing pushes up the debts and thus the interest payments. They restrict the room for maneuver of fiscal policy, and on the borderline, even jeopardize the solvency of states. In addition, government Ponzi financing promotes income inequality, firstly through profit–investment interdependence (Eq. 3.28), where ongoing deficits strengthen the flow of profits, and secondly through credit accumulation, which mainly leads to interest payments for profit earners, more on this later. Initially, deficit spending policies stabilize the economy and tend to reduce inequality through employment effects. But its continued application leads to the opposite.

In the recent crises, states have only limited scope for deficit policy because of their high debt levels. They must increasingly leave the field to the central banks. Central banks are *lenders of last resort* for governments, not only for private banks, but increasingly also for states. However, as we know from the ISLM discussion, their monetary policy has only an indirect influence on employment with little impact. Thus, the central objective remains to ensure the functioning of the financial market and to support bond and stock prices through the policy of cheap money. The direct beneficiaries of cheap money are the private banks. For they can invest the cheap central bank money profitably. And other profiteers are the richer ones, the households of the upper income stratum, whose assets are secured by the central banks. For central banks are primarily concerned with the functioning of the financial market. And this requires, first of all, the securing of financial assets and thus the accumulation of wealth Σ.

3.2.6 Minsky's Approach and the Changes in Economic Activity

Minsky's approach changes the view of macroeconomic processes as described by the ISLM model. The change in perspective is also due to changes in economic processes. Like Keynes, many economists see the economic process as *inherently stable*, and exogenous shocks can throw it off balance in the short term. But the forces at work within it can bring it back into equilibrium. Minsky, by contrast, sees the process as *inherently unstable*. The instability stems from the increasing debt financing that private banks are pushing. Private banks, the driving force, play only a rudimentary role in the traditional macroeconomic literature.

Minsky's ideas about the functioning of the capitalist system recall the "panta rhei" of Heraclitus-Platon: "everything moves on, everything changes, and nothing remains as it is; it is an eternal becoming and changing". In his economic world, change is manifested in an ongoing and accelerating process of innovation which is restructuring the overall economic structure worldwide. Innovation is not limited to the goods market, where it enriches the supply of goods with new products and increases the efficiency of production. It increasingly extends to the financial market. New financial products make credit risk tradable. To this end, private banks are creating new markets worldwide, constantly expanding their business areas, and driving forward financing globally. These innovations, together with debt financing, the "financialization" of the economy, are the cause of economic instability, and this is in the nature of the capitalist system. Minsky speaks of an "*intrinsically unstable economy*". The instability manifests itself in economic crises. The earlier employment crises with inflation and deflation have recently been followed by real estate, banking, and public debt crises. In contrast to earlier crises, it is now primarily central banks that are called upon to stabilize.

Minsky's approach is based on the division of sales revenue PQ between variable labor costs WN and profit Π according to Eq. (3.30). With this division, he brings the profits Π into play. According to Minsky, companies make profits by means of the price mark-up (Eq. 3.32) on the technically determined variable labor costs. The profits also include the high salaries of the large number of highly qualified specialists who provide new competitive products that can compete on the world market. The distinction between low-skilled and high-skilled workers opens up a view of the economic inequality that results from the payment for unequal work. Rajan (2010), who sees education as a cause of inequality, also highlights this. The gap between "rich" and "poor" is also becoming more pronounced in the old industrialized countries as a result of globally oriented production, "*global supply chain management*"—compare Sect. 2.13.2 "Globalization and the economic change to the disadvantage of the old industrial nations".

Minsky, in his profit–investment interdependence (Eq. 3.28), orients investment I to the expectation of future profits Π and emphasizes, like Keynes, that investments depend on the constellation of return, market interest rate, and risk assessment. They are increasingly debt financed. Debt financing increases the opportunities and risks of an investment project, thus increasing uncertainty and volatility.

The Keynes-Minsky momentum describes processes in the world of expectation that affect the real world and vice versa. It captures the psychological perception of opportunity and risk in economic upheavals. In an upswing, opportunities come into focus, and in a downturn, risks. The actions of market participants resulting from this perception can thus reinforce upswings and downturns. Detailed examples of how debt financing increases opportunities and risks are explained later in Tables 4.4, 4.5, 4.6 and 4.7 in Sect. 4.6 "Debt financing and risk: good times and bad times".

The examples in Tables 4.4, 4.5, 4.6 and 4.7 will further illustrate that debt financing dramatically increases the risks and uncertainties in the markets. And the increased risks and uncertainties, together with the Keynes-Minsky momentum, can exacerbate the crises in the capitalist economy to such an extent that market forces are no longer able to resolve the economic crises. Overcoming the crises must come from outside, as the massive state interventions worldwide in the recent crises have shown. In this sense, the highly debt-financed economy is inherently unstable.

With his price mark-up hypothesis (Eq. 3.32), Minsky departs from the traditional money supply approach to explain price levels and inflation. Consequently, he turns away from the Keynesian money market modeling (Eq. 3.8) and turns to the financial market with private banks. They channel the money into the economic cycle, they stimulate *credit expansion* among all market players, they create new products for risk protection, which ultimately increase the systemic risk within the financial sector and thus force the state, especially the central bank, to intervene in the economic process so that the economy can function at all in crises.

With new products, it is not only the new quality, but also the price that determines whether a new placement on the market will be successful or not. The importance of pricing for innovations is evident in the case of option papers, whose successful marketing has contributed to the above-average growth of the financial market, particularly in the UK and the US, in the last two decades before the financial crisis of 2007/2008. We will deal with option pricing later.

The economic process and its stability have changed. This change is due to a variety of factors. They interact and can reinforce each other. To be mentioned:

- Innovations
- Education
- Globalization
- Debt financing
- Economic instability
- Systemic risk
- Social inequality

Companies are constantly striving to increase their profit margins, their return on equity, and thus the market value of their business. According to the price mark-up hypothesis (Eq. 3.32) and profit–investment interdependence (Eq. 3.28), they can increase their profit margin by producing more cheaply on the one hand and by stimulating demand on the other. To reduce unit labor costs $NW/Q = W/A_p$ they will start with wages W and labor productivity A_p. They will have innovation and globalization on their side. They will be able to reduce labor costs WN through *global supply chain management* and increase labor productivity A_p through *innovative production processes*. An essential element of global production is, on the one hand, the "outsourcing" of simple manufacturing work to low-wage countries, and on the other hand, the increased worldwide recruitment of highly qualified, expensive skilled workers for the domestic development and marketing centers of the western industrialized countries. In this way, these countries *strengthen their global competitiveness.* International competitive struggle requires investment in innovation. Companies, therefore, develop products with new properties and new production processes. They secure patents worldwide and prepare themselves for global competition through company acquisitions. They rely on headhunters to attract the best minds to their companies. After all, in addition to technical progress, which manifests itself in innovations, progress in knowledge counts, which unfolds in education and training. The fight for the best minds worldwide with high pay is particularly characteristic of the financial market, which has been able to expand considerably, thanks to numerous innovations, new financial products, especially in the USA and Great Britain. The English language as the "lingua franca" helps in this respect worldwide, cf. The Economist (2014b).

The struggle for the best, creative minds for the domestic centers, and the outsourcing of simple manual work to low-wage countries are causing profit margins to rise, and with them, economic inequality, whether measured by the gap between lower and upper quantiles or by the Gini coefficient. Domestic wages are drifting down so far that many workers are not even able to secure the subsistence minimum from current labor income, not to mention the low pension income; today, this is a fact that not even Karl Marx could have imagined at the time of the Industrial Revolution—because according to the neoclassical theory of marginal productivity, which is common today, wages do not have to secure the subsistence minimum.

Studies discussed in The Economist use the Gini coefficient to illustrate the growing inequality within many countries. But they also indicate that global inequality is declining. This can be seen as a positive effect of globalization, see The Economist (2012).

According to the profit–investment interdependence (Eq. 3.28), government deficit policy favors profit development. Moreover, its permanent application increases the credit demands of the richer ones and provides them with additional income in the form of interest payments, which they would not have if the national budget were balanced in the longer term. Here a paradox of fiscal policy becomes apparent: in the short-term fiscal policy stabilizes demand Y on the goods market, employment N, and thus the wage income WN of the less qualified; in the long term the interest payments Z resulting from the national debt D diminish their effect on the demand for goods and labor, and the long series of deficits Df favors the accumulation of credit claims and interest income Z of the richer, whose profits they also increase because of the profit effect of Df in Eq. (3.28). Furthermore, central bank policy also reinforces *economic inequality* by supporting bond and stock prices and thus assets of the richer. This is because falling share prices are said to have a negative "wealth effect" on consumption. This is particularly true in the USA, where the economy is heavily based on domestic consumption. The Fed, therefore, not only monitors growth, employment, and inflation, but also supports real estate, bond, and equity prices, and thus wealth Σ.

Debt levels are growing, and not only for the government. *Debt financing* is generally increasing at the expense of provisions for future eventualities.

In the case of investments and financial assets, the leverage effect of debt financing increases the opportunities and risks. Uncertainty grows, and with it, instability. As a result, trend extrapolations of subjective expectations à la Keynesian are becoming shorter and shorter and the danger of stronger trend corrections in the Keynes-Minsky momentum is growing, instability is increasing.

Private banks are the driving force behind credit expansion. They get rid of costly local credit monitoring, create new collateral, and benefit from their global marketing. Many of these securities remain within the financial sector. Internal trade increases interdependence between banks and creates a systemic risk that affects the entire economic process. The final security is provided by the government, mainly the central banks, but ultimately it is the society that bears the risk, which it may no longer wish to bear.

Schumpeter saw the situation quite differently in his time. In his approach to economic evolution, it is the entrepreneur who bears the risk. Schumpeter (1939, p. 104) states: "It is the capitalist who bears the risk".

Private banks stimulate debt and thus increase uncertainty. They channel the money from the central bank to finance lucrative investments. They have a key privilege, which ensures them a basic return. It is difficult to explain to society why private banks are able to make a profit thanks to this privilege, even though they can now dispose of most of their risks.

The extension of debt has two aspects. Firstly, as explained using the example of the Keynesian liquidity function $L_2(i)$, it is at the expense of providing for bad times, and thus exacerbates the Keynes-Minsky momentum, i.e., it increases instability. On the other hand, government loan financing with interest payments increases inequality. What richer citizens were saved in tax payments yesterday, they now receive in interest income from the taxation of the broad masses. As leading economists also practice, the effect of debt on inequality can be dismissed on the surface by explaining that debt does not make society as a whole poorer; for example, Krugman (2012, p. 43) notes "debt does not make society as a whole poorer: one person's debt is another person's asset, so total wealth is unaffected by the amount of debt out there". But in the case of inequality, *the distribution of credit claims* is of interest, and as with wealth in general, it is concentrated on the richer. Thus, we have to differentiate: *it is different groups that bear the burden and reap the rewards, both today and tomorrow*. It is, therefore, too simplistic to say that future generations must bear the burden of debt. Because even among future generations, there is one group that bears the fruits and another that has to shoulder the burden. We will refer to the topic again in Sect. 4.11.3 "Profits and losses of central banks".

If we look at the variables that determine economic events, we see a change over time. After prices—the price mechanism in microeconomics—and flows—such as income Y, consumption C, and investment I in the ISLM model—accumulated variables, stock variables such as debt D and wealth Σ, play an increasingly important role in economic processes. This is not quite correct. Karl Marx already emphasized the accumulation of capital, but what is meant is rather the accumulation of production capital K through fixed capital formation I. What gnaws at it is, especially the innovations which, over time, weaken the efficiency of established plant and machinery, leading to considerable depreciation. Nevertheless, the value of the capital stock is growing. This is complemented by the stock of real estate and works of art. And unlike the price level P of consumer goods, the price level of asset values is currently increasing, sometimes with strong inflationary tendencies. The growth in wealth Σ is continuing and is becoming a non-negligible factor in economic activity.

Less favorable than the ISLM model is the second conclusion about state intervention in a world that has changed so much in the meantime: *Fiscal policy expands debt financing and thus promotes instability. It has lost much of its impact on the stabilization of the goods and labor markets due to its permanent deficits. The public debt built up by the long succession of deficits restricts fiscal policy's ability to act and makes it dependent on the central bank. The growth in wealth Σ increases economic inequality. The central bank remains the main player.*

Its attention is focused on the financial market and its stabilization. This is because it considers the functioning of the financial market to be a "conditio sine qua non" for the functioning of the economy as a whole. Central bank policy also increases inequality. This is because its measures are aimed at supporting wealth Σ at risk during crises and strengthening the weakening flow of profits Π so that current investments I can be profitable in the future.

Central bank policy is increasingly revealing the less attractive sides of capitalism. *Unlike Keynesian policy, it is less concerned with the common welfare and more with the mere functioning of the economy.* Here, one can guess that the state's stabilization policy will end in a dead-end.

3.3 Summary

In Minsky's novel economic paradigm, unlike the Keynesian-influenced ISLM model, profits, private banks, and debt financing play a central role. Minsky replaces the Keynesian relationship between investment and saving with the future-oriented interdependence between investment and profit. Profit is ultimately the focus of economic activity in the capitalist market economy. In good times, debt financing increases the chances of profit drastically through its leverage effect, but in bad times the risk of loss is even more drastic. It increases the economic risks and makes the economic process inherently unstable. And private banks are driving forward debt financing. The change in the economic process goes hand in hand with the change in state stabilization. With its permanent deficits, the Keynesian economic stabilization promotes debt financing and thus instability, and favors inequality. What debts are for some, assets are for others. Keynesian fiscal policy has first successfully stabilized the economy for the common welfare and then rendered itself ineffective through its debt accumulation, and together with the private banks, has shifted the focus from the real economy to the financial market. The ineffective central bank remains the main stabilizing actor.

References

Fisher, I.: The Debt-Deflation Theory of Great Depressions. Econometrica 1, 337–357 (1933)
Hayek, F. A.: The Constitution of Liberty, London (1960)
Keynes, J.M.: The General Theory of Employment, Interest, and Money, New York (1936)
Keynes, J.M.: Some Economic Consequences of a Declining Population. Eugenics Review XXIX, 13–17 (1937)
Krugman, P.: End this Depression now!, New York (2012)
Le Monde: France: les salaires réels à la hausse, 12 December 2014
Minsky, H.P.: Stabilizing an Unstable Economy, Yale (1986)
Rajan, R.G.: Fault Lines, How Hidden Fractures Still Threaten the World Economy, Princeton (2010)
Schumpeter, J. A.: Business Cycles. A Theoretical, Historical, and Statistical Analysis of the Capitalist Process, New York (1939)
The Economist: Special Report: For Richer, for Poorer, October 13th 2012, 3–26
The Economist: Risk off, January 25th 2014a, 60
The Economist: The English Empire, February 15th 2014b, 57
The Economist: Debt Calm, August 2nd 2014c, 56
The Economist: Wage Stagnation. The Big Freeze, September 6th 2014d, 65–66
The Economist: The World Economy's Strange New Rules, October 12th 2019, 13.

4 Outlook on the Transformation of the Market Economy and Its Stabilization

Abstract

Central banks remain the main players. Without a viable concept, they must intervene in the financial market in a variety of ways, with uncertain outcomes. Their actions are aimed at assuming economic risks from the private sector, encouraging the flow of profits and safeguarding wealth. Their interventions benefit the richer, the profit takers and the owners. They thus promote inequality. The capitalist market economy shows significant weakness. The state can only worsen the situation with its traditional stabilization policy. It must change its politics and find a new orientation.

4.1 Interest Rate Effect on Minsky's Profit–Investment Dynamics, on Inequality, and on Monetary Policy

In times of crises, such as the current ones, the Fed buys large amounts of newly issued government securities, thereby lowering the interest rate on government bonds to an extremely low level. The Fed's low interest rate policy thus favors monetary budget financing and thus increases the scope for further borrowing without directly increasing government interest payments Z. It thus facilitates Ponzi government financing in the USA with the risk of rising interest payments Z when the Fed exits the low interest rate policy.

However, the US government has set itself self-imposed limits on the expansion of the debt, and Congress and the President negotiate the new definition of these limits in sometimes difficult voting processes. Political players disagree on the impact of the Ponzi scheme. Some would like to use this financing to overcome current crises as quickly as possible, while others warn of future economic risks of debt expansion with rising interest payments Z and the resulting future instabilities. Moreover, some argue that the Fed is losing flexibility. It is unlikely to be able to

R. Pauly, *Economic Instability and Stabilization Policy*,
https://doi.org/10.1007/978-3-658-33626-4_4

abandon its policy of low interest rates in the future because interest payments Z would rise enormously.

In the current crises—and probably also in the future—central bank policy dominates fiscal policy. It supports the deficit policy of the state by purchasing government securities. The ongoing deficits Df have caused the government's debt D_g to increase dramatically over time and with its government interest payments Z_g, which now represent a considerable chunk of government spending, even though current interest rates are low.

The interest payments Z_g *weaken* the effect of the deficits Df on the Π−I dynamic. This is because, unlike transfer expenditure Tr, interest Z_g *only partly affects demand on the goods market, while much of it flows to the financial market, where it is mainly used to trade existing assets* Σ. This means that the goods market no longer benefits from the entire deficit, and consequently, its effect on the profit–investment dynamics of the goods market is reduced.

We want to make this fact clear by adding interest expenditure Z_g to government expenditure—by explicitly listing interest payments Z_g with the government, we separate them from the profit Π to which they actually belong. With the explicit consideration of the interest payment Z_g and its taxation $T(Z_g)$, the government deficit Df from Eq. 3.20 now results in the form

$$\begin{aligned} Df_z &= W_g N_g + \Pi_g + Tr - T_w - T_\pi + Z_g - T_z(Z_g) \\ &= G + Tr + Z_g - T_w - T_\pi - T_z \end{aligned} \tag{4.1}$$

and taking into account the propensity to consume from interest income $c_z(Z_g - T_z)$, the goods market equilibrium (Eq. 3.18) in the form

$$P_c Q_c = c_w W^* + c_\pi \Pi^* + c_z Z_g^* + Tr \text{ with } Z_g^* = Z_g - T_z. \tag{4.2}$$

This model extension is necessary because of the meanwhile considerable amount of interest payments Z_g. The transfer expenditure Tr of the state benefits primarily the poorer people. We have, therefore, set the savings ratio s_{tr} for transfers to zero and have not assumed any tax payment from transfer revenues. The interest payments Z_g are mainly income of the richer. In contrast to wage income W, opportunities for tax evasion open up to a not inconsiderable extent for recipients of interest income, so that taxation $T(Z_g)$ will not effectively reduce interest income Z_g significantly. On the other hand, richer people are expected to have a high savings ratio s, so that the savings from net interest income $s_z Z_g^*$ will significantly reduce the deficit of Df_z. And only the surplus of deficits over interest savings $Df_z - s_z Z_g^*$ has a stimulating effect on profit–investment dynamics.

We can see this if, analogous to the derivation of Eqs. 3.26 and 3.27, we use the transfers Tr from Eqs. 4.1 to 4.2 and then transform it. The modified Π−I interdependence results from the transformation

$$\Pi^* = (I + [Df_z - s_z Z_g^*] - s_w W^*)/(1 - c_\pi) \tag{4.3}$$

and the modified traditional savings-investment equation

$$I + Df_z = s_\pi \Pi^* + s_w W^* + s_z Z_g^* = S. \tag{4.4}$$

If we consider the foreign trade relationship in Eq. 4.3, we get the extended modified Π–I interdependence

$$\Pi^* = (I + [Df_z - s_z Z_g^*] + Ex\ddot{u} + (c_w - 1)W^*)/(1 - c_\pi). \tag{4.5}$$

Compared with Eq. 3.28, the saved interest payments $s_z Z^*$ reduce the stimulating effect of the Df_z deficits on the profit–investment dynamic.

Public debt D_g weakens the growth impact of deficit policy through high interest payments Z_g. The permanently applied deficit policy weakens itself and its remaining room for manoeuvre depends on central bank policy. In addition, rising debt D_g further increases external financing and thus instability, and via interest payments Z_g and rising private credit claims, the backside of government debt D_g, inequality. The growing inequality is hampering society's acceptance of the market economy.

If we associate a reduction in inequality with transfers Tr, then a strengthening with interest payments Z_g. As usual, we have set the propensity to spend c_{tr} from transfer income Tr at one, that from wage income W will be close to one and that from profit Π and interest income Z will be well below one. A large part of the profits and interest income will not be consumed and can be invested in the real estate and financial markets. Through these ongoing real estate and financial investments, recipients of profits and interest income can accumulate considerable financial assets; in connection with comments on Piketty (2013), we will go into more detail on the accumulation of wealth Σ.

If the profit–investment dynamic gets going in the future, as is intended, and the economy enters an upswing phase, a growth phase, then the central bank will intervene even more selectively in economic activity in the event of high national debt D_g. If consumer confidence and the willingness of companies to invest increases during the boom phase, then, according to the price mark-up hypothesis, companies can push through higher prices P: the risk of inflation increases. To avert this risk, the central bank would have to abandon its policy of cheap money and raise interest rates in order to slow down the Π–I dynamic and thus also the P–Π dynamic. However, with a high debt level D_g, higher interest rates, starting from the extremely low level of the last years, can cause government interest payments Z_g to soar, and thus, according to Eq. 4.1, also the government deficit $Df_z = G + Tr + Z_g - T$, even if tax revenues T will bubble up more strongly and transfer expenditure Tr will decline. If the central bank wants to prevent interest payments Z_g and government debt D_g from rising sharply during the boom, it will have to grant special conditions to the state.

In the next upturn with the threat of inflation, the CB may withdraw its support from the commodity and housing market and the banking sector and raise interest rates in the private sector, but probably not to the same extent interest rates for the state. It will want to prevent the cost of public debt from exploding and thereby preventing another sovereign debt crisis from erupting, with fatal consequences, especially in the eurozone. It will see itself obliged to act *asymmetrically* and to continue to provide monetary budget financing for the state by keeping interest rates low, which, despite the high level of D_g debt, will encourage a further increase in debt. And with monetary budget financing, it will undermine the budgetary rights of the parliament.

As we can see, central banks will find it difficult to break away from the low interest rate policy into which they have slipped in times of crises.

4.2 Inequality of Income and Wealth

Nicholas Kaldor, Hungarian economist (1908–1986), has cited as one of the few economic constants, "stylized facts", the ratio of wage income to total income, cf. also the comments on Bowley's law in Sect. 2.13.6 "Economic concepts and traditional economic policy". The Economist compiles the percentage of wage costs to nominal gross domestic product for a number of countries in the period from 1970 to 2012, cf. The Economist (2013d, p. 65). After that, the wage share decreases. This means that the share of capital income increases. He also points out that within the wage-earners, the highly paid have had far greater income increases. The Economist cites three factors as reasons for the growing inequality: international trade, technological development, and the increased demand of companies for highly qualified workers. The Economist also sees this trend for the future: "Most jobs will not be on the factory floor but in the offices nearby, which will be full of designers, engineers, IT specialists, logistics experts, and other professionals". Furthermore: "The revolution will affect not only how things are made, but where. Factories used to move to low-wage countries to curb labor costs. But labor costs are growing less and less important: a $499 first-generation iPad included only about $33 of manufacturing labor, of which the final assembly in China accounted for just $8", see The Economist (2012, p. 13).

Logistics promotes the international division of labor and expands national to global markets, compare Sect. 2.13.1 "ICT revolution (Baldwin and Milanovic)". As a result of globalization, the less qualified workers N of the industrialized countries enter into direct competition with low-paid workers in less developed economies abroad, as the example of Apple production shows. Competitive pressure reduces the increase in wages W at home. The situation is different for highly qualified workers. Globalization expands their field of activity without creating competition from outside. This asymmetry makes low-paid workers N the losers and high-paid workers the winners of globalization. It makes the share of wage income WN in total income Y shrink in favor of profits Π. It thus promotes inequality, which calls for compensation. Samuelson already pointed out the inequality resulting from globalization at the beginning of 2000 and pleaded for a fiscal redistribution, cf. Der Spiegel (2005, pp. 86–90).

International trade, through supply chain management, makes it possible to increasingly relocate simple production abroad, and robot and computer technology creates the conditions for increased automation of simple work processes, with the effect that this technological development reduces the demand for simple work N, cf. The Economist: "Special Report: Immigrants from the future" (2014c). Germany wants to push ahead with the automation of production, and under the banner of "Industry 4.0", the computerization of industry is to be further expanded. In the future, "things" will communicate with each other to a greater extent; for example, a workpiece orders a robot to move to the next production phase, which will allow the production process to run largely autonomously. Automation is also likely to turn the low-skilled workers N into losers.

In view of the declining wage share and growing inequality, the market-liberal Economist sees a need for government action on minimum wage rules, see The Economist (2013e). The Economist discusses income inequality in detail in a review article. According to the article, in many countries inequality measured by the Gini coefficient is growing. Taking the income share of the 1% richest as the inequality measure, inequality increases from 1980 onwards. For example, starting from 1980, the 1% richest Americans doubled their income share within 30 years from 10 to 20%, see The Economist (2013c, p. 6). Saez and Zucman (2019) come to a similar conclusion. We have compiled the following data from their graphical analysis in Fig. 1.1 "The rise of inequality in the United States, 1978–2018, 7":

	Share of national income earned by	
	1980 (%)	2018 (%)
Bottom 50%	20	12
Top 1%	10	20

The overview "Global Wealth" in The Economist (2014e, p. 85) provides information on global wealth inequality. According to this, 0.7% of the world's richest people own 44% of global wealth and 69.8% of the poorest only 8.9%.

As we know from Chap. 1 Introduction, Rajan points to the increasing income inequality. He sees the reason for this in education and professional qualifications. Minsky's approach provides a framework to illuminate this growing social problem. In the production of goods, he separates the technologically determined variable wage costs NW for less qualified workers N from profits Π. The profits Π contain the general costs, which, as mentioned above, are becoming increasingly important with the increase in highly qualified specialists—here Minsky deviates from the usual national accounting definition of wage income. In order to survive in global competition, company managers in industrialized countries employ a large number of highly qualified specialists such as engineers, logisticians, controllers, designers, computer scientists, lawyers, and other experts such as financial analysts; robots are increasingly replacing simple manual activities in the production process, many stages of which are outsourced to low-wage countries.

On the one hand, general costs, which are fixed in the short term, are thus becoming increasingly important, while on the other hand the importance of variable costs, which are shifted abroad via outsourcing at the expense of domestic workers but in favor of foreign workers, is declining. For example, the development centers with highly qualified employees of the Spanish fashion companies Zara and Mango are located in Galicia and Catalonia, whereas production is largely outsourced to low-wage foreign countries. The same applies in other sectors of the economy, for example, the development and production of the iPad, and also to medium-sized companies such as the Italian company Moleskine. Due to supply chain management—low transport costs and strong international production interdependence—the low-skilled workers are in global competition with each other, and global competition even threatens the subsistence level in Western industrialized countries.

The upheaval in the cost structure corresponds to an upheaval in the remuneration structure. This upheaval increasingly reinforces income inequality. The same applies to the financial market, where highly paid managers, financial analysts, and investment bankers are receiving a large part of the proceeds as salaries and bonuses.

To illustrate household inequality, we take a closer look at household income and expenditure. Households differ in their income, both in terms of amount and type. So far, we have looked at households as a whole. Their disposable income Yv is

$$\mathrm{Yv} = \mathrm{Tr} + \mathrm{W}^* + \Pi^* + \mathrm{Z}^*. \tag{4.6}$$

Here too, we list interest income separately from profits. The total interest income Z contains, among other things, the state interest payments Z_g.

Of disposable income, they have after consumption expenditure

$$\mathrm{C} = \mathrm{c_{tr}Tr} + \mathrm{c_w W}^* + \mathrm{c}_\pi \Pi + \mathrm{c_z Z}^* \tag{4.7}$$

the savings

$$\mathrm{S} = \mathrm{Yv} - \mathrm{C} = \mathrm{s_{tr}Tr} + \mathrm{s_w W}^* + \mathrm{s}_\pi \Pi^* + \mathrm{s_z Z}^*. \tag{4.8}$$

Households either keep the money they save as a *cash* reserve, which includes short-term bank deposits, or they invest it in *financial assets* for longer-term returns. Households use their financial means to build up their wealth Σ.

The view of all households blocks the view of differences, of inequality in income and wealth. Only disaggregation and strong accentuation make differences visible. We, therefore, make a rough distinction between "poorer" households, households in the lower income bracket, and "richer" households, households in the upper income bracket. These two extreme groups of households differ not only in the amount of income they receive, but also in the type of income and financial investments they make.

Poorer households have predominantly low income from low-skilled labor Ws and from transfer income Tr. Despite a low tax rate t_w = Tw/Ws on wage income, poorer households have hardly any money left after consumption C_u to build up a significant wealth. On the contrary, for the majority of poorer households, income is below the subsistence level. They need state support to live. Often there are not enough resources left to provide for illness, unemployment, and for their life as pensioners, so the state has to fill gaps in their provision. The state must intervene for social reasons and take corrective action in the economic process.

Richer households generate high income from highly skilled workers as well as from actual company profits such as dividends. The progressivity of taxation formally ensures higher taxation of higher incomes. However, compared with wage income W, there is considerable scope for taxing profits Π. Supported by highly qualified specialists, profit recipients can use this leeway to their advantage, compare, for example, Saez and Zucman (2019), "The triumph of injustice". Even EU states play an active role here by helping economic entities within the EU to reduce their tax bases at the expense of national tax revenues through tax competition. The same applies worldwide. A considerable part of the profits Π also escapes the knowledge of the tax offices, so that the effective progressiveness is significantly lower than the *formal* one of the tax scale. Thus, after taxation T(Π), a high net profit Π* remains. The same applies to the interest income Z*. Due to the lower propensity to consume, the households of the richer class have considerable amounts of money left over which they can invest profitably in the long term. This investment is reflected in their *asset change account*.

If we take a closer look at consumption propensities, they fall away from transfer income Tr to interest income Z*

$$1 = c_{tr} > c_w > c_\Pi \approx c_z.$$

With c_{tr} = 1 we take over the Minsky propensity to consume from transfer income Tr. The propensity to consume c_w from wage income W* is unlikely to be significantly lower, so that we can *neglect the asset change account of households in the lower stratum*. This is because the net income from wage income W* and transfer income Tr is almost entirely used by lower-class households for their consumption C_u. This means that they have *no significant savings S_u for wealth formation*.

Our example of saving and accumulating wealth confirms a detailed empirical study of wealth inequality in the US by Saez and Zucman (2014). They analyze savings behavior as a function of wealth and arrive at the following result for the savings rate s = S/Y, here in percent.

	Saving rate s in the USA	
Wealth holders	1929–1986 (%)	1986–2012 (%)
All	12	9
Bottom 90%	6	0
Top 10%	24	22
Top 1%	24	36

Overall, the savings rate s decreases from 12 to 9% between 1929–1986 and 1986–2012. The decrease is more drastic in the lower 90% of wealthy owners. For them, the savings rate s falls from 6 to 0%. At present, this group of 90% hardly forms any wealth from savings. Their share of wealth falls from around 35% in 1986 to almost 20% in 2012, and their share of income falls from around 70% to 60% during this period.

A completely different picture emerges for the top wealth holders. The savings rate s of the 1% richest increases from 24 to 36%, their share of income from 10% to almost 20%, and of wealth from 25% to more than 40%. The trend toward inequality is clear. The data are taken from Table 2: Rates of Growth, Saving, and Return by Wealth Group and Fig. 1.2: Income and Wealth Share of Bottom 90% and Top 1% Wealth Holders in Saez and Zucman (2014).

Now back to our example and here to the situation of the upper stratum. According to the above empirical analysis, it looks completely different from the situation for the lower stratum and is reflected in the accounts in Table 4.1.

The savings S_o are considerable in the richer class. The income of an upper-class household considerably exceeds the income of a lower-class household. And the low propensity to consume c_π and c_z leave the richer households considerable money S_o for accumulation of wealth, changes in the stocks "cash" and "financial assets", symbolized by Δ.

Financial assets include the purchase of securities such as bonds, shares, and derivatives. Expenditure on residential real estate from current production is included in consumption C_o in national accounts, but it also increases the wealth of upper-class households.

The accumulation of assets Σ consists of real estate, bonds and shares, and other assets. Real estate prices, bond, and share prices fluctuate. And this volatility, as we know from the Keynes-Minsky momentum, increases the uncertainty in the financial, goods, and thus labor markets.

Table 4.1 Current account and asset change account for households in the upper income stratum

Current account	
Expenditure	Revenue
Consumption C_o	Profits Π^*
Savings S_o	Interest income Z^*
Asset change account	
Δ Cash	Savings S_o
Δ Financial assets	

Table 4.2 Bank balance sheet

Assets	Liabilities
Cash	Loans from the central bank
Deposits to the central bank	Deposits from customers, e.g., from
Loans to customer, e.g., mortgage loans	Household (cash from A.A. Stone in
(For Kate in our example)	Harari's example)
Trading assets like corporate and government	Trading liabilities
bonds and securities like ABS, MBS, and CDO	Equity

A lot of money goes into trading stocks, be it assets on the property market or assets on the financial market. The trade in the existing real estate and existing securities is likely to exceed the trade in new construction and in newly issued securities significantly.

The accumulation of wealth increases the importance of stocks for the economic process. The interdependence between markets has recently been increasingly joined by the *interdependence between flows and stocks*. As a result, balance sheets are becoming increasingly important. They compile central stocks whose values are largely determined by the financial market. It is, therefore, not surprising that Admati and Hellwig (2013) base their analysis of the recent financial crisis on balance sheets. We will discuss the banking business in more detail using a schematic bank balance sheet in Table 4.2 "Bank balance sheet".

In times of crises, central banks support asset trading and thus the development of wealth holdings Σ. In doing so, they keep an eye on the functioning of the financial market. If trade collapses and prices collapse with it, confidence in the economy dwindles, and with it the prerequisite for the Π−I dynamic. However, it is doubtful whether the "wealth effect" actually supports the propensity to consume. In any case, the support of assets Σ favors the richer and thus increases inequality.

By strengthening the assets Σ, the central bank is also increasing the equity ratio. Falling securities price led to lower equity ratios and thus to a lower risk cushion. Central bank policy thus embellishes the situation of private banks. This can be seen as support for a balance sheet policy, on the border of a balance sheet manipulation. The central bank makes private banks appear more secure and thus restores confidence in the financial system, which is what it is trying to do.

4.3 Piketty on Inequality

Piketty (2013) comprehensively examines inequality. His Graph 1.1 "L'inégalité des revenues aux Etats-Unis, 1910–2010" on p. 52, which shows the development of the income share of the 10% richest income earners, is an eloquent testimony to the resurgence of income inequality since 1980. Piketty also analyses in detail the long-term development of wealth and wealth inequality for numerous countries in a large-scale historical study. He provides a comprehensive definition of economic wealth. In addition to the production capital K, which promotes long-term growth g, it also includes the real estate assets of private households and corresponds to the wealth Σ. He relates wealth Σ to the current income Y and compiles long time series for the ratio $\beta = \Sigma/Y$. This shows that at the end of the nineteenth and the beginning of the twentieth century the assets Σ in France and Great Britain were more than six times the current income Y and that after 1910 the ratio β had fallen to well below four times by 1950. After that, wealth grows more strongly again, so that the wealth ratio β rises more than fivefold in 2010, almost reaching the level before the First World War again. Germany has a similar pattern of development, see Fig. 1.2 "Le rapport capital/revenu en Europe, 1870–2010" in Piketty (2013, p. 54).

The inequality in favor of wealth increases if the wealth Σ grows faster than income Y. According to Piketty in his retrospective analysis, this is the case if the national economic return $r = \Pi/\Sigma$ is significantly higher than the growth rate $g = \Delta Y/Y$ of income Y; if r clearly exceeds g—Piketty then speaks of the "force de divergence fondamentale". It should be noted here that Piketty defines profit Π more narrowly than Minsky, in line with the national accounts. According to Piketty, growth rates g will remain low in the future after the phase of high growth rates in the years 1950 to 1980, cf. "La fin de la croissance?" in Piketty (2013, pp. 156–159). And low growth rates g of income Y will increase inequality in wealth ratio β.

Piketty uses an example to illustrate the effect of the "force de divergence fondamentale $r > g$" on wealth inequality. In this example, he sets g at 1% and r at 5%. According to him, it is then sufficient for owners of high net worth to save and invest more than a fifth of their current income so that their wealth grows faster than the average income of society, cf. Piketty (2013, p. 573).

We can easily understand this statement of Piketty's by referring to the accounts of the upper income bracket in Table 4.1 and including interest income Z in the profits Π, as is customary in national accounts. The assets Σ of the upper income stratum grow with the savings S_0, i.e. $\Delta\Sigma = S_0$. The growth rate of wealth $g_\Sigma = \Delta\Sigma/\Sigma$ is, therefore, $S_0/\Sigma = S_0/\Pi \cdot \Pi/\Sigma = s_\pi \cdot r$. If $s_\pi > 0.2$, then for $r = 0.05$ the growth rate $g_\Sigma > g = 0.01$.

However, the growth in wealth is not only due to savings, but also to enormous increases in the value of private households' property holdings. According to Koo, this has been relatively low in Germany, unlike in many other countries, at 10% from 1995 to 2014, cf. Koo (2015, p. 2). This also explains why in 2010, in relation to income, the value of the real estate stock in France alone is roughly as large as the value of the total asset stock in Germany, cf. Graph 3.2 "Le capital en France, 1700–2010" and Graph 4.1 "Le capital en Allemagne, 1870–2010" in Piketty (2013, pp. 189 and 225).

The difference in the asset structure between Germany and France makes it obvious that real estate assets can cause a *considerable gap between production capital K, the capital stock in classical growth theory, and national wealth Σ.* Production capital K grows with tangible investments I of the companies, which promotes the growth g of income Y in the short and long term. The increase in assets Σ is inflationary in some economies, partly because of the real estate prices. This increase has no significant growth effect, at least not a lasting one. And CB measures strengthen not so much the $\Pi - I$ dynamic, and thus growth g, but rather the price increase in assets, so that they increase Piketty's wealth ratio $\beta = \Sigma/Y$ and thus inequality in wealth. Critical comments on Piketty in The Economist (2015, p. 70) also point to rising house prices as a major factor in the increase in inequality.

The capital stock K accumulated from the past will have less impact on the growth g of today's production Y because of innovation, see Sect. 2.13.1 "ICT revolution (Baldwin and Milanovic)". In contrast, due to rising prices, wealth Σ will play a major role in inequality.

The Economist notes that inflation in the real estate market is the main reason for the rise in yields. It states: "In fact, surging house prices are almost entirely responsible for growing returns on capital", see The Economist (2015, p. 70). Bastagli and Hills (2012) come to a similar conclusion in their study for the UK, where, according to their study, the increase in assets is primarily due to property assets. They substantiate the trend with the following figures:

Housing wealth of households in Great Britain (£000, 2005 prices) (according to asset percentiles)			
	10	50	90
1995	0	27 [73%]	121 [64%]
2000	0	44 [81%]	197 [80%]
		{63%}	{63%}
2005	0	102 [90%]	306 [79%]
		{278%}	{153%}

Square brackets indicate the share of real estate assets in total assets and curly brackets indicate the increase in value compared to the base year 1995. The figures are taken from Table 1.1: Net Household Worth in 1995, 2000, and 2005 from Bastagli and Hills (2012, p. 10).

As the data show, the median household (asset percentile 50) can already participate in the increase in the value of assets, and real estate assets account for a very considerable proportion of this; this is illustrated by the percentages in square brackets. The increase in the value of real estate is largely due to price increases. Of the enormous percentage increases of 278% and 153%, respectively, only 8% and 9% are due to property growth in real terms, according to the figures from Table 2: Net Household Worth in 1995 and 2005 from Bastagli and Hills (2012, p. 12).

The increase in the value of the asset stock Σ, which is often emphasized here, is not taken into account in the growth formula $g_\Sigma = s_\pi \cdot r$. The extension $g_\Sigma = p_\Sigma + s_\pi \cdot r$ formally emphasizes the relative increase in value of the wealth Σ with the summand p_Σ; it follows from $\Delta\Sigma = p_\Sigma \Sigma + S_0$. And as we have seen, it is above all the price increases of real estate that are responsible for the increase in value.

Piketty provides information on the inequality in the personal income distribution but not on the inequality in the personal wealth distribution. His relationship r > g relates to income and wealth in each case, and thus, says little about the inequality in personal wealth distribution.

In contrast to the personnel income distribution, a much smaller increase in inequality can be observed in the personnel wealth distribution in recent years. Atkinson, therefore, advises caution when speaking of an increase in inequality in terms of wealth, cf. Atkinson (2015), Reducing Inequality: Sharing Capital, pp. 71–72, referring to a detailed study by Roine and Waldenström (2014). According to this study, inequality in wealth increases again from 1970 onwards in Australia and the USA, but not in Denmark, France, the Netherlands, and Sweden, cf. tables and charts in Roine and Waldenström (2014). The result for the USA is confirmed by Saez and Zucman (2014).

Of particular interest is the distribution of personal wealth in France. Jorda et al. determine the composition of the asset portfolio for France, Germany, Japan, Great Britain, and the USA. Real estate ownership accounts for almost 50% of this, cf. Jorda et al. (2017). Household real estate ownership in France is high and widely dispersed. This means that a large proportion of French people could participate in the enormous rise in property prices in recent years and are, therefore, less dependent on economic development. Broad access to real estate ownership can thus ensure long-term participation in prosperity for many in the population.

"Life can only be understood backwards in the show but can only be lived forward in the show" is a sentence attributed to Sören Kierkegaard. Although one may not agree with Piketty's interpretation of his data study, it must be conceded that he has made a considerable contribution to knowledge about the past with his *comprehensive data analysis* and that he has brought the important issue of economic inequality to the fore in research and in the public eye.

He uses IT technology to create a comprehensive inventory of economic inequality, helping us to know more about what has actually happened in this important area. This also applies, for example, to the major data analyses by Roine and Waldenström, Saez and Zucman, Jorda et al. and Milanovic, who use modern information technology to provide us with comprehensive information on historical facts in the form of tables and graphs. Tirole even talks about the "*Big Data*" studies beginning to change the economic discipline, cf. Tirole (2016), where he states on page 117: "Aujourd'hui, le Big Data commence à chambouler la discipline". He also refers to applied microeconomic studies such as the studies by Levitt, cf. Levitt and Dubner (2005).

The large data analyses are a reminder of the extensive data collection of the Danish astronomer Tycho Brahé (1546–1601). He himself was not able to extract his data treasure. He had to wait for the astronomer and mathematician Johannes Kepler (1571–1630). In economics, we must persevere until a second Schumpeter provides us with a concept of economic evolution, where flow and stock variables interact and helps us to be more forward-looking in the show. We come back to this in methodological part 4.10 "Economic processes and their analysis".

4.4 Scheidel on Inequality

Scheidel's long-term analysis reinforces Claude Lévy-Strauss' presumption of exploitation that hierarchical social orders serve not so much the enlightenment as exploitation. He examines inequality from the Stone Age to the present day, i.e., also over a longer period of time before the capitalist system was established. Smith's "invisible hand", which leads the self-interest of many individual actors to the general welfare of society, is not very effective in the early days. According to Scheidel, it is rather the compulsion of the ruling class that has been a dominant factor in society and the economy. And the ruling class exploits its supremacy to enrich itself, see Scheidel (2017, p. 73): "And indeed, our sources emphasize the paramount importance of coercion as a source of top incomes and fortunes", and p. 84: "In premodern societies, very large fortunes regularly owed more to political power than to economic prowess". Scott (2017, pp. 150–182) expresses a similar view, for example at the beginning of his "Chapter Five, Population Control: Bondage and War".

Both authors use the terms "subsistence" and "surplus" in their comments. If we use *min* as the minimum subsistence level and *de* as the average income, then $\alpha = de/min$ is an *indicator for surplus*. This surplus indicator α is included in a modified Gini coefficient developed by Milanovic, Lindert, and Williamson (2011), which is also used by Scheidel to measure income inequality in preindustrial societies. At that time, the surplus and thus the potential for inequality was significantly lower, and this will be taken into account in long-term studies.

The traditional Gini coefficient Gk is between 0 and 1, the lower limit is reached when the distribution is equal and the upper limit when the income or wealth are in one hand. This extreme concentration is conceivable for wealth, but not for income. In order to survive, people need a minimum income, the subsistence minimum.

Taking into account the minimum subsistence level min, Milanovic, Lindert, and Williamson reduce the maximum Gini coefficient Gk to

$$Gk^* = (\alpha - 1)/\alpha$$

The maximum Gk* increases with α In the course of economic development, the surplus, the potential for inequality, rises and thus α. And the maximum Gk* increases with α. Milanovic, Lindert, and Williamson call the curve the "Inequality possibility frontier (IPF)". Information on the course of the IPF curve is provided by Graph A.1 in Scheidel (2017, p. 446) and Graph 1 in Milanovic et al. (2011, p. 258). The closer the measured Gini coefficient Gk is to the IPF curve, the greater the inequality in society. Figure 3 in Milanovic et al. (2011, p. 258), shows that in preindustrial societies the Gini coefficient Gk is much closer to the IPF curve than in modern societies. According to this, inequality does not increase over a long period of time, but rather decreases.

The decrease is particularly evident in the "Inequality extraction ratio (IER)". It puts the measured Ginikoeficient Gk in relation to its maximum Gk*. This quotient is the "Inequality extraction ratio (IER)"

$$\mathrm{IER} = \mathrm{Gk}/\mathrm{Gk}^*$$

The quotient measures the degree of inequality caused by the unequal distribution of the surplus over the subsistence level. According to Table 2 in Milanovic et al. (2011, p. 263), the value of the Inequality extraction ratio IER drops significantly from 77 to 44% from preindustrial to modern societies. There can, therefore, be no talk of a particular inequality in the capitalist economy. The results of Piketty's analysis, which takes a critical look at the capitalist economy, are thereby presented in a different light. Scheidel (2017, pp. 445–456) has taken over most of the findings of the three authors Milanovic, Lindert, and Williamson in his appendix "The limits of inequality".

With regard to the siphoning off of surpluses by the ruling class in early agricultural societies, Scheidel (2017, p. 47) comments as follows: "Rulers, their agents, and large landowners, categories that commonly intersected, were locked in conflict over the control of the surplus that could be siphoned off through state taxes and private rents". Although society today is more open and innovative entrepreneurs can often create huge fortunes from nothing, the enormous inequalities in income and wealth are a barrier to equal opportunities. Atkinson points to this (2015, pp. 10–11). Inequality weighs on economic activity, all the more so because people no longer want to accept it as acceptable. For then it reduces people's willingness to cooperate, which is the basis for the economy based on the division of labor and economic progress.

Even though Scheidel's historical study is skeptical about the effects of redistribution measures, there is still a need for action in modern industrialized countries. This will show whether the state can reduce the gap between society and the economy. Certainly, it will have to rethink its approach and come up with innovative concepts in education and taxation, especially in the taxation of inherited wealth. There is also a new role for central banks which may be promising for the development of a strong, autonomous society, see Sect. 1.7.2 "Reorientation of economic policy in democratically constituted states" and Chap. 5 "Conclusion: changing economic policies".

4.5 Private Banks: Equity Ratio, Banking Business, Risks, and Regulation

4.5.1 Equity Ratio

Along with the stock data, balance sheets, and in particular, balance sheets of banks are also of increasing interest. *Traditionally, private banks do not play a significant role in macroeconomic models*. Minsky opens his macro approach to private banks and points out that banking is central to the modern economy. Admati and Hellwig (2013) focus on balance sheets in their analysis. They argue for higher equity ratios. On the one hand, this means that less funds are available for risky financial investments, and on the other hand, the buffer is larger to absorb any losses that arise. Strengthening self-liability also reduces the systemic risk.

The equity ratio EQ is the quotient of equity and total assets in the balance sheet. The higher the equity ratio, the higher the buffer against risks/losses. If the share price falls and the lower price is recognized in the balance sheet, the equity ratio is reduced. It increases if a rise in the share price is recorded in the balance sheet. Profits/losses from the profit and loss account increase/decrease equity and thus the equity ratio. The equity ratio is a residual figure. It is the result of changes in accounting, as indicated in Tables 4.2 "Bank balance sheet" and 4.3 "Bank profit and loss account (P&L)". It is subject to market risks due to price fluctuations. As a residual figure, it is, therefore, hardly controllable, not even by a bank supervisory authority.

ABS Asset backed securities, MBS Mortgage-backed securities, and CDO Collateralized debt obligations.

The business segment with *trading assets* is typical for investment banking and marks an expansion compared to the traditional commercial bank in Schumpeter's time.

Equity capital is a buffer against possible future losses. The higher the equity ratio EQ, the more losses a company can absorb from its own resources. The equity ratio is, as mentioned above, a residual figure. Other variables determine its value. Admati and Hellwig (2013) have illustrated how this happens in numerous balance sheet examples for households, companies, and banks.

According to Tables 4.2 "Bank balance sheet" and 4.3 "Profit and loss account (P&L)", two determinants influencing the change in the equity ratio EQ should be highlighted:

- the performance of the securities portfolio,
- the profit development in the profit and loss account (P&L).

If the prices of bonds and shares in the bank's portfolios rise and the bank generates profits, the equity ratio EQ rises. In the opposite case, it falls. If it is too low, the Basel regulation requires the bank to take measures to strengthen its capital ratio again. For example, it can sell securities and thus reduce its securities portfolio, and to a corresponding extent, its liabilities.

Table 4.3 Bank profit and loss account (P&L)

Expenses	Revenues
Interest and similar expenses	Interest and similar income
(Among others risk premium payments)	(Among others risk premium income)
Credit loss provision	
Non-interest expenses	Non-interest income
Profit/Loss	

To illustrate the effect of sales on the EQ, we use an example, discussed in detail in Admati and Hellwig, which deals with the property ownership of a woman named Kate. Here we assume that Kate is buying a house with two flats of equal value. The house costs €500,000. She finances the purchase with a €400,000 mortgage loan and €100,000 equity. Her equity ratio EQ is, therefore, 20%

Assets	Liabilities
500,000 € Value of the house	400,000 € Mortgage loan
	100,000 € Equity

A real estate crisis surprises Kate after her purchase decision. The value of her house falls by 10% and her EQ falls to 11.1%.

Assets	Liabilities
450,000 € Value of the house	400,000 € Mortgage loan
	50,000 € Equity

With the lower EQ, Kate's credit rating drops. Her bank charges higher interest rates for the follow-up financing of her short-term loan. She can no longer cover the higher interest payments from her current income. She, therefore, sells one of the two flats and repays €225,000 of her mortgage loan. Her EQ rises to 22.2%, and so does her credit rating. Even if her bank raises the interest rate in the real estate crisis, her interest burden will still fall because of the halved debt and will be affordable for Kate.

Assets	Liabilities
225,000 € Value of the flat	175,000 € Mortgage loan
	50,000 € Equity

Kate has solved the financing problem that the real estate crisis has created. She has "shrunk back to health". Healthy shrinking has worked for Kate. She remains solvent.

However, the real estate crisis will not only affect Kate, but a large number of property owners, many of whom are not in the comfortable position of being able to part with a piece of real estate. Many go bankrupt and have to part with their entire property. And a drastic increase in forced sales causes property prices to fall further. A downward price spiral can set in and destroy assets to a considerable extent.

Similarly, the effect of a wave of sales of securities must be assessed if the Basel banking regulations strictly insist on compliance with their required equity ratio in a banking crisis. We will go into this later, but first, we will take a closer look at the banks' business.

But before that, we will discuss the case that Kate cannot "shrink back to health" by selling one flat of her house. And let us take a closer look at her situation before and after the real estate crisis. Kate earns well, let's say €3,000 € net per month after taxes, social security contributions, and health insurance payments. She has €100,000 in equity. Property prices are rising—according to Koo, for example, from 2000 to 2006 in the USA by 120%, from 1995 to 2007 in Ireland by 400%, in Greece by 240%, and in Spain by 200%, see Koo (2015, p. 2). Kate buys the house for €500,000 in this favorable situation. She takes out a loan of €400,000, say at a mortgage interest rate including repayment of 4.8%. Her equity ratio is 0.2, and after interest payment and repayment she has €1,400 net at her disposal. On this, she can live well and is carefree if everything remains as it is.

However, the situation tilts on the property market and the Keynes-Minsky momentum takes effect. Property prices fall dramatically—according to Koo (2015, p. 2), for example, in Ireland from 2007 to 2012 by almost 50%. In the case of Kate, we assume a price collapse of 10%. She has financed her house purchase in the short term and needs follow-on financing in the now unfavorable situation. The lower property price lowers her EQ and thus her credit rating. The banks see risks in her credit claim, which could lead to increased provisions. They raise the interest rate for Kate, say to 6.9%. This brings their monthly interest payments to €2300 and leaves Kate with only €700 left to live on. Whereas she previously had 47% of her net income at her disposal, the disposal rate is now drastically reduced to 23%. Kate now has to align her expenses to the strongly decreased income.

If a large number of economic subjects are affected, then the general economic spiral turns downwards: household consumption falls, entrepreneurs postpone their investment plans, outstanding debts of private banks are endangered, risk increases and pessimism spreads. Now the central bank feels called upon to stop the downward spiral. It lowers the central bank interest rate, buying real estate bonds and government bonds, and hedging assets. Private banks can receive central bank money meeting lower security requirements—their liabilities to the central bank in Table 4.2 "Bank balance sheet" increase. The private banks will use central bank money to restructure their balance sheet holdings in order to reduce their risks and open up new profit opportunities. They are less concerned with expanding credit to households and firms than with investment banking, with their trading asset activity.

Koo points out that a lot of money remains within the banking sector, and that, despite low central bank interest rates, little money from private banks flows to consumption C and investment I. This is because loans to the private sector will not increase as desired due to the low central bank interest rates, since the burden of debt financing still lies on private households and companies, see Koo (2015, p. 2): "The private sector is minimizing debt because liabilities incurred during the bubble remain, while the bubble bursts, leaving balance sheets deeply underwater. While everyone is saving or paying down debt and no one borrowing, even at zero interest rate (of the central bank), the economy started shrinking". In his analysis,

Koo sees central banks' QE policies as not very effective and advocates fiscal policy.

4.5.2 Banking Activities

Banks ensure efficient payments, facilitate purchases and sales, and favor market transactions (*Transaction banking*).

Traditionally, commercial banks collect money from a large number of depositors, especially households, and grant loans with the deposits. For example, banks provide mortgage loans to households to finance the purchase of a house and loans to businesses to finance the purchase of efficient manufacturing equipment and high-performance IT products, compare Harari's example in Sect. 2.8 "Economic evolution through innovation and credit creation (Schumpeter)". Before granting loans to households, they check whether future income flows will be sufficient to meet future interest and principal payments. In the case of companies, they check to what extent the expected profitability from their investment projects has been substantiated or not.

The monitoring is costly, and despite thorough examination, future uncertainties remain in relation to loans granted, with the result that banks include provisions for loan losses in their profit and loss accounts, see Table 4.3 "P&L account". Lending is the central activity of commercial banks. They check the creditworthiness, grant the loans and set the loan conditions, and monitor compliance with the conditions, interest, and redemption payments. Traditionally, they use their funds for lending and their funds come mainly from money deposits of private households (*Traditional Commercial Bank, Financial Intermediaries I, Risk assumption)*.

Banks incur short-term liabilities, either by taking deposits from households or by borrowing short-term from the central bank, and use these funds to grant longer-term loans, for example, for the purchase of cars and houses by households or for longer-term investment projects by companies. This maturity transformation is seen as one of the sources of instability of private banks, the "mismatch between 'long-term loans' and 'short-term deposits'", see The Economist: The inevitability of instability (2014a, p. 56) (*Maturity transformation, risk assumption*).

Traditional commercial banks expand their lending business and take over the asset management of wealthy major customers, trade in securities and support companies in financing projects and capital increases and create new securities and thus new markets (*Investment banking*).

The change from commercial banks to investment banks is reflected in the extension of the bank balance sheet beyond loans to customer, cf. Table 4.2 "Bank balance sheet". For example, they take over issues of securities at their own risk and resell them at a profit, listed there under "trading assets".

Investment banks create new securities with option papers and for these new issues, they need an appropriate price. Options are bets on the future development of prices, in the financial market of prices of, for example, shares, bonds, and currencies. Fluctuations in prices mean opportunities to make a profit and options can be used to buy future profit prospects. In order for banks to successfully market options, they need, as I said, an adequate starting price for their option offering. This is provided by the Black–Scholes formula published in 1973, and thus enables the successful marketing of options, a financial innovation with a considerable market volume. Robert C. Merton has also contributed to the development of the financial mathematical model. Myron S. Scholes and Robert C. Merton were awarded the Nobel Prize in 1997 for the development of the model (*Creating new products*).

Banks have a *special privilege*. It enables them to channel central bank money M into the economic cycle. They receive the money at an interest rate set by the central bank against certain collateral. As with household deposit money, they grant loans with central bank money. They finance profitable projects, be they real or financial investments; they invest the money profitably by buying securities and other financial securities for themselves or third parties. Banks buy government and corporate bonds, grant consumer and real estate loans to households, and buy shares in companies. This involves considerable risks. Companies, governments, and households can go bankrupt, and thus no longer meet their payment obligations (credit risk). Share prices can fall drastically and foreign government bonds can also lose considerable value due to price fluctuations (market risk). Banks want to protect themselves against risks.

Private banks are the main players in the transmission mechanism through which central bank money flows into the economy. In times of crises with a low interest rate policy of the central bank, private banks, in particular, can benefit from their privilege. The low interest rate policy makes central bank money cheap. In that case, deposits from private households become less attractive. There is then a structural shift away from private deposits and toward liabilities to the central bank, see under liabilities of the bank balance sheet in Table 4.2 "Bank balance sheet" (*Financial intermediaries II, Banking privilege*).

Banks are expanding their fields of business by systematically extending debt financing. They can earn money on every loan they grant and every bond they place. Debt financing increases the opportunities and risks, both for banks as creditors and for debt financiers as borrowers (*Increased debt financing, Increased financialization of the economy*).

As financial intermediaries, banks take risks, which are amplified by maturity transformation. A classic example of this is the Bank Run. In crises, private households fear for the security of their deposits and withdraw them at short notice. Banks' hands are tied by longer-term loans. They do not have sufficient funds to cope with the rush of households. They are unable to pay, become insolvent. A Bank Run thus leads to insolvency because of the differing deadlines for the use of funds and the raising of funds. The risk vis-à-vis the Bank Run has been reduced by the deposit insurance provided by the state. The creditor risk remains with the banks. They want to get rid of this risk. Banks are increasingly innovative. They create new products for this purpose, with which they make risks tradable. In doing so, they create new markets and new profit opportunities. Securitized bonds such as

ABS papers and the insurance products Credit Default Swaps (CDS Papers) are of particular economic relevance (*Business with risks*).

Banks collect comprehensive information in the course of their activities, whether in connection with the granting of loans or in connection with investment as a financial investor. Similar to management consulting and auditing companies and rating agencies, they are well informed about economic events. The subject matter of information is changing, namely from the procurement of information for the granting of credit—the main interest of commercial banks—to the procurement of information for the investment of money—the main interest of investment banks (*Banks as information centers*).

4.5.3 Risks and Risk Management

We want to take a closer look at the risks and the business with them because of their economic significance. Lending by banks is associated with the risk that the borrower, the debtor, will not be able to meet its future interest and redemption payments. In advance, therefore, the bank as creditor checks the creditworthiness of the debtor. The examination incurs costs, and despite a thorough examination, the bank cannot exclude the possibility that the borrower may not be able to pay his debts in the future. He may become insolvent and in case of default, the bank makes provisions and creates reserves in the profit and loss account, compare Table 4.3 "P&L account". In the event of insolvency, the risk takes the form of losses. The lender bears the audit costs and the costs in the event of the risk occurring, namely the losses from the outstanding payment obligations and possibly also the costs from the insolvency settlement (*Risk costs of the creditor, provisions for credit default risks*).

The securitization of receivables enables the Bank to sell its risks by means of the ABS securities. With the ABS paper, the receivable becomes a commodity. On the one hand, the bank can use the ABS paper to reduce its risk costs—there is no need for detailed risk assessment—and on the other hand, it can sell the risk to third parties and even earn money from the sale [risk shifting and reduction of credit costs]. As a commodity, ABS papers such as bonds and shares are subject to market risk. Because they have a price. It can fluctuate and is, therefore, volatile (*Market risk*).

The CDS-papers make the risk tradable. Here, credit default swaps are the traded commodity. We will illustrate the construction of this good with a simplified example. Deutsche Bank (DB) subscribes to a €10 million bond issued by Siemens or Greece and wants to hedge against the default of its claim against Siemens or Greece. This hedging is made possible by the CDS market, where CDS securities are traded between protection buyers, here DB, and protection sellers, an insurance company for example. DB, as the collateral taker, buys "collateral" against the loss of receivables from the borrower Siemens. It consists of the fact that the guarantor compensates DB for the loan loss in the event of Siemens' insolvency. For this compensation payment, the insurance payout, DB pays *a price, a premium,* to the guarantor, which may be another bank or an insurance company, such as the US large insurance company AIG.

The amount of the premium is based on the probability p that the insured event will occur. The higher the probability of default is considered, the higher the premium that DB has to pay. Let us substantiate the example further by setting the term to two years. The price for CDS is given in basis points bp. Let us say that the price is 400 bp. DB then pays €400,000 in premiums for €10 million, divided into quarterly premium payments of €100,000:

1. If the debtor goes bankrupt after one year, the insurance company/other bank pays DB € 10 million. These insurance payments are offset by premium payments of € 400,000.
2. If the debtor remains solvent for more than two years, no compensation payments are due to DB, which pays €800,000 in insurance premiums.

The insurance premiums correspond to implicit credit default probabilities. If we remove the division of the two years into quarters, and for the sake of simplicity, compare the expected premium payments with the expected insurance payment for the two years as a whole, we obtain the implied credit default probability p over

$$(1-\mathrm{p})800,000=\mathrm{p}(10,000,000-800,000).$$

The resolution of the equation yields $p = 0.08$. If market participants consider the probability of default to be too low and increase the probability of default to $p = 0.10$ in their risk assessment, then the premium payments rise according to

$$0.9\mathrm{Premium}=0.1(10,000,000-\mathrm{Premium})$$

from €800,000 to €1 million. This will also increase the price of the CDS- paper.

If the risk increases, the CDS price will rise. In the case of the bond that DB buys, the reverse effect occurs. The risk premium rz, the credit risk spread, increases, and thus the bond price falls. Due to the compensatory effect of the CDS prices, DB can, however, hedge against falling bond prices by purchasing CDS securities on the corresponding bond. It thus concludes a hedge transaction and can thus pass on its risk. An example may illustrate this. DB buys a newly issued bond at a price of 100 and with a nominal interest rate of 3%. If the issuer loses creditworthiness after selling it, a risk premium rz = 1.33 leads to an increased interest rate of 4%. The increase in the interest rate is accompanied by a price loss from 100 to 75. If DB has purchased a CDS security issued on it, at the same time as the bond in times of low risk, i.e., if it has hedged its bond purchase, it can offset its price loss in times of higher risk by the increase in the price of its CDS security. With this hedging, DB can continue to take risky transactions (*moral hazard*). And so, the overall risk increases in national economies, and globally because of international trade.

The hedging aspect is one factor of the innovation "CDS paper". The other factor is that the innovation has created a new financial product, the purchase of which can be worthwhile independently of hedging transactions. If market participants speculate on future increasing risks, on rising CDS prices, they buy CDS paper, possibly debt financed with a high leverage. The CDS market thus quickly takes on a life of its own with supply and demand like any other market.

In the financial crisis at the beginning of this century, the prices of CDS paper skyrocketed—similar to the risk premiums on market interest rates, for example, for CDS on Greek government bonds. The higher prices reflect the higher estimated probability of credit default with the consequence that the now increased caution reduces lending. The flow of credit is coming to a standstill. In bad times, panic breaks out not only among depositors, as the example of Bank Run teaches us, but also among other players, such as banks, which then become over-cautious in granting loans.

There is a significant difference between traditional life and damage insurance and the new type of credit default insurance. Although both insurances are based on probability considerations, in the case of classic insurance the probability can be objectified from historical values—in the case of motor vehicle accident insurance, from the frequency of accidents in the past—in the new type of credit default insurance, it is *based solely on the subjective assessment* of risk. And here we know from the Keynes-Minsky momentum that when a crisis occurs, the risk can be *overstated.*

The CDS market has developed magnificently since 2000. In the financial crisis of 2008, the outstanding insurance claims threatened the solvency of the major American insurance company AIG, among others. The US government intervened to support the insurance company because without state intervention the global financial system and thus the world economy threatened to collapse.

From the perspective of an individual financial institution, financial innovations such as ABS and CDSs have the advantage that the individual institution can transfer risks to third parties and reduce the costs of risk assessment and monitoring. These favorable circumstances encourage financial institutions to enter into riskier financial transactions with higher interest rates in good times (*moral hazard*). However, trade within the financial sector has increased its interdependence, creating *systemic risk*. In bad times, this risk threatens the financial system worldwide, and through increased debt financing, the financialization of the economy, also the global economy. And to avoid global economic collapse, governments, and central banks must intervene massively, individually, and in a coordinated manner, including in coordination with international organizations such as the IMF and the World Bank.

Until the introduction of ABS and CDS securities, banks used risk premiums to hedge against an increase in risk. Now they can act more quickly with the new securities and banks with *good information* can react particularly quickly and profit from situational upheavals.

It is not surprising that financial innovations such as the ABS papers, and especially the CDS papers, are considered *toxic products*. Banks get rid of the costs of credit monitoring, make money from risk trading and increase the *systemic risk*, which ultimately, if it occurs, has to be borne by society.

If the subjective probability of default p rises—favored by the Keynes-Minsky momentum, the prices of risk papers skyrocket, and because of enormous stocks, so does the risk potential. No wonder that the then ECB President Trichet warned of a collapse of the CDS market. This clearly shows the systemic risk that risk trading in new financial products has created. This is because trading takes place largely within the financial system and thus leads to a networking of the financial industry and to the systemic risk that has been mentioned several times.

Admati and Hellwig (2013), like Minsky, see the instability of the economy threatened by the financial market, especially through banking transactions. They point out in detail that in bad times, banks are often no longer able to cover risks arising from their equity capital. The two authors argue strongly in favor of self-insurance for banks and call for an increased equity ratio to cushion losses in crises. We believe that a better capital base is a suitable means of absorbing increased losses of individual badly managed banks in *normal times. In crises, however, the bank's own protection* via *the equity ratio will be insufficient*. This is because the equity ratio drops drastically in crises. As a residual figure, it is hardly controllable because, as we have seen, it depends heavily on market and credit risks, which can rise dramatically in crises. Moreover, systemic risk exacerbates the crisis in the entire banking sector. The protection can only come from *outside*, be it in the EU through a financially strong EU banking union or from other government institutions, including international institutions such as the World Bank or the IMF, as we know, as Rajan has already pointed out.

Our concerns about the equity ratio as collateral in crises are confirmed by a proposal of the ECB to establish a "bad bank" in view of a "fragile EU banking sector, with rock bottom equity", see A. Enria: "ECB: the EU needs a regional 'bad bank'", Financial Times, October 26, 2020.

Bankers are determined to make profits by expanding their lending business, creating new financial products, and thus creating new markets. And they are highly motivated because the rewards in the form of bonus payments are quickly apparent. Some speak of greed as the driving force that turns bankers into gamblers. This driving force can develop freely. The risks only become apparent with a considerable delay, as Rajan already points out. And it is not the innovative bankers who bear the risks, the costs are borne by society. Society must bear the losses in a downturn, in a crisis. So, there is an asymmetry in two respects, *firstly in time and secondly in the consequences for the bankers. This asymmetry favors moral hazard behavior*.

4.5.4 Basel Banking Regulation and EU Banking Union

Private banks are subject to a capital requirement. A sufficiently high EQ should protect them against risks. The Basel Committee on Banking Supervision specifies the requirements in the so-called Basel capital rules. In these rules, market risks are recorded using the "value-at-risk (VaR)" risk measure. The financial institutions concerned can, under their own responsibility, select a model to forecast their market risk "VaR" one day in advance. The financial institutions must subsequently verify their short-term forecast using a so-called "backtesting procedure". If their forecasts underestimate the risk in a statistically significant way, they must increase their EQ according to the extent of their underestimation. Banks can, as explained above, increase their EQ by selling securities from their portfolio or by issuing new shares. However, banking self-regulation has not been very effective in the recent financial crisis and we will discuss this in more detail in Sect. 4.10.2 "Quantitative numerical analysis".

The EQ is a residual figure which, as explained above, depends largely on the performance of securities holdings in bank balance sheets and on the profit performance of banks. The Basle rules aim at obliging financial institutions with higher risk to make higher own provision, to provide a stronger buffer against possible losses. In times of crises, risk increases and a large number of banks are affected by the rising risk. This is because profits generally fall during a crisis and then the prices of securities, and consequently, the EQ of many banks also fall. They are forced to strengthen their equity base. But if there is a wave of sales of securities, prices will continue to fall. As a result, the value of the remaining securities holdings in the bank's balance sheet will continue to fall and, consequently, the EQ. In a crisis, therefore, the Basel self-regulation of banks can trigger a wave of sales, exacerbate the crisis and reverse the self-provision for risk cases that the EQ is aiming for. The crisis calls for external intervention. This has also been the case in the recent financial crisis. The international community has, as I said, supported the global banking system in coordination with central banks and international organizations such as the World Bank and the IMF.

The short-term forecast of market risk contained in the Basel regulation has a time horizon of one day and is *symptomatic of the short-term orientation in the financial market.* This short-term orientation spills over to the real economy with the financing flows, and also the increased "tail risk" of the financial market, the particularly *extreme risk.*

With the Banking Union, the EU is establishing a new institution that can intervene from outside in future crises. It is intended to stabilize the EU banking system in times of emergency and, if necessary, wind up individual ailing banks without endangering the financial system as a whole. To this end, EU banks are to raise a €55 billion liquidation fund with their own resources in eight years from 2015 onwards. Necessary interventions are to be initiated by the ECB. It must then present alternative courses of action because times of crises call for quick decisions. This gives the ECB a new task which has nothing directly to do with its primary task of stabilizing the price level P. Under President Draghi, the ECB is expanding its scope on its own initiative in order to ensure the functioning of the EU economy and prevent the break-up of the eurozone.

With its "Outright Monetary Transactions OMT Decision", it indirectly grants cheap budget financing to the euro countries. And by tying the financing to ESM conditions, it actively supports the EU's hesitant economic policy. It has usurped the law of action and created facts. It is extending its powers in the direction of the American Fed. It is not surprising that the Federal Constitutional Court of Germany classifies the ECB's action as an unauthorized appropriation of competence, as an ultra vires act, cf. Federal Constitutional Court: Main proceedings ESM/EZB (2014). The Federal Constitutional Court made detailed comments on the Public sector Purchase Programme (PSPP) in 2020. We will return to this in an excursus in Sect. 4.11.3 "Profits and losses of central banks".

With the close link between the EU banking union and the ECB, and with its autonomous OMT policy, the ECB is moving away from its originally clear simple objective of maintaining price stability. However, it remains to be seen whether this newly established EU banking union buffer will be sufficient for times of crises.

4.6 Debt Financing and Risks: Good Times and Bad Times

In the following section, we would like to illustrate the effect of credit leverage in debt financing by means of selected examples. Credit leverage increases opportunities and risks, both in good and bad times. Market participants are not guided by statistical expectations. They do not form the mean value of opportunities and risks. They see both sides, just not at the same time. In the course of the economy, the direction of vision changes. If investors have their eyes on the opportunities in the upswing, they fear losses in the downturn. According to the Keynes-Minsky momentum, the turnaround from good times to bad turns the focus from opportunities to risks, and the turnaround at recovery from losses to profits. The momentum thus reinforces the interdependence of profits and investment, compare Eq. 3.28.

The following examples refer to an investment project. The project can be a real investment by a company, for example, the purchase of robots for a production line or the purchase of IT equipment for new logistic processes. Similarly, debt-financed financial investments, debt-financed purchases of shares or CDS-papers have a similar effect.

Investment I depends on the constellation between project return r_p, market interest rate i, and risk premium rz. The market interest rate i and the degree of debt financing v, as well as the risk premium rz, are the central factors of debt financing. The factors r_p, i, v, and rz determine the future return on equity r_e

$$r_e = r_p + v(r_p - i \cdot rz). \tag{4.9}$$

The higher the expected return on equity r_e, the greater the propensity to invest I and the stronger the $\Pi - I$ dynamic in Eq. 3.28. The project return r_p must be greater than the market interest rate i increased by the risk factor rz if debt financing is to be worthwhile.

In the course of the business cycle, good times alternate with bad. With this alteration, the constellation also changes between project return r_p, market interest rate i, and the risk premium rz, as well as the debt financing ratio v, the leverage ratio. Two examples illustrate the situations in good and bad times.

In good times, debt financing opens up brilliant prospects for the future and is then the main focus of attention, i.e., here on Table 4.4 "Version: Opportunity/Profit in good times [bright side]". The increase in credit leverage from 0 to 3 increases the return on equity by a factor of 2.5 from 10 to 25%. If an investor invests €10,000 of his own money for one year, then, according to Table 4.4, he will make a profit of €1,000, i.e., a return of 10%. If he has financed three-quarters of the investment with a loan at 5%, the investment of €2,500 will yield a return on equity of 25%. From the €1,000 profit, he pays €375 interest and the remaining net amount of €625 on the €2,500 invested equity gives the 25% return.

According to Table 4.5 "Version: Risk/Loss in good times [bright side]", in good times the rise in credit leverage from 0 to 3 increases the loss by a factor of 5.5. Return on equity falls from −10 to −55%. However, this risk is largely ignored in good times, it is largely disregarded.

Table 4.4 Effect of the credit leverage for an investment project/a financial asset amounting to €10,000

Version: Opportunity/Profit in good times [bright side]			
Equity capital EC	10,000	5,000	2,500
Debt capital DC Interest rate i = 0,05	0	5,000	7,500
Leverage v = DC/EC	**0**	**1**	**3**
Earnings before interest	1,000	1,000	1,000
Project return r_p in %	**10%**	**10%**	**10%**
Interest payments	0	250	375
Earnings after interest	1,000	750	625
Return on equity r_e in %	**10%**	**15%**	**25%**

Table 4.5 Effect of the credit leverage for an investment project/a financial asset amounting to €10,000

Version: Risk/Loss in good times [bright side]			
Equity capital EC	10,000	5,000	2,500
Debt capital DC Interest rate i = 0,05	0	5,000	7,500
Leverage v = DC/EC	**0**	**1**	**3**
Earnings before interest	−1,000	−1,000	−1,000
Project return r_p in %	**−10%**	**−10%**	**−10%**
Interest payments	0	250	375
Earnings after interest	−1,000	−1,250	−1,375
Return on equity r_e in %	**−10%**	**−25%**	**−55%**

Table 4.6 Effect of the credit leverage for an investment project/a financial asset amounting to €10,000

Version: Opportunity/Profit in bad times [dark side]			
Equity capital EC	10,000	5,000	2,500
Debt capital DC, interest rate i = 0.08 *and risk premium rz = 1.6*	0	5,000	7,500
Leverage v = DC/EC	**0**	**1**	**3**
Earnings before interest	800	800	800
Project return r_p in %	**8%**	**8%**	**8%**
Interest payments	0	400	600
Earnings after interest	800	400	200
Return on equity r_e in %	**8%**	**8%**	**8%**

Table 4.7 Effect of the credit leverage for an investment project/a financial asset amounting to €10,000

Version: Risk/Loss in bad times [dark side]			
Equity capital EC	10,000	5,000	2,500
Debt capital DC, interest rate i = 0.08 *and risk premium rz = 1.6*	0	5,000	7,500
Leverage v = DC/EC	**0**	**1**	**3**
Earnings before interest	−1,200	−1,200	−1,200
Project return r_p in %	**−12%**	**−12%**	**−12%**
Interest payments	0	400	600
Earnings after interest	−1,200	−1,600	−1,800
Return on equity r_e in %	**−12%**	**−32%**	**−72%**

In bad times, the outlook for profits clouds over and the impending risks increase.

The declining profit prospects are reflected in Tables 4.6 and 4.7 in the project returns $r_p = 0.08$, which are reduced by 20%. With the credit leverage v = 3, the profit outlook turns drastically during the transition from good to bad times. Tables 4.4 and 4.7 illustrate this with the return on equity r_e, which drops from 25% to −72%. The poorer market outlook is compounded by less favorable financing conditions. These are manifested in the risk premium rz, which increases the market interest rate i by 60%. A worsening market outlook and less favorable financing conditions reduce the return on equity and thus the willingness of companies to invest.

In bad times, the outlook for profits clouds over and the risks become more apparent.

With a credit leverage v = 5, equity no longer covers the loss. According to Eq. 4.9, the return on equity is then

$$r_e = -0.12 + 5(-0.12 - 0.08) = -1.12$$

At −112%, the loss exceeds the equity capital, so the equity capital is no longer sufficient to offset a loss. In banks, the equity ratio is often very low, in other words, the credit leverage is high. If the equity ratio is low, it can often no longer serve as a buffer for losses in crises. Then banks are threatened with insolvency, and because of the strong financialization, companies in the real economy are threatened with collapse. Amati and Hellwig (2013) see a sufficient equity ratio as a significant contribution to risk provisioning. The Basel rules for banks also focus on capital regulation. As explained in Sect. 4.5.4 "Basel banking regulation and EU banking union", we are skeptical whether the residual figure "equity ratio" can be a controllable variable.

The weighting of opportunity and risk, of expected profit and impending loss, is subjective. The subjective assessment changes during the transition from "good" to "bad" times. In good times the "opportunity/profit" version is highly weighted, i.e., the main focus is then on the version in Table 4.4 In bad times the "risk/loss" version is highly weighted, i.e., the main focus is then on the version in Table 4.7. This change in weighting corresponds to the Keynes-Minsky momentum. The change from "overconfidence" to "over fear" in the transition from "boom" to "recession" underpins behavioral studies, studies in "behavioral economics". The Economist states: "Risk aversion, ..., rose sharply after the crash, even among investors who had suffered no losses in the stock market. The reaction to the financial crisis, the authors concluded, looked less like a proportionate response to the losses suffered and more like old-fashioned 'panic'", The Economist (2014b, p. 60).

Table 4.8 shows how profit and loss can develop as in relation to debt financing, the leverage ratio v, where we have taken values for return on equity from Tables 4.4 and 4.7. They reflect the changing perspectives.

Credit leverage increases opportunities and risks, profits and losses (*leverage effect that magnifies the gain and the risk)*. It increases the range from [10, −12] at v = 0 to [35, −112] at v = 5.

The above example is an illustration of the investment risk (business risk). It becomes visible in profit and loss, in fluctuations in market results. Without external financing, v = 0, the investor takes a manageable risk. With increasing credit

Table 4.8 Range of profit and loss in % of return on equity r_e

Leverage ratio v	Profit	Loss
0	10	−12
1	15	−32
3	25	−72
5	35	−112

leverage v the risk increases, the credit risk is added to the business risk. Loans increase the chances of profit, but also the risks of a loss, which the borrower, the entrepreneur, has to bear. If v = 5, the entrepreneur can no longer cover his losses from his own funds. He goes bankrupt, and the lender, the bank, must also record a loss in his profit and loss account (P&L).

The market risk is reflected in fluctuations in prices, be they of goods, interest rates or the prices of shares and bonds, and the credit risk is the risk of the borrower's insolvency. Debt financing is directly linked to the credit risk. As the example shows, it has a direct impact on the investment risk to a considerable extent. It also has a similar effect on financial investments, in the case of debt-financed investments in shares and bonds. It has an indirect effect on market risks. This is because the expansion of debt financing has led to the creation of substantial asset portfolios. One need only think, for example, of claims on the state; its debt D has risen sharply in industrialized countries in recent decades, and so has the stock of government bonds. And the prices of equities, bonds, ABS, and MBS papers are volatile and thus risky. As already mentioned, ABS and MBS securities not only carry market risk, but also credit default risk, generally in bonds and even in equities, since companies can go bankrupt.

In principle, Keynesian deficit policy can directly influence the macroeconomic Π−I relationship, because in it the government deficit Df is a determinant of profits and thus of investment I. However, the increased debt level limits its scope for action. The central bank alone must now shoulder the burden of economic stabilization. It acts *indirectly* at the microeconomic level by improving the financing conditions for investment projects and also for financial assets. It aims to improve the return on equity, which has deteriorated during the recession, and thus to strengthen the propensity to invest, ultimately boosting the Π−I dynamic. To explain the effectiveness of the CB's low-interest policy, we use the return of equity formula from Eq. 4.9

$$r_e = r_p + v(r_p - i \cdot rz)$$

The project return r_p cannot be influenced by the CB. It reflects the market opportunities for innovations. And the development and marketing of new products is the business of entrepreneurs. Their business can flourish if they have sufficient entrepreneurial freedom and if free markets increase their sales opportunities. Private banks control the flow of money, which is reflected in the degree of external financing v, and the risk premium rz as well. Thus, the focus of the CB is on the market interest rate i, which it wants to depress by means of its central bank interest rate and its bond purchases. We will use two examples to illustrate how much it has to cut the interest rate i to compensate for the less favorable conditions for investment in a recession.

In a recession, sales opportunities and thus project returns r_p decline. Private banks become more cautious in granting loans and as cash flow decreases, so do the degree of leverage v. In addition, banks increase the risk premium rz. Let us take the "Opportunities example" from Table 4.4 as a basis. With the project return $r_p = 0.10$, the leverage v = 3, the market interest rate i = 0.05 and no risk premium, rz = 1, the return on equity is $r_e = 0.25$. In bad times the project return drops to 0.08 and the risk premium rz rises to 1.6. In order to restore confidence and turn the tide with a constant leverage ratio v = 3, the central bank must keep the market interest rate i low by lowering central bank interest rates. According to Eq. 4.9, it would have to lower the market interest rate i from 5 to 1% in order to turn the "bad" situation back into a "good" one. For according to Eq. 4.9

$$0.08 + 3(0.08 - i \cdot 1.6) = 0.25$$

the market rate i is i = 0.01.

In bad times, the leverage ratio v will also fall, say to v = 2. This is due to the decreasing propensity to borrow and more cautious lending—in uncertain times, private banks are reluctant to lend and the credit mechanism falters. If we also take this "deterioration" into account, then the central bank would have to lower the market interest rate i to 0. From

$$0.08 + 2(0.08 - i \cdot 1.6) = 0.25$$

results i = 0.00.

If the CB actually succeeds in significantly reducing market interest rates i by means of a strong CB interest rate cut, it can indeed improve the propensity to invest and give the Π−I dynamic a boost.

However, it cannot be ruled out that the drastic intervention on the financial markets will benefit not so much Investment I, and thus the Π−I dynamic so central to growth rate g, as the price on the securities markets and the price of real estate, very much to the benefit of richer households. Moreover, even a drastic cut in central bank interest rates need not yet have the necessary effect on the market interest rate i.

While direct government intervention in the goods market in the form of deficit policy with debt levels and interest payments has already had significant knock-on effects on the economic process, the knock-on effects of indirect intervention by the central bank are likely to be even more significant. It is an illusion to believe that interventions in a dynamic and interdependent economy in constant change could be targeted without having significant unintended consequences, for example, instability and inequality. And financialization is likely to further strengthen interdependence and thus the risks of unintended consequences. As we will see later in Sect. 4.12 "Consequences of economic change and state stabilization: instability and inequality, distorted markets, and intertemporal imbalance" the interventions of the central bank strongly affect the intertemporal balance between "Much Credit" and "High Growth".

4.7 Inflation and Deflation: Good Times and Bad Times

According to Minsky, the central bank does not have a direct effect on the price level P via the money supply M, as in money supply-based approaches, but it influences the return on equity r_e and profits Π via its low-interest policy, and thus indirectly influences the development of the price level P via the profit mark-up m according to Eq. 3.32

$$P = (W/A_p)[1 + m], m = \Pi/NW$$

In it, labor productivity A_p is strongly *technically* determined and *technical progress* largely determines its development. Innovations open up new ways for entrepreneurs to move forward into the future, and new opportunities arise in a more or less strong continuous process that develops separately from cyclical processes. These, on the other hand, have a strong impact on wages W and the profit mark-up m. The extent to which trade unions can enforce their wage demands depends to a large extent on the *economic situation*. The same applies to the enforcement of profit mark-ups by companies.

In addition to the business cycle, globalization has recently started to influence price formation. We have dealt with this in connection with the so-called "second unbundling" in the form of the global chain production processes in Sect. 2.13.1 "ICT revolution (Baldwin and Milanovic)".

In a recession with high unemployment and low growth, workers have little chance of pushing through their demands for higher wages W; the P-W spiral stressed by Hayek does not get off the ground. In this bad economic situation, entrepreneurs are forced to grant price reductions in the short term and thus accept a loss in their return on investment. Through price discounts, they try to stimulate the demand for their products. By doing so, they lower the profit mark-up m and thus push down the price level P. Deflation threatens. In deflation, households postpone their consumption decisions in anticipation of further price reductions. The intended stimulation of demand through price discounts does not materialize. This is because, according to Eq. 4.5, the propensity to consume c declines and thus weakens the already sluggish $\Pi-I$ dynamic even further. Deflation thus exacerbates the recession. And it further lowers the already low returns r_e in bad economic situations. According to this, the $\Pi-I$ and $P-\Pi$ interdependencies *interlock in the recession and reinforce the downward spiral.*

Now it is up to the central bank. It must intervene to prevent a looming economic crisis and to reverse the downward spiral. As we know from the examples in Sect. 4.6 "Debt financing and risks", it must cut its interest rate sharply so that it can even bring the market interest rate i to a sufficiently low level to allow the return on equity r_e to rise again. This low interest rate policy supports the weakening $\Pi-I$ dynamic and stops deflationary tendencies. According to Eq. 4.9, a low market interest rate i increases the return on equity r_e and this stimulates investment I; low market interest rates i also increase the propensity to consume c, and thus, according to Eq. 4.5, profits Π. If the outlook for profits is better, companies can renounce their discounts and the expected stable prices allow the propensity to consume c to return to its normal level.

Even if the low interest rate policy drastically expands the money supply M, there is no reason to fear that this could lead to inflation during a recession according to the Minsky approach. This is because the money supply M has no direct effect in this case. *A lot of money flows into the securities and real estate markets. There it causes share prices and also property prices to rise.* Money deposits at private banks are no longer worthwhile and insurances are also less worthwhile. If interest rates remain low for a longer period of time, private banks no longer need to solicit money deposits from private households. They can now simply be financed to a greater extent by the central bank. *And, so, the low interest rate policy increases the dependence of private banks on the central bank and weakens the precautionary efforts of private households.* It restructures the source of funds on the bank balance sheet in favor of central bank financing, see Table 4.2 “Bank balance sheet”.

Inflationary tendencies arise in boom periods when high Π−I dynamics lead to considerable growth rates with low unemployment. This is because then the trade unions can push through higher wages W and the entrepreneurs higher profit mark-ups m, which in turn further accelerate the Π−I dynamics. The inflation, which then increases, devalues the financial assets of private households and endangers the growth of real wages W/P. The P-W spiral outlined by Hayek is now starting to move. The central bank then has to slow it down by raising its interest rate in order to curb the Π−I dynamic and thus also the P−Π interdependence via rising market interest rates i.

Profits are currently buoyant, but investment I in the real sector remains at a low level. A lot of money flows into unproductive assets in the stock economy. Real estate prices are rising there. By contrast, inflation in the circular economy remains low, and real wages are falling here, see The Economist (2018b).

Property prices continue to rise, even during the Corona crisis. In the G7 countries, the inflation rate for houses was 5% on average per year between 2013 and 2020, and in Germany, it was 11% in 2019. The share price index of globally listed residential firms rose from 110 to 220 in the period from 2013 to 2020, i.e., by 14% annually, compare The Economist: “The house party returns”, October 3rd, 2020, p. 10, and The Economist: “The three pillars”, October 3rd, 2020, p. 57.

4.8 Capital, Growth and Sluggish Growth

Keynes has analyzed economic developments in the short term for a depressed economic situation. In his analysis of underemployment, he excluded the effect of fixed capital formation I on the accumulation of productive capital, on the capital stock K. He was not interested in growth. Minsky also excluded capital accumulation in his analysis of progressive debt financing and its instability effect.

Not so Smith and Marx. They deal with the longer-term evolution of the economy. As we read in Chap. 2 "A review of the history of the economy and its concepts: change is a constant", Smith sees capital accumulation as the basis for the growth of an economy. Accumulation promotes the division of labor and thus labor productivity, which ultimately underpins growth. Marx places the long-term development of wages at the center of his analysis and predicts the impoverishment of the working class. He sees the long-term decline in the returns on capital and thus the rate of profit of capital. In order to compensate for the declining tendency and yet still secure profits and returns, entrepreneurs strive to reduce production costs, especially wage costs.

Falling marginal returns in capital accumulation are shown in Fig. 2.4 in Sect. 2.2 "Capital accumulation, economic growth and industrial revolution (Smith)". Along the production function F(K) in Fig. 2.4, as indicated there by arrows, we can roughly imagine the Marxian long-term view, where capital accumulation with falling marginal returns leads to a long-term impoverishment of the worker. However, Marx has a different concept of capital, he does not measure capital in constant prices, see Sinn (1975). But we must note that today's poverty is manifested above all in unemployment, and the poverty of the less qualified is also caused by their low assets and their low pension entitlements in old age and illness. In reference to Marx, the Economist says: "In Britain house prices are so high that people under 45 have little hope of buying them. Most American workers say they have just a few hundred dollars in the bank. Marx's proletariat is being reborn as the precariat", The Economist (2018a, p. 72).

In neoclassical growth theory, capital K plays a central role. It is connected with Solow. In its growth approach, production capital K, together with labor N and technical progress TF, determines the level of production Y, Y = F(N,K,TF), and its growth g, cf. Solow (1957).

Gordon uses Solow's concept of total factor productivity (TFP) to demonstrate the current weakness of growth, see Gordon (2016). His core thesis is that it is primarily innovation that drives growth—here he refers to Schumpeter, cf. the section on "Innovation through history: the ultimate risk-takers" in Gordon (2016, pp. 568–574)—and that innovation has been declining more recently, causing growth to weaken. The effect of innovation on growth should be measured by total factor productivity. The TFP results from a marginal consideration, typical of the neoclassical approach, as a residual variable, and thus as an estimated variable with little reliability. In addition, the estimate is based on the assumption of a constant and differentiable production function, and on the fact that the factors labor N and capital K are paid according to their marginal product and that production Y is distributed in constant proportions between the two input factors. Gordon himself is critical of the measure TFP, see Gordon (2016, p. 569). But he sees it as the best substitute, cf. Gordon (2016, p. 16).

Gordon bases his long-term analysis not only on total factor productivity, but also supplements it with labor productivity. According to his Chart 1.1, the growth rate of labor productivity measured in hours worked in the US declines from 2.82% to 1.62% between 1920 and 1970 and the more recent period 1970 to 2014, see

Gordon (2016, p. 14). This declining trend in labor productivity is confirmed by the graph "Not what it used to be" for Japan and Germany in the period from 1970 to 2015, cf. The Economist (2016a, p. 69); see also The Economist (2016c, p. 68). As already mentioned in Sect. 2.10 "Sluggish growth and social inequality", according to the graph "Where is the tech?" contained therein, the average growth rate of labor productivity in the period 1970–1996 to the period 2004–2014 falls from almost 3% to 1% in Japan, France, the UK, and Germany, and even more sharply to almost 0% in Italy.

Gordon points to current unfavorable conditions that stand in the way of a promising future development. Growing inequality weakens the willingness of society to cooperate. The high level of debt continues to create instability. Insufficient pension provision is forcing states to increase transfer payments, and the taxes required to do so then weigh on private economic activity. Recently, national trends in world trade have added to this.

Now a word about the concept of capital, as it is sometimes used in inequality analyses. In his work "Le capital au XXIe siècle" Piketty uses the term "capital" neither in the sense of production capital K nor in the sense of Marx. He means wealth Σ, which includes the enormous property holdings of private households or art collections of rich households. They do not constitute the capital stock K that promotes growth in an economy. Atkinson addresses this fuzziness in Piketty and uses the term "wealth" in his analysis of inequality, see the section "The drivers of wealth accumulation" in Atkinson (2015, pp. 158–166).

And one more word about the production function F(N,K,TF) and the new type of technical progress as described in 2.13.1 "ICT revolution (Baldwin and Milanovic)". We remember here the words of Baldwin. He sees the impact of the ICT revolution as "transformative, revolutionary, and disruptive" to previous economic processes. The ICT revolution is restructuring production processes globally. Thus, the concept of national production functions will hardly be tenable. And globally, as we know from Milanovic, the blessings of technological progress can now be seen in the form of economic prosperity outside the traditional industrialized countries, and within these countries, among the richer stratum of the population.

4.9 Globalization: Good Aspects and Bad Aspects

Smith saw the division of labor and productivity as directly related to market size. The larger the market, the more pronounced the division of labor can be, which promotes productivity and growth in an economy. International trade enlarges the market. Ricardo has shown the advantages for trading partners by giving a simple example of two countries. Both produce the goods cloth and wine. He argues convincingly that even if one country can produce the two goods more cheaply, the trade will benefit both. Both countries win, it is a win–win situation for both, as we know from Sect. 2.3 "Invisible hand, market, profit, division of labor, productivity, and international trade (Smith and Ricardo)". Industrialized countries have actively pursued the expansion of markets, especially with their imperialist policies, see Rodrik (2011, pp. 52–63): "Trade and Institutions in the 19th Century" and "The (limited) triumph of free trade".

More recently, globalization has been based on multilateral trade agreements and new international institutions. Keynes was one of the driving forces behind the creation of the World Bank and the International Monetary Fund (IMF), an organization which has been instrumental in helping to resolve the recent euro crisis. What the IMF is at the international level, the ESM is and will be for the euro area, a powerful stabilizing factor in the face of uneven economic developments. At the international level, the GATT round is added, which culminated in 1995 with the creation of the World Trade Organization (WTO). Commenting on these international organizations, which pave a new path to multilateralism, Rodrik (2011, p. 107) notes: "Multilateralism meant that the enforcement of rules and beliefs would be done through international institutions—the International Monetary Fund, the World Bank, and the GATT (General Agreement on Tariffs and Trade) rounds of talks—rather than with the tools of naked power politics or imperial domination. This was a most significant innovation".

International trade has, until recently, been a driving force for global growth. China, for example, is an eloquent example of how globalization has turned a developing country into an industrialized nation through years of growth, a success story from a global perspective. There, export-led growth and foreign investment have lifted hundreds of millions of Chinese out of poverty, see The Economist (2016h, p. 9).

From a global perspective, globalization also reduces inequality. Milanovic uses a graph to illustrate that, from a global perspective, it is not only the super-rich who are winners from globalization, but above all the middle classes, see Milanovic (2011, pp. 10–45), Chap. 1 "The rise of the global middle class and the global plutocrats". It states on page 19: "Who are the people in this group (the global middle class), the obvious beneficiaries of globalization? In nine out of ten cases, they are people from the emerging Asian economies, predominantly China, but also India, Thailand, Vietnam, and Indonesia". And on page 20 he concludes: "In short: the great winners have been the Asian poor and middle classes; the great losers, the lower middle classes of the rich world".

Globalization also has its dark sides, with the losers of the middle class in the rich industrialized countries. The Stolper–Samuelson Theorem already pointed out more than 50 years ago that free trade with low-wage nations could hurt workers in high-wage countries. According to it, one could derive protection for workers in industrialized countries, see The Economist (2016e, pp. 52–53), where the significance of the theorem for the current economic situation is discussed.

Globalization makes the world a field of action for companies of the industrialized countries, and also for countries such as we know from Sect. 2.13.7 "Globalization and the international competitive struggle (Marx)". Logistics allows networked production worldwide. To save costs, many companies can outsource numerous production steps to low-wage countries. On the other hand, they can expand their domestic development departments with highly qualified minds from all over the world. This leads to an enormous restructuring in global production processes—one could say upheavals. For example, of the 6 million jobs in manufacturing, the USA lost over 1 million to China, see The Economist (2016h, p. 9): "Perhaps a fifth of the 6 m or so net job losses in American manufacturing between 1999 and 2011 stemmed from Chinese competition". The risk of losing one's job increased considerably in the USA between 1965 and 2015, especially for the less qualified. The employment rate fell from around 95% to below 85% over this period, less so for the more highly skilled, see the chart "The risks of dropping out", p. 6 in the "Special Report: An open and shut case" in The Economist (2016i). With the outsourcing of production processes with low-skilled labor from industrialized countries to other countries, international competitive pressure in the low-wage sector is growing, at the expense of workers in the low-wage sector of industrialized countries. Thus, not everyone is a winner under globalization. Gordon comments on wage trends in a globalized world: "Globalization works as in the classic economic theory of factor prize equalization, raising wages in developing countries and slowing their growth in the advanced nations", cf. Gordon (2016, p. 633).

The extent to which employment restructuring in industrialized countries can take place in the long term is shown by Gordon for the US. He illustrates development trends by showing the level of employment for three widely differing years, namely 1870, 1940, and 2009. We summarize his main findings in Table 4.9.

The data is taken from Table 2.3, respectively, Table 8.1 in Gordon, cf. Gordon (2016, p. 53 and p. 255).

Here, the development of management and specialist staff is of particular interest. The employment of managers and skilled workers increased dramatically from 1940 to 2009, from 10.8% to 34.9%. They are highly qualified and highly paid. And this increase is one reason why inequality is rising sharply in the US. There, American companies are currently generating extraordinary returns that they can distribute among their managers and experts.

The graph "Ever better at making money" shows the distribution of returns of US companies. It shows that the percentage of firms that generated a return of more than 50% grew from almost 0% to almost 20% in the period from 1965–1967 to 2011–2013, see The Economist (2016b, p. 22). In a "Special Report", this magazine states that global companies are the winners: "The superstar effect is particularly marked in the knowledge economy. In Silicon Valley a handful of giants are enjoying market shares and profit margins not seen since the robber barons in the late nineteenth century. "And further on:" There are good reasons for thinking that the superstar

Table 4.9 Distribution of occupations 1870, 1940, and 2009 in the USA

Labor force in %	1870	1940	2009
Agriculture	46.0	17.3	1.1
Industry			
Blue Collar	33.5	38.7	19.9
White Collar	12.6	28.1	41.1
Managers, and Professionals	4.6	10.8	34.9

effect will gather strength. Big and powerful companies force their rivals to bulk up in order to compete with them. They also oblige large numbers of lawyers, consultancies, and other professional-services firms to become global to supply their needs. Digitalization reinforces the trend because digital companies can exploit network effects and operate across borders", cf. The Economist (2016f, p. 5).

The results of world trade are currently increasingly viewed from a national perspective and are, therefore, no longer readily accepted by a large number of people in the industrialized countries. Tensions are rising between society and the market economy. If the business is interested in further shaping globalization, many people in industrialized countries see themselves as being dependent on economic development and more likely to be threatened by globalization. They see themselves as the losers of globalization because many of them are threatened by a drift into precarious living conditions. In the political sphere, this means a return to the emphasis *on the national and a return to national power politics.* In Rodrick's trilemma of globalization, the nation-state and political democracy, the last two are thus increasingly gaining weight at the expense of globalization.

The EU and the euro are examples of globalization. They restrict the room for manoevre of national governments and national parliaments in Europe. Power-political aspects are involved in the creation of the eurozone: the monetary power of the German Bundesbank has been brought into the EU. Here the calculations of the political elites have played a decisive role. They are interested in influence. They want to shape and steer and also to participate in economic growth. This is an age-old concern of the ruling class, as we know from Scheidel's long-term analysis, see also Marx's remarks on the ruling class in Sect. 2.13.7 "Globalization and the international competitive struggle (Marx)". Here too, the decision is made at the expense of the low-skilled, especially in the European southern states with little innovative industry.

For decades the European South has been able to secure its competitiveness by devaluing its currencies. This is now denied to them with their entry into the eurozone. Initially, the rigid framework of the common EURO currency did not have a negative impact on economic development. Wages are rising and, what has been disastrous, in some cases much faster than productivity, see "Fig. 1.1. Salaires et évolution de la productivité en Europe (1998–2013)" in the section "La compétivité" in Tirole (2016, pp. 354–357), and the graph "For richer and poorer" in The Economist (2017, p. 6). In countries with large disparities, such as Greece, Portugal, Spain, and Italy, competitiveness has deteriorated drastically, and this economic weakness has come to light abruptly with the financial crisis. The weakness has been demonstrated by the financial distress and the rise in unemployment, particularly youth unemployment. Even without the financial crisis, entry into the euro area has been accompanied by the risk of increased unemployment. Many economists have warned against this. They have pointed out that workers will have to pay the price for giving up currency flexibility. They must look to work and live where the industry is competitive. This can be a high price to pay, especially for those who are not very flexible and have few qualifications. We recall Polanyi's critical remarks on labor as a commodity. People in the political sphere can show their refusal to pay the price, and they do.

National trends are strengthening protectionism and thus weakening globalization, which, in turn, clouds growth prospects. On the other hand, IT giants from the USA and China will find huge markets in India and South-East Asia, possibly later in Africa with its enormous population growth, see The Economist (2018c).

With the recent emergence of the international competitive struggle, globalization will take a new direction. Sections 2.13.2 "Globalization and economic change to the disadvantage of the old industrialized countries" and 2.13.7 "Globalization and the international competitive struggle (Marx)" deal with this. Cooperation between innovative leading countries will increase in world trade and states will be involved in this international competitive struggle.

4.10 Economic Processes and Their Analysis

4.10.1 Levels of Economic Processes

The state intervenes in economic processes that take place on three intertwined levels:

- Development level with the project return r_p,
- Microeconomic level with the return on equity r_e,
- Macroeconomic level with Minsky's $\Pi{-}I$ and $P{-}\Pi$ interdependence.

These three levels of real economic processes are meshed with the level of expectation that we have come to know in Keynes-Minsky momentum, among others. In addition, there is a developmental tendency in the variables in economics. At first, "*price variables*" played a dominant role, as we have seen in Sect. 2.6.1 "Market equilibrium, price mechanism, competition, and profit". With Keynes, "*flow variables*" have been added. And now "*stock variables*" have a strong impact on the economic process.

The first level, the level of research and development, precedes the actual economic processes at micro- and macroeconomic level. This is where different specialists such as chemists, physicists, engineers, IT specialists, and designers drive technical progress. It manifests itself in innovations, such as new products, novel services and concepts, and new production processes. This level creates the basis for lucrative sales opportunities and worthwhile project returns r_p, which, unlike returns on equity r_e, are not debt financed.

Innovations are the basis for high project returns r_p. If innovations fail to materialize, then the returns r_p shrink. Entrepreneurs take advantage of the opportunities offered by technical progress in the form of product innovations such as explorers, who are moving on uncertain terrain. Entrepreneurs have the talent to take risks and the stamina to withstand setbacks, see Stefan Zweig's story of C.W.

Field, who tenaciously pursued his cabling project from the USA and England. They test in an uncertain world whether their new products will be accepted on the market and, whether their offer will be profitable. The market offers them the freedom to experiment. According to Hayek, this freedom must be protected, because entrepreneurial activity drives economic development. And their actions open up profit prospects for them, but also a prospect of growth for society. Trade and change bring social prosperity.

Despite the recent severe financial crisis, there is no denying that economic growth in the US, the EU countries, China, India, Brazil, and many other countries has been sustained over the past decades. However, world trade and thus sales opportunities have been growing at a much slower rate than the global economy in recent years. Whereas the growth rates of world trade in the period from 1987 to 2007 were almost twice as high as those of world gross domestic product, in 2012 and 2013 the rate of world trade falls below the rate of the global economy, see Le Monde (2014).

Innovations open up new ways for societies to move forward in time, into uncertain environments. The market is setting the course for this. In the market-place, it is the buyers who decide which of the products offered by the companies are successful and which are profitable. It is here that the path that innovations will take is decided.

Despite a significant entrepreneurial effort, innovation does not have to be profitable. And profitability only becomes apparent after a considerable time. Entrepreneurial activity at the development level is uncertain and risky. However, it is essential and is a long-term determinant of entrepreneurial success, and ultimately of economic growth and public welfare. Companies want to maintain the developmental advantage that they have over their competitors through costly innovations. With the help of marketing experts, they transform their products into brands and thus set themselves apart from the competition. They create a product image and thus give the product an additional appeal. According to The Economist, this assessment is supported by W. Ohlins, one of the great marketing experts: "… consumers are not just looking for utility in the things they buy. They are also looking for meaning", cf. The Economist (2014d, p. 59).

It takes a long time before innovations can be brought to market.

Nevertheless, entrepreneurs dare to invest money in longer-term development of new goods if they can expect a return on their investment. A variety of microeconomic processes determine profitability. It is at the heart of the capitalist economy. Profitability is achieved when income, expenditure, and financing flows generate substantial profit streams over a long period of time, which are reflected in high returns on equity. Formally recorded Eq. 4.9

$$r_e = r_p + v(r_p - i \cdot rz)$$

the return on equity r_e. It shows that the financial market influences the return on equity r_e via the debt financing ratio v, the market interest rate i, and the risk premium rz. This influence links the financial market with the real economy. The link is so strong that one speaks of a "*financialization*" of the economy. The interdependence transfers the short-term time horizon of the financial market to the real economy, and in addition, the increased risk there, which goes by the name of "tail risk".

Investments with a high return on equity r_e lead to profits Π at the macroeconomic level. It is the level at which economic policy measures are discussed. Politicians use historical data from national accounts. Many of the discussions still dwell on the ISLM model attributed to Keynes but which has been overtaken by economic change. The Minsky approach, with the $\Pi{-}I$ interdependence Eq. 4.5

$$\Pi = T_\pi + (I + [Df_z - s_z Z_g^*] + Ex\ddot{u} + (c_w - 1)W^*)/(1 - c_\pi)$$

and its interaction with the $P{-}\Pi$ interdependence Eq. 3.32

$$P = \left(W/A_p\right)[1 + m] \text{ with the profit mark-up } m = \Pi/NW$$

creates a new open framework, a new paradigm for discussing processes at the macro level, such as the impact of fiscal and monetary policy. In it, the return on equity r_e from the micro level has an effect on the $\Pi{-}I$ dynamics of the macro level. Expectations of high returns on equity promote the $\Pi{-}I$ dynamics and thus economic growth. Growing prosperity favors an increase in consumer propensity c and gives companies greater scope for the profit mark-up m, which causes the price level P to rise and thus inflation. Not only do they further promote propensity to consume c, but they also reduce the burden of real debt D/P. In the case of deflation, the effect is reversed. The propensity to consume c falls and slows down the $\Pi{-}I$ dynamic. The burden of debt increases. Then the paradox described by Fisher can occur despite nominal debt relief, the real debt burden D/P, "*real debt burden*", can rise.

Two further levels need to be distinguished in economic processes, namely the real level and the expectation level. They too are interdependent. Real events take place in the current present, whereas expectations relate to the future. The world of real decisions, which is manifested at the macro level in consumer spending C and investment activities I and at the micro level in returns on equity r_e, is preceded by the world of expectations, which affect precisely these decisions.

The development of the return on equity r_e depends on income and expenditure flows. In crises, current revenue flows usually do not cover expenditure flows. The gap is closed by financing flows. It widens during crises. Financial flows begin to dry up and assets have to be adjusted downwards and even sold when insolvency threatens. Expectations change, plans are corrected. The assessment of the future tilts from "*over confidence*" to "*over fear*". With the growing financial flows, the financialization of the economy, the short-term orientation of the financial market with its increased risks spills over to the real economy and intensifies the Keynes-Minsky momentum and thus instability. Central banks have recognized in recent crises that they can dampen this momentum by giving the economy longer positive expectations.

The state intervenes in these complex economic processes. Numerous illustrations in Sect. 3.1 "Main principles of Keynesian macroeconomics" illustrate how the instrument variables "deficit Df" of fiscal policy and "money supply M" of monetary policy previously acted on the demand for goods Y and for labor N in the ISLM model, thus making the economic stabilization at that time comprehensible. The ISLM paradigm no longer bears fruit. Compared to then, economic conditions have changed. The specific, clearly defined objective of stabilizing the demand for goods Y and the demand for labor N has been replaced by the general, much broader objective of stabilizing the instability of the economy caused by the financial market. Fiscal and monetary policy lacks effective instrument variables at the macro level for this purpose, as we have described in the Minsky model of the open framework of interdependencies (Eqs. 3.32 and 4.5).

The economic processes at the macro level are based on economic processes at the micro and development levels. They interact with expectations. In addition to the flow variables Df, Y, and N, important stock variables such as wealth Σ and debt D are now added. To better understand the effects of government measures in these interdependent complex processes, we distinguish between numerical quantitative and formal quantitative, qualitative effects.

4.10.2 Quantitative Numerical Analysis

In crises, politics is under considerable pressure of public expectations. It should take appropriate measures to overcome them quickly. The state sees itself called upon to intervene in a stabilizing way in complex, interlinked economic levels, *in a dynamic and interdependent economic process in constant change*. But where is the leverage to intervene quickly and effectively? It does not exist! The state would also have to be able to assess the possible consequences of its interventions, for example on inequality, if it did not want to be surprised by unintended effects, to which it would then have to react. *Quantitative numerical estimates would be desirable.* There is no basis for this. Keynes' fundamental reservations about quantitative macroeconomic analyses are still valid, despite considerable progress in econometrics.

With his formal explanations in his "General Theory", Keynes not only gave the impetus for the formulation of the Hicks–Hansen ISLM model, but with his circulation model and the flow variables occurring in it, such as consumption C, savings S, investment I and production Y, he also provided impulses for the development of the System of National Accounts (SNA). It is a quantitative review of an economy and makes it possible to describe the development of an economy and the differences between economies in the past in quantitative numerical terms. For example, time series of growth rates g of national output Y from two economies, such as France and Germany, provide information on historical differences in economic performance.

The SNA developed in detail by the UN contains a large number of economic variables. Their definitions are boxes for statisticians around the world to fill with the relevant data from their national economy, thus producing time series for a large number of macroeconomic variables. This enables a wide range of time series and cross-sectional analyses to be carried out.

The data collected by statistical offices are *ex post variables* and will differ from the *ex ante variables*, plan variables as we have seen in the ISLM model and the Minsky approach. If entrepreneurs underestimate household consumption C, their investment I according to SNA will be larger than their ex ante planned investment I. Goods planned for sale are then stockpiled, thus increasing the investment in inventories according to SNA and thus the ex post investment. The unplanned investment in inventories leads to planning corrections in the business calculation with further effects on business decisions. However, no data is available on unplanned factors in SNA, so the correction cannot be captured in empirical analyses.

Nevertheless, the Dutch Nobel Prize winner Jan Tinbergen (1903–1994) saw an opportunity early on in the extensive data collections to form quantitative macroeconomic models and to use them for quantitative numerical economic analysis and forecasting, as well as for macroeconomic management of the economy and policy advice. Keynes expressed fundamental reservations about these econometric studies in his article "Professor Tinbergen's Method" (Keynes 1939). They should be seen in connection with Keynes' remarks in Chapter 18 "The General Theory of Employment Re-stated" in his "General Theory" (Keynes 1936). They concern both statistical analysis and economic modeling. Keynes is particularly critical of statistical business cycle analysis. Although econometrics has made enormous progress in some areas since Keynes' time, his reservations about the quantitative analysis of interdependent economies, which is of interest here, remain valid. Above all, the constancy in the change of economic processes speaks against a structural constancy necessary for statistical analysis. As Minsky's work points out, change is reflected in new paradigms with new structures.

According to Keynes, the economist would have to provide the statistician with a correctly specified model. The list of variables would have to be *complete*, the functional form in which they operate would have to be *correct*, and also the specification of their operation in time, the specification of dynamics, the so-called "time lag" structure. The economist cannot fulfill these requirements for modeling. And he does not need completeness for formal quantitative, qualitative analyses that are of interest to him. Keynes, for example, has *mentally isolated* the events that are central to his research from the rest. For example, he disregards the effect of production capital K, which grows as a result of Investment I. And he identifies central determinants of production Y and employment N in the propensity to consume c, the attitude to liquidity $L_2(i)$, government demand G and in the money supply M. These determinants, he admits, can, in turn, be the subject of further studies and are thus by no means the finally independent factors. However, this *conceptual isolation* of the event of interest *cannot be transferred to quantitative empirical analysis. For it cannot be ruled out that the interactions cut off by the isolation may distort the quantitative statistical analyses of economic processes.*

Now the problem is with the statistician. In a *sequential search process,* he would have to find the "correct" model from a series of falsified analyses in a statistically reliable way, a difficult if not impossible task for the statistician.

After Keynes, he is confronted with further problems that are hardly easier to solve. Not all significant factors can be *measured*, and there are *interactions between factors*, such as the profit–investment interdependence (Eq. 4.5) and its interaction with the price level profit interdependence (Eq. 3.32). Interactions also exist in many ways between the different levels of economic processes.

In the case of factors that cannot be measured, Keynes thinks, among other things, of the psychological attitude to liquidity and the subjective formation of expectations that we know from the Keynes-Minsky momentum. But it is precisely the omission of these factors, which are central to the economic movement, that distorts the results of empirical analysis, and it is not clear how these distortions could be corrected retrospectively. Therefore, according to Keynes, econometric models à la Tinbergen are not applicable for the statistical quantitative analysis of economic processes. Despite these fundamental reservations about distortions due to the lack of non-measurable variables, econometric modeling and statistical analysis methods have been further developed in the Tinbergen approach. However, these developments have so far proved to be of little use in predicting turnarounds. They have also provided little insight into quantitative economic processes.

It is not surprising that important recent economic analyses are based on tables and graphs, as is the case in Piketty (2013), Baldwin (2016), Milanovic (2016, 2019), Iversen and Soskice (2019).

According to Keynes, the interactions are not compatible with the sequential statistical analysis method using regression. In a regression equation, so-called explanatory variables determine the movement of the variables to be explained. If, for example, we choose consumption C as the variable to be explained, then income Y is the explanatory variable, and in the linear form $C = b + c\,Y$, the parameter c is the marginal propensity to consume. It indicates that consumption increases by c units if income Y increases by one unit: the coefficient c thus captures the quantitative effect of the explanatory variable Y on the variable C. The statistician also speaks of Y as an exogenous, independent variable and of C as an endogenous, dependent variable. The exogeneity of the explanatory variable is indispensable for the correct statistical measurement of its quantitative effect on the endogenous variable, i.e., in the example for the unbiased estimation of the propensity to consume c. The variables Y and C should, therefore, not influence each other.

The *unbiasedness* of the estimate thus depends on whether the *explanatory variables are exogenous or not.* However, this cannot be decided a priori for economic variables because of the *interdependence typical in economic processes.* Caution is, therefore, required to assume that economic variables interact with each other. Keynes does this in his criticism of Tinbergen's statistical analysis, pointing out that because of interdependence, Π profits cannot be an exogenous variable in Tinbergen's explanation of Investment I; Minsky's $\Pi{-}I$ interdependence points in the same direction. Tinbergen's regression analysis, therefore, leads to a distorted analysis of investment activity. The estimation of the coefficients informing about quantitative effects is, therefore, systematically distorted and useless for a quantitative empirical analysis.

The Dutch American Nobel Prize winner Tjalling Koopmans (1910–1995) explained the bias using the simple example of consumer goods demand $C = b + cY$, which we know from the ISLM model. The explanatory variable Y is not exogenous in economic terms in that consumption has an impact on income via the goods market equilibrium $C + I = Y$. This feedback effect leads to the so-called "simultaneous equation bias", which, as already mentioned, calls into question a sound quantitative analysis of economic processes based on sequential partial analyses.

Econometricians subsequently proved to be creative. They developed asymptotically unbiased estimators for global analyses of interdependent economic models. Theoretically, this made the criticized sequential approach superfluous if the models were clearly classified into endogenous and exogenous variables. A priori, however, it cannot be decided whether a variable is undoubtedly exogenous or not, independent or not. In empirical analyses, this has the consequence that the list of endogenous variables becomes more and more comprehensive and thus the system of multi-equations for the entire economy becomes very extensive. These global models have not become any more useful for forecasting purposes, nor have they been able to contribute to greater insight into quantitative processes. In many cases, they are also referred to as "*black boxes*" because of this *lack of insight*.

ARIMA time series models prove to be more accurate in forecasts, but also less accurate in turnarounds. In the form of their manageable multi-equation approaches —the so-called vector ARIMA models—they enable the "time lag" structure to be analyzed statistically and also the exogeneity and the "spurious correlation" mentioned by Keynes in his criticism of Tinbergen. The concepts for this go back to the British statistician Clive Granger (1934–2009), both the analysis of the "spurious correlation" by means of cointegration and the exogeneity in the form of the "Granger causality" named after him. The limitation of the analytical framework to a small number of selected central economic variables is, however, a step backward with regard to comprehensive structural multi-equation models.

Granger received the Nobel Prize in Economics in 2003 together with the American statistician Robert Engle (∗1942). Engle has been honored for his ARCH approach. It is a successful tool for statistical analysis and forecasting of financial market volatility, which is important in the context of the Basel banking regulation. With the generalized GARCH approach, it is possible to statistically test whether the market risk of financial institutions remains within a desirable range, more specifically whether a certain VaR value is not exceeded too often. If a statistical "backtesting" procedure indicates an increased risk, then, as we know, international self-regulation of banks—the Basel regulation—stipulates that the banks concerned must increase their equity capital share to cover their increased risks. However, banking self-regulation is not very effective. On the one hand, financial institutions use simpler procedures than the GARCH model, which tend to systematically underestimate risk, and on the other hand, the mechanism in self-regulation for increasing capital proves to be too weak for a sufficient correction, see Sect. 4.5.4 "Basel banking regulation and EU banking union".

Despite the progress made in many sub-areas in the statistical analysis of economic phenomena, Keynes' reservations about quantitative numerical analyses of macroeconomic processes remain. At present, Romer's criticism reinforces Keynes' concerns. Romer received the Nobel Prize in 2018.

In the economy, a large number of players interact with each other in a complex way. The interaction takes place over time and is increasingly oriented toward the future. Today's decisions have a delayed effect later. Economists have few ideas about the temporal chain of effects, the time lag. This is where statisticians and econometricians should help. With them, stochastics comes into play more and more. Their stochastic assumptions are based little on economic considerations or empirical evidence. Nevertheless, these assumptions can seriously influence the empirical results of the analysis. Small modifications in the dynamics and in the stochastic embedding can lead to completely different results. The results are, therefore, not very robust, which they should be if they are to have more general validity.

Even newer approaches, known as "Dynamic stochastic general equilibrium models (DSGE)", suffer from the fact that they are not very robust. These models, be they new classical or neo-Keynesian models, hardly provide insights into the interdependence and dynamics of macroeconomic processes, but results based on uncertain foundations.

Romer's criticism of the DSGE models starts with stochastic assumptions, and more precisely with identification assumptions, see Romer (2016). Identification precedes estimation. No matter how much data statisticians may have, the results of their analyses are worth nothing unless they have first ensured, by means of suitable identification assumptions, that their data can actually be used to estimate the economic structure they are looking for. After all, that is the prerequisite for them to be able to reveal structures that could help, for example, to recommend targeted policy measures.

Romer points out that estimation results depend heavily on identification assumptions, which are, however, insufficiently verifiable—identification assumptions which he calls "fed in as facts with unknown truth value (FWUTV). The results are, therefore, not very robust, or as the Economist puts it: "And an arbitrary assumption in one part can affect everything else in it", The Economist (2016g, p. 68).

It is interesting to see how Romer starts his critical remarks. He juxtaposes a partial analysis *in the form of two graphs*, which he finds fruitful, with the less informative residual analysis with "imaginary shocks" of stochastic global models. He concludes his criticism of the DSGE models by looking back at the Keynesian models: "The situation now is worse. Macro models make assumptions that are no more credible and far more opaque", Romer (2016, p. 19). And he cannot conclude his critique without referring to the misleading remark by Lucas: "My thesis in this lecture is that macroeconomics in this original sense has succeeded: Its central problem of depression prevention has been solved, for all practical purposes, and has in fact been solved for many decades", Lucas (2003, p. 1). And what a contrast to Minsky (1986). On the one hand, comprehensive dynamic models tend toward equilibrium, and on the other hand the partial view with profit and with debt financing supported by private banks, which lets the economy slide into instability, cf. also The Economist (2016d).

The fierce and also personal criticism is probably an appeal by Romer to get away from these unfruitful macroeconometric models. In any case, these interdependent econometric models are of little use for macroeconomic management of the economy. And as already mentioned, nowadays it is mostly analyses with tables and charts that provide insight into economic processes.

We have to admit that empirical quantitative analyses of global economic systems have little statistical basis. We know little about how strong and how quickly fiscal and monetary policy measures work. We also know little about longer-term consequences. A quick and well-intentioned measure dictated by impatience can have fatal effects in the longer term, for example, on economic instability and inequality. *Hayek warns against denying our ignorance*, and in response to hasty short-term interventions, he says: "To the ambitious and impatient reformer, filled with indignation at a particular evil, nothing short of the complete abolition of that evil by the quickest and most direct means will seem adequate. If every person now suffering from unemployment, ill health, or inadequate provision for his old age is at once to be relieved of his cares, nothing short of an all-comprehensive and compulsory scheme will suffice. But if, in our impatience to solve such problems immediately, we give government exclusive and monopolistic powers, we may find that we have been short-sighted" (1960, p. 227).

Interdependence, dynamism, and change are arguments against a sound quantitative impact analysis. But we also have to admit that the capitalist market economy tends toward underemployment, instability, and inequality. Corrective external measures are, therefore, essential. And, as said before, they are also vehemently demanded by the state in public. However, we must also recognize that state intervention is now hitting the fruitful market economy at its core by distorting market mechanisms and by threatening its intertemporal balance.

4.10.3 Understanding Using Partial Models

Comprehensive interdependent econometric models are primarily used for numerical forecasting. Even in the form of simulations, they provide little reliable insight into economic interrelationships and are certainly no paradigm by which politicians can orientate their decisions; the previous section has dealt with these models critically in detail.

The Keynesian approach is quite different: it is a partial model. In limited consideration, it focuses on the goods market, supplemented by the money market in a rudimentary form. The labor market is exogenous. Private banks play no role.

Growth is excluded. The manifold decisions at the microeconomic level are only subliminally present, as we know from the Keynes-Minsky momentum. Nevertheless, or perhaps precisely because of his isolated approach, Keynes created a paradigm for economic policy—see Fig. 2.8 in Sect. 2.7 "Economic crisis and macroeconomic stabilization by the government (Keynes)". The circular flow model has served politicians as an orientation guide for several decades. Keynes created the state as a compensatory agent: If in the private sector the economic entities spend too little, the entrepreneurs subsequently cut back their production and lay off workers, then the state should not reduce but rather expand its demand. It should close the expenditure gap in the short term and thus stimulate the demand for labor and keep the economic cycle in motion.

Minsky, too, takes an isolated approach, for example, he leaves the labor market and growth out. He puts profit and private banks at the center of his partial view. In this, the banks go beyond the limits that Schumpeter saw as a secure framework for capitalist evolution. They market loans, they get rid of their risks, and create new financial products and new financial markets. They increase debt financing and favor indebtedness. They burden the whole economy with systemic risk. Minsky made this burden, which continues today, clear as early as 1986. He opened up the Keynesian circular flow paradigm to a paradigm of interdependence between key flow and stock variables. In it, the dominance of the financial market leads to instability. However, his approach has not had the penetrating power of the Keynesian one and has not led to a new convincing concept.

One of the reasons for this is that the state can no longer play the role of a compensatory agent under the changed economic conditions. According to this, if economic entities in the private sector were to finance their expenditures more and more through borrowing, the state would have to limit its debt financing. However, an austerity policy would lead to enormous political tensions, which the state wants to avoid. And the states have not yet found a new leading role in the finance-dominated economy, for example, in international banking regulation, as we know from Sect. 4.5.4 "Basel banking regulation and the EU banking union".

Nevertheless, partial analyses can be useful. Tyrol, a French Nobel prize winner, is of a similar opinion. He comments on insights into the impact of private banking activities as follows: "il (l'économiste) peut comprendre que les expositions mutuelles entre banques et d'autres facteurs sont susceptibles d'engendrer une crise systémique sans pour autant saisir la dynamique complexe de propagation d'une telle crise", Tirole (2016, p. 129). Propagation is dealt with by econometric models, which, however, provide little insight into the economic process.

However, the ex ante abundance of conditions is great and so are the possibilities for partial considerations. Before economic processes become history, *it is an art to select an appropriate partial analysis*. In retrospect, ex post, the abundance is limited and only then can we say with much greater reliability which analysis helps our understanding to comprehend past processes. In retrospect, we can more easily recognize which approach helps us to order what happened into a meaningful context.

4.10.4 Formal Quantitative, Qualitative Analysis

The formal quantitative method of analysis in Keynes' "General Theory" led to a new key paradigm for successful economic policy over a longer period of time, despite the lack of numerical estimation at the time. It has led to a deeper understanding of the underemployment equilibrium in which an economy can remain in a cyclical downturn with high unemployment for a prolonged period. It has provided an approach, through deficit policy, to how government intervention can effectively stabilize the business cycle and overcome unemployment.

Keynes's state intervention is clearly targeted on the one hand: it is intended to eliminate the temporary under demand on the goods market and thus the under demand on the labor market; it is intended to support the weakening market forces toward equilibrium, to strengthen the "mean reversing" forces. And secondly, Keynesian fiscal policy has an effective instrument variable in the form of government expenditure G, or more precisely government deficits Df. It directly fills the gap of under demand in the goods market and can prevent serious unemployment because of the close link between aggregate demand Y and the demand for labor N. The effect of the state's economic stabilization is thus directly benefiting workers in precarious employment, especially the less qualified workers N, the less well-off. Fiscal policy supports the functioning of the market economy on the one hand, and on the other, by supporting the labor market, has a *social aspect* which has been essential for Keynes. Minsky emphasizes this: "Keynes defined the political problem as a need to combine three things: economic efficiency, social justice, and individual liberty", Minsky (1986. p. 9).

As we know, according to the Keynesian narrative and to the first thesis in Sect. 1.8 *"Key thesis": The market can fail and the government can fix it with its fiscal policy. The state can manage national economies for common welfare.*

The scourge of underemployment remains with the market economy, and now economic instability and social inequality, distorted markets, and intertemporal imbalance add more social burdens. This puts economic efficiency, and to an even greater extent, social justice at risk. State intervention, on the other hand, has become less effective.

This is because the instrument variable Df has now lost its effectiveness, and with it, fiscal policy. All that remains is the *relatively inefficient* central bank policy. Unlike the ISLM model, however, as Minsky's approach makes clear, the central bank does not have the instrument variable "money supply M". *It also lacks a theoretical concept that could guide its actions in the long run.* And in its objective, it must be modest and concern itself primarily with the functioning of the financial market. To this end, it has recently been intervening in the economic process in a variety of ways, in the hope that employment could also benefit from it, especially the low-skilled workers N.

In view of underemployment, instability, and inequality, however, the state's fiscal policy should remain capable of action. Fiscal policy can possibly regain this ability if it returns to the original concept of Keynesian countercyclical economic policy. It would have to give up its permanent debt financing, finance its expenditure from taxes in the long term, and even make financial provisions in good times in order to be able to act quickly in crises. Sovereign wealth funds, replenished in upswing periods, could then be used in a targeted manner in times of crisis. In this sense, the ESM program, which emerged in the recent crisis, represents a sovereign wealth fund that can be developed into a powerful regulatory instrument for securing the euro.

Minsky's qualitative analysis is based on Π−I and P−Π interdependencies. In the next section, we follow the intervention of CB policy in economic processes against the background of Minsky's Π−I and P−Π interdependencies, the microeconomic Eq. 4.9 on return on equity and the Keynes-Minsky momentum.

Similar to Minsky's qualitative analysis, the abovementioned qualitative analyses with tables and graphs are convincing evidence of informative and substantial contributions to economic understanding.

4.11 Stabilization Policy in the Post-Keynesian Era

4.11.1 Central Bank Policy

Even if the central bank lacks an instrumental variable in Minsky's formal macroeconomic order, one goal is clear in crises: to boost the then sluggish Π−I dynamic. When the phase of prosperity comes to an end and the economy enters a crisis, as has been the case recently, business, credit, and market risks increase, and finally, systemic risk in the financial system. For investment projects, the risk premium rz increases and the debt financing ratio v decreases. As a result, the return on equity r_e falls. Profits Π flow more sparsely and the Π−I dynamic at the macro level loses momentum. Higher credit risk is associated with the threat of insolvencies. Greater market risks cause security prices to fall and asset portfolios to shrink. Banking crises threaten. The confidence of market participants is waning. From the outside, the impetus must come for a turnaround. The central bank, in particular, has a vocation to do so, as it can improve financing conditions and give new impetus to the Π−I dynamic. However, it should not be overlooked that project returns r_p—the very basis of Π−I dynamics and economic growth—may be declining. This would diminish the central bank's impact since the central bank has hardly any influence on it. The Economist examines the question of whether the innovative power for growth tends to weaken, see The Economist (2013a); see also Piketty (2013, pp. 156–159).

Central bank policy is primarily focused on the financial system. The financial activity increasingly dominates economic processes worldwide. It increases credit risks and thereby the business and market risks as well as the systemic risks. It stresses the stability of the financial market, and through "financialization", the stability of the economy as a whole.

Market transactions in both the real and financial sectors are increasingly profit-driven. In addition to investments in tangible assets, investments are increasingly being supplemented by financial investments, with companies, banks, and private households—mainly from the richer income and wealth stratum—acting as money investors. Together with profit flows, debt financing leads to considerable assets that are unequally distributed. *Trading in stocks has become an important factor in the economic process*, be it transactions in the property, securities or art markets. And the volatility of stock prices, especially property and securities prices, further increases risks and thus instability. The trading of securities, in particular, of financial investments such as ABS and CDS securities, increases the interconnectedness of the global financial system and thus creates a systemic risk.

The task facing the central bank is broader than stabilizing demand for goods. In many ways, risk has made the whole economy more unstable. In an unstable economy, crises can endanger the core of the capitalist market economy. It is geared to making profits Π. Economic subjects have the expectation that they will achieve lasting prosperity, lasting wealth Σ, by their own efforts, and that they will be able to maintain this prosperity for a long time. Crises in an unstable economy can shake this basic expectation of the capitalist market economy.

Four lines of action can be identified in central bank interventions:

(1)	Promoting return on equity r_e and profit Π,
(2)	Securing wealth Σ,
(3)	Stabilizing expectations,
(4)	Preventing deflationary tendencies

In the case of the ECB, it should be added:

(5)	Preserving the euro and the eurozone

Minsky's new macroeconomic paradigm, together with the return on equity, makes the workings of central bank policy understandable. Let us start with the formula of return on equity in Eq. 4.9

$$r_e = r_p + v(r_p - i \cdot rz).$$

In crises, the risk premium rz increases. It makes debt financing more expensive. In addition, the flow of loans from private banks to investors, be it for investments in tangible or financial assets, decreases. The debt financing ratio v decreases. Central banks want to reverse this development. They are lowering their central bank interest rate, lowering the security requirement for private banks, and thus facilitating the flow of central bank money M to private banks. At the same time, they buy bonds to depress the market interest rate i.

In this way, the central bank is counteracting the deterioration in debt financing conditions during the crisis. Whether its intervention is effective depends on how private banks assess future yield developments. If they do not see a positive trend in project yields r_p in the foreseeable future, and if they continue to regard economic development as uncertain, they will continue to lend cautiously despite favorable financing conditions from the central bank. The loans will not flow abundantly, as necessary, and the effect of central bank policy on the credit lever v will then be insufficient. The return on equity r_e will remain at a low level, and it will then not be able to stimulate the Π−I dynamics in Eq. 4.5

$$\Pi = T_\pi + (I + [Df_z - s_z Z_g^*] + Ex\ddot{u} + (c_w - 1)W^*)/(1 - c_\pi)$$

Growth is stalling and prosperity is at risk.

Over time, the Keynesian liquidity trap, which is due to the behavior of private households on the money market, no longer plays a role in explaining economic events, but the investment trap does. However, the causes of this trap have changed fundamentally. In the change in economic processes, profit Π emerges as the central factor in Investment I, firstly at the macroeconomic level in the form of Π−I interdependence (Eq. 4.5) and secondly at the micro level in the form of return on equity r_e in Eq. 4.9.

Let us look at the right side of Eq. 4.5. If the variables "Df", "Exü" and "c" do not stimulate profits Π, i.e., if fiscal policy, foreign demand and household consumption demand do not have a positive impact on profits Π, and according to Eq. 4.9, technological development and debt financing factors no longer favor expectations of returns, then the economy is caught in an investment trap despite massive central bank intervention and the desired economic growth fails to materialize. During a crisis, central banks' QE policies do not sufficiently succeed in improving the constellation of debt financing, which depends on factors v, i, and rz, in such a way that the private sector is prepared to increase its demand. But this would be necessary to boost the real economy.

And with the money flowing into the economy, it is to be feared that it is not driving the Π−I dynamic. After all, large parts of the cheap money are likely to flow into the purchase of existing assets. According to The Economist, for example, only 15% of British bank lending is used for real investment I: "... only 15% of British bank lending is used for capital investment", The Economist: "The inevitability of instability" (2014a, p. 56). The fact that the Π−I dynamic is indeed not picking up is shown in Chart 3 "Boom deferred" in The Economist (2013b, p. 26). According to this chart, investment I as a % of GDP has been declining in the euro area and the UK since 2007. In the US, despite an increase, investment I remains well below precrisis levels. Koo argues similarly (2015). In his critical analysis of central banks' QE policies, he points out that in good times the private sector invests massively in asset portfolios, especially in real estate assets, and that in bad times prices of assets Σ are threatened by decline. According to Koo, the private sector seeks to reduce the burden of debt D built up in the process before it is tempted by lower central bank interest rates to increase its spending. In this behavior, even a massive QE by central banks cannot increase the private sector's cash flow for investment I and consumption C.

The central bank intervenes massively in bond markets, seriously disturbing the market mechanism there. It is becoming a key player in the financial market not only to keep market interest rates low, but also to keep bond prices high. The same applies to share prices, which it supports with its cheap money. It is less concerned with the "wealth effect" on consumption than with *safeguarding the core of the capitalist economic system, the pursuit of profit and ownership*. By securing the assets Σ, it supports a basic expectation of economic subjects to the capitalist market economy: the expectation that the capitalist market economy can lead to long-lasting prosperity. The central bank must act under this public pressure of expectation. And the public assumes—in a sense an echo of the long successful Keynesian fiscal policy—that the market can fail and the state can fix it for the common welfare; as the first conclusion on state intervention policy put it.

Central banks are not only increasingly intervening in the market mechanism. With their "long-term forward guidance", they also stabilize market expectations by structuring the expectations of market players over the longer term. They also continue to push forward debt financing through their cheap money policy in order to counteract feared deflation. In Minsky's explanation pattern, money supply does not play a role in the development of the price level. For in its pattern, the profits Π have an effect on the price level P via the profit mark-up, see Eq. 3.32

$$P = \left(W/A_p\right)[1 + m] \quad \text{with profit mark-up } m = \Pi/NW$$

There the debt financing has an effect on the profit Π via the return on equity r_e and on the price level P, i.e., on inflation and deflation, via the profit mark-up m = Π/NW. By favoring debt financing, the central bank aims to stimulate the Π−I dynamic in crises, thereby boosting economic growth and counteracting threatening deflationary tendencies.

Crises reveal a paradox of risks. Central bank policy may take on private sector risks by making massive purchases of securities, but it also increases market risks, because economic players know that central bank intervention alone cannot overcome crises. This assessment is familiar to us from the ISLM approach. It remains valid, even if the way central bank policy works has changed.

According to Sect. 1.8 "Key thesis", In a third conclusion we can state here: *Like fiscal policy, central bank policy continues to strengthen debt financing, which according to Minsky is the source of instability, and the "financialization" of the economy, and thus ultimately the instability of the economy as a whole. Instability reveals striking weaknesses in the capitalist market economy. It can no longer function without state support. State intervention deepens the interdependence between market and state. And as a result, economic inequality increases, which can become a further source of instability through social conflict. And as a result of its massive interventions in the financial market, it disrupts the market mechanism and its credit expansion causes an intertemporal imbalance.* More on this later in Sects. 4.11.3 "Profits and losses of central banks" and 4.12 "Consequences of economic change and state stabilization: instability and inequality, distorted markets and intertemporal imbalance".

Recent market interventions by the central bank overshadow traditional Keynesian market interventions. The central bank's massive buying up programs and drastic interest rate cuts undermine the open market economy with free competition. It is the decisive determining factor in the financial market. It allows private banks to market the risk, and it allows it to become a systemic risk that ultimately has to be borne by society. It structures future market expectations. Signals that usually come from the market are increasingly sent by the central bank. The central bank is also the determining factor for the development of values in the capital markets. In crises, it supports the asset portfolios, the wealth Σ. It thus favors the owners, the richer ones.

And by supporting assets, the central bank promotes economic inequality. This is also pointed out by The Economist (2014f, p. 73). And Piketty (2013) provides evidence for this in his historical studies. According to his "force de divergence fondamentale: r > g", inequality in wealth increases if the economic rate of return $r = \Sigma/Y$ exceeds the growth rate $g = \Delta Y/Y$ of income Y. The CB policy promotes these forces of divergence, because with the money that flows into portfolio trading it supports above all the development of assets Σ and less the growth g. And growing inequality can reduce the acceptance of the capitalist market economy.

The fact that the state favors inequality is an argument for a more progressive design of inheritance tax. The resulting additional revenues could ultimately give fiscal policy back the urgently needed room for manoeevre. With regard to inheritance tax, a minority vote in the Federal Constitutional Court ruling on the new inheritance tax system refers to the German Sozialstaatsprinzip (welfare state principle) contained in the German Grundgesetz (Constitution). The vote states that inheritance tax not only serves to generate tax revenue, but also to ensure equal opportunities, cf. Federal Constitutional Court: Privileged treatment of business assets in inheritance tax, judgments of 17 December 2014, p. 4.

4.11.2 Monetary and Fiscal Policy in the Eurozone

Under the Maastricht Treaty, the ECB is clearly committed to price stability. It is in principle not allowed to provide Ponzi scheme financing, and it is not allowed to provide monetary state financing.

The economic crisis that began in 2008 affects the euro countries to varying degrees. The crisis hits countries with different levels of competitiveness. In addition, they differ in the efficiency of tax collection and administration, some have a bloated state apparatus and thus relatively high administrative expenditure, which is reflected in relatively high government spending G. The crisis causes overall demand Y to fall and thus also the demand for labor N, so that unemployment rises. As a result, tax revenue T falls and transfer expenditure Tr rises, and with it the deficit Df_z, especially in countries with low competitiveness and low government efficiency.

The situation becomes critical if investors fear that the Ponzi financing will jeopardize their outstanding interest payments, i.e., if the government primary surplus Pü = Tw + Tπ + Tz−G−Tr is not sufficient to pay the interest Z and that the deficit Df_z that then arises can only be financed by increasing debt. Risk premiums increase and there is a risk of sovereign default. The Keynes-Minsky momentum is set in motion.

The risk that the countries affected by this will no longer be able to pay their interest and repay their maturing debts, therefore, increases and causes interest rates on their government bonds to soar by means of risk premiums. The rise in interest rates pushes up interest payments Z and thus deficits Df_z and, consequently, government debt D. The spiral of loss of confidence continues, exacerbated by the rise in the price of risk on CDS papers. The euro countries concerned are helplessly exposed to this dramatic downward trend. For they can no longer act effectively against this sovereign debt crisis. They gave up the means of currency devaluation when they entered the euro currency. They can therefore no longer strengthen their competitive position. Moreover, their national central banks can no longer provide them with cheap money. Unlike in the USA, they do not have a central bank that could serve them as a *lender of last resort.*

The introduction of the euro has increased the interdependence between the euro countries. Nevertheless, the Maastricht Treaty, with its "no bail-out" clause, stipulates that each euro state must look after itself and not expect help from others. As mentioned before, this clause turns out to be untenable in crises. The banking crisis in the USA, sometimes exacerbated by banking or real estate crises in their own countries, plunges Ireland, Portugal, Greece, Crete, Spain, and Italy into a sovereign debt crisis. The euro monetary union is at risk and a break-up threatens the economic stability of the remaining countries. A rethink of euro policy and swift action is called for. The reorientation takes place in several stages:

- Foundation of the EFSF on a temporary basis,
- Permanent establishment of the ESM,
- Addition of the European Fiscal Compact, the Fiscal Stability Treaty TSCG, to the Maastricht Treaty,
- Creation of the OMT program by the ECB,
- Establishment of the EU banking union.

The development from the temporary European Financial Stability Facility EFSF to the permanent European Stability Mechanism ESM shows the reluctance of EU politicians to act. Only under pressure are they prepared to create a permanent institution that can actively support an EU economic policy with its own financial resources.

However, the ESM soon proves to be inadequate to deal with the euro sovereign debt crisis, especially after the crisis had reached the large countries Spain and Italy. The downward spiral leads to rising interest rates with drastic price falls, i.e., substantial asset losses for creditors of Spanish and Italian government bonds—for example, if interest rates rise from 3 to 6%, their issue price is halved from 100 to 50 and so are their fixed assets. This downward trend undermines creditors' confidence in the Spanish and Italian governments and in the euro and must be stopped. Despite the ESM, it threatens to break the monetary union and pull the economy of the entire euro area down.

Further action is urgently needed. An increase in the ESM proves to be lengthy and difficult to implement in parliament. In this emergency situation, the ECB is inventive and seizes the reins of action. On 6 September 2012, it adopted the "Outright Monetary Transaction Programme (OMT)". Under this program, the ECB is empowered to intervene massively in bond markets to support the euro.

The OMT program aims to reduce market interest rates for euro countries threatened by insolvency and to restore their creditworthiness on the financial market by reducing interest payments. Ultimately, it is intended to prevent the eurozone from breaking up as a result of a withdrawal from the eurozone. The OMT program envisages buying government bonds of endangered euro countries with a residual maturity of up to three years on the secondary market. It requires these countries to submit to the conditions of the ESM rescue fund.

Its President underlines the determination of the ECB with the slogan: "*Ready to do what ever it takes*". The massive purchase of Spanish and Italian bonds on the secondary market and the determination to continue the buying up have an effect: the rise in interest rates on the secondary market for old bonds and on the primary market for new issues has been halted. It remains to be seen whether this effect will last.

Let us take a closer look at how the OMT program works in the secondary market. The falling trend in the prices of existing bonds means an increasing loss of assets for creditors. They want to get rid of the risk of rising losses, and therefore, offer their bonds. Since risk assessment is generally shared, prices continue to fall as a result of the increased supply. Now, with the ECB, an additional buyer is appearing on the secondary market, which can stop the falling trend in bond prices through massive purchases and thus also the rise in interest rates. The existing private sector creditors are thus largely rid of their risky securities and the creditor risk is transferred to the ECB: the ECB assumes the risk and relieves the private creditors.

However, with its large-scale purchases, the ECB intervenes massively in the price mechanism of individual financial markets in the euro area and, like the Fed, dominates the market. The question is whether the ECB is still acting "in accordance with the principle of an open market economy with free competition".

Nevertheless, the ECB's action must not be enough to restore the confidence of private investors and to make countries that appear to be at risk today appear solvent in the future. This is because structural reforms are needed to boost confidence and reduce the risk of insolvency. This is where the link between the OMT program and the ESM, monetary and fiscal policy, comes into play. The ECB combines its bond purchase program with the condition of reforms to be introduced under the control of the ESM. In the absence of reforms, the ECB has had its last shot and the President's bold slogan may turn out to be a hollow phrase.

The ECB has engaged in a risky game. For its outcome depends on the success of reforms in risk countries, namely on the weakest euro member state. If it does not achieved, mistrust and risk will return to the primary and secondary markets, and then another wave of selling will put pressure on the euro. And the OMT action has in the meantime created new unfavorable facts. By cutting interest rates, it has encouraged deficit policies and the expansion of debt in risk countries; in fact, it has indirectly supported Ponzi financing of governments, which it is not allowed to do; and it has high-risk bonds on its balance sheet to a considerable extent. It has nationalized private risk. The Community bears the risk, and risk has its price, as the CDS papers teach us. Yet the risk does not appear in any government budget.

The risk is that countries with higher interest payments Z and large debt rescheduling and repayment needs may become insolvent. In the event of acute insolvency, the public call for debt relief is reinforced. If it occurs, the risk becomes apparent that the ECB's authorization has violated the budgetary rights of parliaments. Debt relief means, on the one hand, public financing through monetary policy, and on the other hand, transfers from solvent states to insolvent states in the euro area. This is because debt relief will at least be at the expense of the ECB's profits and thus ultimately at the expense of the taxpayer, as explained in more detail in the next section.

However, under Draghi, the ECB turned out to be an innovator and compensated for weaknesses in EU economic and monetary policy—in this context the German Federal Constitutional Court speaks in 2014 of an arbitrary assumption of competence (Ultra-Vires Act). In 2020, the German Constitutional Court has again dealt with the ECB's bond purchase program. We discuss this in an excursion at the end of the next section.

Looking back, one might later celebrate the ECB's OMT policy as a major step toward EU integration. Probably less so the fiscal compact that was supposed to strengthen the Maastricht Treaty. For, like the Maastricht Treaty, it will turn out to be insufficient. Here we recall Rajan's words about politics from a national perspective: "Politics is always local, there is no constituency for the global economy. Change will come only when countries are forced to change, or decide it is their best interest to do so" (2010, pp. 208 and 2010). If constitutional concerns were to restrict ECB policy, the euro countries could make a virtue out of necessity and develop the ESM into a more powerful regulatory institution, and with sufficient resources, direct it toward the stability of the euro.

Regulatory rules alone are not enough to stabilize the situation. That is the lesson of the failure of the Maastricht rules for coordinating European fiscal policy. The self-regulation of the international Basel banking supervisory authority will also fail in crises. There is also skepticism about the supplement to the Maastricht Treaty in the form of the Fiscal Stability Treaty [Treaty on Stability, Coordination, and Governance in the Economic and Monetary Union TSCG]. Instead, stabilizing an inherently unstable system requires financially powerful and clearly oriented institutions that can exert a stabilizing influence from outside on money flows, value stocks, and expectations. The emergence of the ESM, the EU Banking Union, and the new type of ECB policy initiated by ECB President Draghi can be seen as the evolution toward a new regulatory policy. However, with the close links between the EU Banking Union and the ECB and with the arbitrary OMT policy, the ECB is moving away from its originally simple and clear objective of price stability.

The Fed has fewer problems with stabilization. It can consistently pursue its low interest rate policy to stabilize growth without having to take account of state-specific problems. And the devaluation effects of the dollar resulting from its low interest rate policy are more welcome in times of crises. After all, the devaluation of the dollar should favor the export surplus Exü and thus help to stimulate growth according to the Π−I dynamic (Eq. 3.28). However, the trends in currency parities can be reversed quickly if the Fed shows that it will abandon its low interest rate policy, which could lead to new distortions, especially in the eurozone.

4.11.3 Profits and Losses of Central Banks

Economic crises, triggered by the real estate market or a pandemic, affect countries to varying degrees. Economically weak countries with high unemployment and debt levels and low growth prospects usually suffer particularly badly from crises, which further worsens their creditworthiness on the financial market. As a result, the prices of their government bonds fall and their effective interest rates rise. The money they need to survive an impending crisis becomes more expensive. They can only issue their bonds at worse conditions, at higher interest rates. However, the rising interest payments will cause their future debt or tax burden to increase further. A downward spiral will develop. The ECB stops their threatening downward movement by buying up the bad bonds of endangered countries. It assumes the repayment risk from the existing creditors. The risks increase considerably from 2007 to 2019. According to the graph "Piling up above junk" in The Economist, the volume of poorly rated corporate bonds is growing much more strongly than better rated ones. BBB-rated bonds more than triple from under $1trn to over $3trn over the period, see The Economist: "Credit-rating agencies. Markers marked", May 9th, 2020, 55–56.

In the pandemic crisis, the ECB remains committed to relieve the financial burden of the EU economy. Under the existing asset purchase program (APP) it starts a pandemic emergency purchase program (PEPP). The PEPP has a volume of €1,850 billion at the end of December 2020. Despite the APP, the ECB considers that the EU banking system is threatened by bad loans as the ECB proposal to establish a "bad bank" indicates, see A. Enria: ECB: the EU needs a regional 'bad bank'", Financial Times, October 26, 2020.

If the repayment risk of a bond occurs in the future, *the ECB bears the loss*. Creditors will therefore receive their money in full from the ECB. *The ECB thus provides creditor protection* and thus supports the richer ones who mainly own the securities. There is, therefore, no debtor other than the ECB who would have to pay for the bond issued earlier. In this respect, *no future generation will be directly burdened* if, as happens in crises, the ECB takes over bad bonds and the losses resulting from them, that is, if the *ECB assumes the redemption risk*.

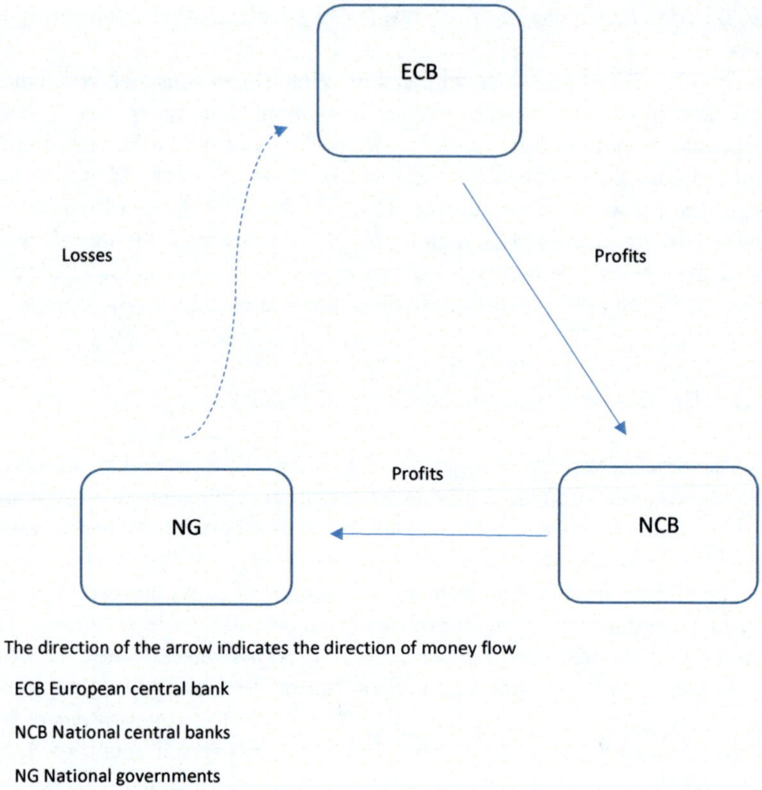

Fig. 4.1 ECB profits and losses

So central banks can make losses, often they show profits. The ECB explains in a diagram what happens when it makes profits, see www.ecb.europa.eu/explainers/tell-me-more/html/ecb_profits.de.html. In a modified form, it is shown here again in Fig. 4.1 "ECB profits and losses", where losses are now also listed. Money flows in the direction of the arrow.

If the ECB makes profits, it may distribute them to the respective national central banks (NCB) in accordance with national shares—Table 4.10 provides information on selected shares. They then pass these on to their national governments (NG). Losses could theoretically be borne by the national governments and thus ultimately by the taxpayers in the euro countries. The same applies to other central banks, as the magazine "The Economist" points out in two articles. In the article "Unprofitable arguments. Losses by central banks are nothing to fear" he explains Britain's Treasury has already promised to compensate the Bank of England for any losses from today's bond-buying. And further in the article "From yields to maturity. The Fed has been supporting markets. Now it must find ways to boost growth: America's central bank has promised to buy up to $750bn in corporate bonds and $500bn

Table 4.10 NCB and their share of profits and losses

Germany	25.6%
France	20.1%
Italy	17.5%
Spain	12.6%
Netherlands	5.7%
Belgium	3.5%
Greece	2.9%

in state- and local-government debt. ... The security, in this case, is mostly a guarantee by America's Treasury to absorb some of the Fed's losses".

It is politically explosive, however, if taxpayers from the euro countries have to take joint responsibility for the debts of an insolvent country. For political reasons, this is to be avoided. Even then, in the early seventies of the twentieth century, the Deutsche Bundesbank did not burden the German government with its losses. But in the end, the government still bore the costs in so far as it had to do without profit transfers for several years. Like the Deutsche Bundesbank at that time, the ECB will now also bear the losses incurred if a country in the Eurozone is unable to repay its bond.

At the latest when the ECB redeems government bonds, it becomes apparent that the central bank supports national governments. Then it would engage in monetary public finance. The community of EURO countries would bear the debts of a country. No matter whether the ECB makes the taxpayers pay for it or whether it books the losses permanently with it—i.e., finances the repayment out of nothing with central bank money.

This scenario becomes more likely if national economies are unable to improve their growth prospects over a longer period of time by their own efforts. What may make sense in the short term—to do whatever it takes to preserve the euro—may prove to be a heavy burden in the long run. This is because *the threat of losses in permanently weakening national economies will put a burden on confidence in the euro economy and the system that supports it. And trust is an essential commodity for economic activity. The ECB's debt policy is therefore risky in socio-political terms.*

Indirectly, however, today's debt can burden future generations. If economically weak national economies are unable to pay off their debts, confidence in their performance and thus their creditworthiness on the financial market declines. Their future financing costs increase and thus the burden that local society will have to bear in the future increases. It is in danger of drifting into an unfavorable economic situation that could have serious long-term consequences.

More general: Central banks, through their financial market interventions, are facilitating a huge expansion of credit. In the long term, it will lead to a serious intertemporal imbalance, an imbalance between today's debt financed expenditure and tomorrow's earnings then needed to cover the finance costs of yesterday's commitments.

With the huge program of buying up bad securities, the clear target-means relationship of bond operations to combat inflation is coming to a troubled end. If low growth is accompanied by inflation and the economy enters a phase of *stagflation*, the ECB is faced with *a dilemma. By buying and selling bonds—its key tool—it cannot fight inflation and boost the economy at the same time.* The fight against inflation requires the sale of bonds at high interest rates to reduce demand and the stimulation of the economy requires the purchase at low interest rates to stimulate demand.

The CB can overcome the dilemma of stagflation by opening up to economic players and providing them directly with central bank money through grants or loans. This reorientation also enables the CB to return to its original simple target-means relationship to combat inflation, namely open market policy with bonds.

Excursus: Federal Constitutional Court ruling of 5 May 2020 on the ECB's government bond purchase program [Public Sector Purchase Programme (PSPP)].

The purchase of assets is intended to expand the money supply. The aim is to increase consumption and investment and to let inflation grow to just under 2%. We discuss the monetary policy of a central bank in detail with the ISLM approach in 3 "Keynes' and Minsky's macroeconomics". There we question the effectiveness of monetary policy for macroeconomic management.

In contrast to the European Court of Justice (ECJ) in its ruling of 11 December 2018, the Federal Constitutional Court of Germany has concluded that the PSPP is to be qualified as an ultra vires measure—a measure that lies outside the ECB's competence. The Federal Constitutional Court criticizes the fact that the ECJ concedes a creeping extension of competence to the ECB and that in its ruling it completely ignored the effects of the program on the economy.

The impact of the PSPP increases with increasing scale and duration. In detail, the Federal Constitutional Court lists a number of harmful effects. The purchase of risky securities helps private banks to improve their balance sheets and thus promotes the "evergreening" of the banking sector in the longer term. The low interest rate caused by the bond purchase weakens the incentive to save and generally weakens the provisioning behavior of citizens. The lack of provision for the future will increase poverty in old age. With the low interest rate, economically no longer viable companies will remain on the market. The "evergreening" thus extends to the entire economy. All in all, the dependence of the economy on politics is increasing. It is becoming increasingly difficult for the ECB to end and unwind its interventions in the financial market without jeopardizing monetary union. This points to an impasse and a dilemma with emerging inflation.

Politics is also becoming increasingly dependent on the economy. "The higher the outstanding QE as a share of total government debt, the more the government is exposed to fluctuations in short-term interest rates", The Economist quoted an English central bank member, see The Economist: "Starting over again. The pandemic has accelerated a rethink of macroeconomics. It is not yet clear where it will lead", July 25th, 2020. If interest rates on the market rise, budgetary policy will come under pressure. Should it raise taxes, continue to increase its debts and hope for further support from the central bank?

Given the considerable scope of the ECB's interventions, it is incomprehensible that the ECJ has left the field open for speculation. In any case, the lack of explanations does not contribute to transparency, and *the ECJ and the ECB have missed the opportunity here to inform society about key economic policy issues. They are, therefore, not promoting the development of a knowledge-based society. On the contrary. Without warning, they allow economically weak societies to lose their creditworthiness, which later generations will have to pay for.*

The newspaper "Le Monde" points out that the weakness of the economically less competitive countries in southern Europe will continue. The recession triggered by the pandemic will hit the most vulnerable countries in southern Europe particularly hard. According to "Le Monde", in 2020 GDP will plunge by 11.2% in Italy, 10.9% in Spain, 9.8% in Portugal, and 9% in Greece. In these countries, moreover, innovation investment is particularly low compared with Germany, for example. Expenditure on research and development in 2018 is 1.39% of GDP in Italy, 1.36% in Portugal, 1.24% in Spain, and 1.18% in Greece compared with 3.13% in Germany, see Le Monde: Les handicaps persistent en Europe du Sud, 21 July 2020, 12.

The ECB meanwhile sees "evergreening" as a burden for the EU economy. The chairman of the supervisory board of the European Central Bank, A. Enria, warns of the "evergreening" generated by bad loans in EU banking balance sheets. This "evergreening" puts the EU banking system itself at risk. He sees the creation of a "bad bank" as a solution for the European banking system threatened by so-called non-performing loans (NPL). In particular, he emphasizes: "The European Central Bank estimates that in a severe but plausible scenario non-performing loans at euro area banks could reach €1.4tn, well above the levels of the 2008 financial and 2011 EU sovereign debt crises." … "we need to be faster in dealing with NPLs." And further: "The result today is a fragile EU banking sector, with *rock bottom equity*", see A. Enria, "ECB: the EU needs a regional 'bad bank'", Financial Times, October 26, 2020.

Enria focuses on a realignment. With regard to the establishment of a "bad bank", he puts less emphasis on the risk relief of banks than on the future refocusing of the banking system: "This is not about helping banks that took excessive risks and managed them poorly. Instead, the aim is to enable EU banks to support viable households, small businesses, and companies, and to bolster the EU's needed transformation to a greener and more technologically advanced economy without banks being weighed down by impaired loans". The extent to which a realignment of the EU banking system can succeed, *particularly in terms of future risk behavior of banks*, must, however, remain open despite the proposed way out of the impasse in form of a "bad bank". Doubts persist aswhether this can be a good sustainable solution. Isn't it more like debt relief—a cure against symptoms?

The overall economic risk associated with "evergreening" and uncontrolled credit expansion is the focus of the intertemporal imbalance in the next section.

4.12 Consequences of Economic Change and State Stabilization: Instability and Inequality, Distorted Markets, and Intertemporal Imbalance

The permanently applied deficit policy causes the national debt D to increase and with it the state interest payments Z. Its effect in the extended Minsky approach shows that debt-financed fiscal policy weakens the $\Pi-I$ dynamics and thus economic growth g in the long run. Its remaining room for manoevre depends on the interest rate policy of the central bank. If it moves away from its low interest rate policy, it further narrows the fiscal policy leeway. Rising debt D increases debt financing and thus instability, and, via interest payments Z and rising private credit claims, the flip side of government debt D, increases inequality.

Interest Z and profits Π mainly flow to households in the upper income bracket, the richer ones. They can invest a large part of it profitably in the financial and property market. These ongoing financial investments from profits Π and interest Z allow richer households to accumulate considerable property and financial assets, widening the gap between richer and poorer people.

Much money from profits Π and interest Z does not benefit the $\Pi-I$ dynamic. A lot of money flows into trading portfolios, be it assets on the real estate market or assets on the financial market. Trading in existing real estate and in existing securities is likely to significantly exceed trading in new buildings and issues. The portfolios are therefore becoming increasingly important. The interdependence between markets has recently been increasingly joined by the interdependence between flow and stock sizes. And the volatility of portfolio prices, above all the fluctuations in real estate prices and securities prices, poses an additional risk that endangers the wealth Σ and thus a core of the capitalist market economy.

Price fluctuations represent a market risk. The business risk and credit risk are illustrated by the example of an investment project in Tables 4.4, 4.5, 4.6, and 4.7, where the Keynes-Minsky momentum is reflected in good and bad times. Without debt financing with the credit leverage $v = 0$, the investor takes a manageable business risk and the entrepreneur should be able to absorb the resulting loss in bad times from his own resources. Debt financing increases the risk, because now the credit risk is added. Loans increase the chances of profit, but also the risks of a loss, which the borrower, the entrepreneur, has to bear. If the debt financing is very high, in the example at the leverage $v = 5$, the entrepreneur can no longer cover his losses from his own funds. He goes bankrupt, and the lender, the bank, has to realize a loss in its profit and loss account (P&L). Bad times affect the trust between creditors and debtors. A lack of trust makes debt financing more difficult. And the regaining of new trust necessary for a turnaround takes time, obviously a lot of time in the recent economic crisis.

The debt financing pushed by the private banks increases their risks. They can pass on their risks, thanks to innovative financial instruments. The innovations give rise to new markets. Trade flourishes and generates systematic risk. Various measures are designed to curb the risk of debt financing. With the EQ, the Basel self-regulation of banks is intended to create a sufficient buffer for losses in a crisis. What is right for an individual bank in a specific crisis does not necessarily apply to a banking system in an economic crisis. And in the recent financial crisis, the Basel rules have also failed. The EQ is a residual figure. It depends, among other things, on the development of securities holdings on banks' balance sheets. If securities prices collapse across the board in a financial crisis, the EQ falls. If, in this precarious situation, the Basel regulation insists on compliance with its EQ rule, it exacerbates the crisis. It will want to avoid a worsening of the crisis. It will, therefore, refrain from strictly observing its rules. With the establishment of the EU Banking Union, the EU is making it clear that it considers the Basel regulation to be less effective. But one can also be skeptical about the effect of the newly created Banking Union. After all, its resources are relatively insignificant compared with the volume of market transactions on the financial markets. The Maastricht rules have also failed. They have not been able to prevent excessive state debt financing. Similarly, the rules of the new European Fiscal Compact TSCG are unlikely to be effective. Here, the trilemma between supranational rules, democracy, and nation-state interests is likely to be an insurmountable obstacle to making supranational rules for state debt financing effective. That leaves the ECB which, in an innovative way and in coordination with the ESM State Fund, may be able to effectively stabilize instability in the euro area and help to overcome the trilemma.

Central banks remain the main players. *Unlike Keynesian fiscal policy at the time, central bank policy today lacks a sound theoretical basis for targeted intervention in economic processes*. Their main focus is on stabilizing the financial system. Broad-based interventions aim to influence the financial factors of the return on equity r_e in such a way that longer-term expectations of profits Π can rise again and wealth Σ remain secure.

The central bank's first priority today is to ensure the functioning of the financial market in order to stabilize the economy as a whole. Stability means that production and its marketing must be profitable and money flows must be unimpeded. Societal concerns take a back seat.

At the same time, the broad-based interventions by central banks continue to strengthen debt financing and thus instability. They become the main financier of private banks, which have less need to solicit private investment. They are thus changing the structure of bank balance sheet liabilities and the private sector's provisioning behavior. The support of asset portfolios benefits the richer and promotes inequality. The interventions will become more selective. If the turnaround comes at good times, central banks will have to continue to keep government interest rates low so that an increase in interest payments Z does not further limit the scope for fiscal policy. The result will be an asymmetric central bank policy, restrictive toward the private sector and rather lax toward the government sector.

The expansion of the money supply is unlikely to have any inflationary effects as long as the $\Pi - I$ dynamic does not kick in. However, they are desirable in view of deflationary trends. And so, it is not surprising that the Deutsche Bundesbank sees scope for higher wages W in 2014. And according to Minsky's price level approach $P = (W/A_p)\ [1 + \Pi/NW]$, wage increases would indeed be a means to raise the price level P and promote inflation. However, the demands made on the unions and employers also show the helplessness of the central bank in steering macroeconomic developments.

State management of the economy is under public pressure to meet the public expectation that the state can quickly take effective measures to stabilize the goods and labor market and to stabilize the unstable financial market. However, the desired successes do not have to come quickly. It is uncertain how the measures will work. And in the long run, it cannot be ruled out that they will promote instability and inequality. State stabilization is a risk; it itself is full of risks. And in the longer term, it will lead to greater interaction between business and government. Left alone, the central bank must intervene in the complex economic processes in many ways to achieve success. It lacks fiscal policy support. Fiscal policy can, however, regain its room for manoevre through more effective taxation of income Y according to the ability to pay and a more progressive taxation of assets Σ in inheritance, which also serves to provide equal opportunities.

A resounding short-term success of the various central bank interventions is still to come, especially in the eurozone. The long-term costs are already becoming apparent. The central banks are assuming classic private sector risks—and in the eurozone, increasingly fiscal risks as well. By assuming risk, the central banks are restructuring the market economy and thus becoming its mainstay. And by supporting asset portfolios, they gloss over the economic situation of private banks on the one hand and increase economic inequality on the other.

We can also conclude that the skepticism already expressed in the paradox of risks that central banks can overcome economic crises on their own is justified. Central bank policy needs the support of fiscal policy, and little has changed from the ISLM approach. The latter has promoted instability and inequality through permanent debt financing of large parts of its expenditures, rendering itself ineffective. However, the state can counteract instability and inequality by means of tax reform by gearing its taxation more effectively to the efficiency principle and to equal opportunities. And, according to Keynes (1937), a more even distribution of disposable income also stimulates the propensity to consume c and thus overall demand Y. Through a tax-financed expenditure policy, fiscal policy can re-establish the economic stabilization originally propagated by Keynes. Support for the euro was provided by an expansion of the ESM, which can help to bridge the performance gap between the euro countries through support programs.

Let us move on to a final assessment of the state stabilization policy. The modern history of state intervention in the capitalist market economy begins promisingly, thanks to Keynes. The market can fail in the short term, fiscal policy can fix it, in the interests of the common interest (First thesis in Sect. 1.8 *"Key theses"). Applied in the long run, also to generate growth, fiscal policy encourages the expansion of credit financing and thus debt and instability. It thereby renders itself incapable of action and must leave the field of stabilization to the less effective central bank (Second thesis in Sect.* 1.8 *"Key theses"). The central bank continues to increase credit financing. Its massive interventions in the financial market are aimed at making the financial system work. It assumes risks that are usually borne by companies. It promotes the development of profits Π and secures wealth Σ and thus inequality. It is increasingly distancing itself from the common welfare that was still associated with Keynesian fiscal policy.*

Their massive and prolonged interventions continue to disrupt market mechanisms, thereby undermining the benefits of the market economy that Smith explained to us. The expansion of credit financing creates an intertemporal imbalance. As outlined above: an imbalance between today's debt-financed expenditures and tomorrow's earnings then needs to cover the finance costs of yesterday's commitments (Third thesis in Sect. 1.8 "Key theses").

This imbalance may jeopardize the vital confidence of economic players in the future. Here we recall Harari's comments on credit creation in Sect. 2.8 "Economic evolution through innovation and credit creation (Schumpeter)": "What enables banks—and the entire economy—to survive is our trust in the future". Chapter 16 "The capitalist creed" in Harari (2011, pp. 341–373), shows the graph "The modern economy" with the three supporting pillars of the modern economy, shown here in Fig. 4.2.

The three pillars are:

- Great trust in the future
- Much credit
- Fast growth.

Central banks, as we have noted in the context of the intertemporal imbalance, provide "Much credit", but through their "evergreening" policies they support unprofitable firms and thus favor "Low growth". "Much credit" and "Low growth"

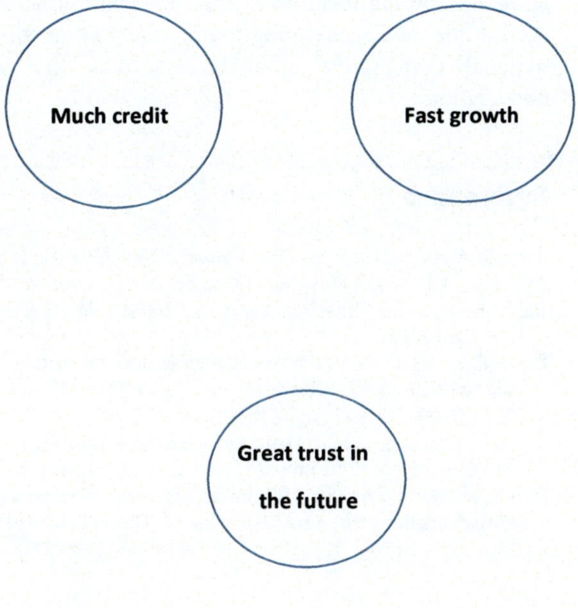

Fig. 4.2 Main pillars of the modern economy: much credit, fast growth, and great trust in the future

are the cause of the intertemporal imbalance. It makes the "Great trust in the future" dwindle, which can have fatal consequences for future economic evolution. Massive state interventions in crises cause loans to rise and growth to slow down and thus an intertemporal imbalance: "Many credits" and "Sluggish growth" with "Low trust in the future".

The impasse in the current stabilization policy calls urgently for a way out (Fourth thesis in Sect. 1.8 *"Key theses"). The way out is outlined in Sect.* 5.3 *"Reorientation of government and social policy".*

4.13 Summary

Central banks remain the main players. Without a viable concept, they must intervene in the financial market in a variety of ways, with uncertain outcomes. Their actions are aimed at assuming economic risks from the private sector, encouraging the flow of profits, and safeguarding wealth. Their interventions benefit the richer, the risk takers, and the owners. They thus promote inequality. Consequently, the beneficiaries of state intervention are also changing. The effective Keynesian fiscal policy has still served the common good. It has benefited disadvantaged workers.

The capitalist market economy shows significant weaknesses. It is still plagued by the evil of unemployment, and two further social burdens, instability and inequality, are added to this. With distorted markets and intertemporal imbalance, two further problems are weighing on the development of the capitalist market economy. The state can only worsen the situation with its traditional stabilization policy. It must rethink. The solution lies in civil society. By strengthening its autonomy on the local level, the state can initiate a new kind of social prosperity. And in the newly emerging international competitive struggle, it can improve the national competitive strength and thus the opportunities for international cooperation.

References

Admati, A.A., Hellwig, M.: The Bankers' New Clothes, Princeton (2013)

Atkinson, A.B.: Inequality. What Can be Done?, London (2015)

Baldwin, R.: The Great Convergence, Information Technology and the New Globalization, London (2016)

Bastagli, F., Hills, J.: Wealth Accumulation in Great Britain 1995–2005: The Role of House Prices and the Life Cycle, Centre for Analysis of Social Exclusion, London School of Economics, 2012, 1–37

Bundesverfassungsgericht: Hauptsacheverfahren ESM/EZB: Urteilsverkündung sowie Vorlage an den Gerichtshof der Europäischen Union, 7. Februar 2014, 1–5

Bundesverfassungsgericht: Privilegierung des Betriebsvermögens bei der Erbschaftsteuer, Pressemitteilung Nr. 116/2014 vom 17. Dezember 2014, 1–4

Bundesverfassungsgericht: Beschlüsse der EZB zum Staatsanleiheprogramm kompetenzwidrig, Pressemitteilung Nr. 32/2020 vom 5. Mai 2020, 1–4

Der Spiegel: Der Markt hat kein Herz, 38, (2005), 86–90

Enria, A.: ECB: The EU Needs a Regional 'Bad Bank'", Financial Times, October 26, 2020

Gordon, R. J.: The Rise and Fall of the American Growth, Princeton (2016)

Harari, Y.N.: Sapiens. A Brief History of Humankind, London (2011)

Hayek, F.A.: The Constitution of Liberty, London (1960)

Iversen, T. and Soskice, D.: Democracy and Prosperity. Reinventing Capitalism Through a Turbulent Century, Princeton (2019)

Jorda, O., Knoll, K., Kuvshinov, D., Schularick, M., Taylor, A.M.: The Rate of Return on Everything, 1870–2015, Working Paper, National Bureau of Economic Research (2017), 1–123

Keynes, J.M.: The General Theory of Employment, Interest, and Money, New York (1936)

Keynes, J.M.: Some Economic Consequences of a Declining Population, Eugenics Review, XXIX, (1937), 13–17

Keynes, J.M.: Professor Tinbergen's Method, The Economic Journal, XLIX, (1939), 558–568

Koo, R.C.: Escape from Balance Sheet Recession and the QE Trap, Singapore (2015)

Lucas, R.E.: Macroeconomic Priorities, American Economic Review, (2003), 93, 1–14

Levitt, S.D., Dubner S.T.: Freakonomics. A Rogue Economist Explores the Hidden Side of Everything, New York (2005)

Piketty, T.: Le capital au XXIe siècle, Paris (2013)

Le Monde: Commerce mondial: la fin de l'âge d'or, Economie & Entreprise, 21.11.2014, 3

Le Monde: Les handicaps persistent en Europe du Sud, 21. Juli 2020, 12

Milanovic, B.: Global Inequality. A New Approach for the Age of Globalization, London (2016)

Milanovic, B.: Capitalism, Alone. The Future of the System that Rules the World, London (2019)

Milanovic, B, Lindert, P.H., Williamson, J.G.: Pre-Industrial Inequality, The Economic Journal, 121, 2011, 255–272

Minsky, H.P.: Stabilizing an Unstable Economy, Yale (1986)

Rajan, R.G.: Fault Lines. How Hidden Fractures Still Threaten the World Economy, Princeton (2010)

Rodrik, D.: Das Globalisierungsparadox. Die Demokratie und die Zukunft der Weltwirtschaft, München (2011)

Roine, J., Waldenström, D.: Long Run Trends in the Distribution of Income and Wealth, IZA Discussion Paper Bonn (2014), 1–151

Romer, P.: The Trouble With Macroeconomics, Stern School of Business, 14th September 2016, 1–25

Saez, E., Zucman, G.: Wealth Inequality in the United States since 1913: Evidence from Capitalized Income Tax Data, Working Paper, National Bureau of Economic Research 2014, 1–65

Saez, E., Zucman, G.: The Triumph of Injustice. How the Rich Dodge Taxes and How to Make them Pay, New York (2019)

Scheidel, W.: The Great Leveler. Violence and the History of Inequality from the Stone Age to the Twenty-First Century, Princeton (2017)

Scott, J.C.: Against the Grain. A Deep History of the Earliest States, Yale (2017)

Sinn H.-W.: Das Marxsche Gesetz des tendenziellen Falls der Profirate, Zeitschrift für die gesamte Staatswissenschaft 131 (1975), 646–696

Solow, R. M.: Technical Change and the Aggregate Production Function, The review of economics and statistics, 39, 1957, 312–320

The Economist: The Third Industrial Revolution, April 21th 2012, 13

The Economist: Has the Ideas Machine Broken down?, January 12th 2013a, 19–22

The Economist: Six Years of low Interest Rates in Search of Some Growth, April 6th 2013b, 24–26

The Economist: Special Report: For Richer, for Poorer, October 13th 2013c, 3–26

The Economist: Workers' Share of National Income. Labour pains, November 2nd 2013d, 65–66
The Economist: Minimum Wages. The Logical Floor, December 14th 2013e, 16–18
The Economist: The Inevitability of Instability, January 25th 2014a, 56
The Economist: Risk off, January 25th 2014b, 60
The Economist: Special Report: Immigrants from the Future, March 29th 2014c, 1–27
The Economist: The Ascent of Brand Man, April 26th 2014d, 59
The Economist: Global Wealth, October 18th 2014e, 85
The Economist: Early Retirement, November 1st 2014f, 73
The Economist: Inequality and Housing. Through the Roof, March 28th 2015, 70
The Economist: Doing Less with More. Low Wages are Both a Cause and a Consequence of Low Productivity, March 19th 2016a, 69
The Economist: Too Much of a Good Thing, March 26th 2016b, 21–24
The Economist: There are More Explanations than Solutions for the Productivity Slowdown, June 4th 2016c, 68
The Economist: Financial Stability. Minsky's Moment, July 30th 2016d, 52–53
The Economist: Tariffs and Wages. An Inconvenient Iota of Truth, August 6th 2016e, 52–53
The Economist: Special Report: The Rise of the Superstars, September 17th 2016f, 1–16
The Economist: The Emperor's New Paunch. No Holds are Barred in Paul Romer's Latest Assault on Macroeconomics, September 24th 2016g, 68
The Economist: Why They're Wrong, October 1st 2016h, 9
The Economist: Special Report: An Open and Shut Case, October 1st 2016i, 1–16
The Economist: Special Report: The Future of the European Union, March 25th 2017, 1–16.
The Economist: Reconsidering Marx. Second Time, Farce, May 5th 2018a, 71–72
The Economist: Wages. The Real Story, June 30th 2018b, 63–64
The Economist: Tech Firms in Emerging Markets. Clash of the Titans, July 7th 2018c, 52–54
The Economist: Seeing red. A Ruling by Germany's Highest Court Undermines the European Central Bank– and with it the EU's Entire Legal Order, May 9th 2020, 16–17
The Economist: Credit-Rating Agencies. Markers Marked, May 9th 2020, 55–56
The Economist: Unprofitable Arguments. Losses by Central Banks are Nothing to Fear, May 9th 2020, 61
The Economist: From Yields to Maturity. The Fed has been Supporting Markets. Now it must find Ways to Boost Growth, June 20th 2020, 61
The Economist: Starting over again. The Pandemic has Accelerated a Rethink of Macroeconomics. It is not yet Clear where it will Lead, July 25th 2020, 13–16
Tirole, J.: Économie du bien commun, Paris (2016)
www.ecb.europa.eu/explainers/tell-me-more/html/ecb_profits.de.html 2017

5 Conclusion: Changing Economic Policies

Abstract

Two narratives tell us about the common welfare. The Smith narrative lets the invisible hand work in the market. In the Keynesian narrative, the state is the visible hand which intervenes in the economy for the common good. Economic change and its continuing stabilization are associated with instability, inequality, distorted markets and the threat of intertemporal imbalance. They narrow future perspectives. To make the future promising again, the state should realign its policies. It can turn its support to a knowledge-based society and innovative companies at a local level. In this way, the state can unleash forces of people at local level for new national welfare.

Only a large-scale popular movement toward decentralization and self-help can arrest the present tendency toward statism. At present there is no sign that such a movement will take place (Aldous Huxley 1946, Foreword to "Brave New World").

5.1 Economic Crises and State Intervention

Various factors drive change in the economy. The classic force is Schumpeterian innovation in production. It changes the range of products on the goods market and the production methods. More recently, with the ICT revolution, this is changing more and more through automation and logistics, which enables coordinated production on a global scale. Baldwin (2016) speaks of a "second unbundling", which transforms national production into global production processes. In addition, product innovations are appearing more frequently on the financial market, which increasingly dominates economic activity. Private banks act as central players there. They drive the credit business and thus debt financing worldwide. They closely link the financial system with the real economy. This link transfers the short-term time

R. Pauly, *Economic Instability and Stabilization Policy*,
https://doi.org/10.1007/978-3-658-33626-4_5

horizon and the increased risks of the financial market to the real economy and is expressed in the term "financialization of the economy".

Debt financing increases uncertainty, especially credit risks but also market risks. The growing risks make the financial market unstable and the Keynes-Minsky momentum increases instability at the expectation level. Minsky qualifies the economy as inherently unstable. In his qualification, he goes beyond Keynes. He sees it as immanently stable. According to Keynes, the market-inherent forces are strong enough to ensure that economic downturns always return to the long-term growth trend. Only, these "mean reversing" forces take too long for this. And the long-lasting lack of demand in the goods and labor market leads to socially intolerable unemployment, which the state can, and according to Keynes, should overcome. Even the market liberal, Hayek, sees the state as having a duty to do so.

Grant (2014) points out that back in 1921, market forces were strong enough to overcome an economic crisis. However, this historical example does little to show a solution for current crises. After all, the economy has changed and has become immanently unstable with the change. Nevertheless, the question arises whether the massive central bank interventions do not severely impair market mechanisms and further weaken the remaining "mean reversing" forces, see also Koo (2015, p. 97 ff.), who points out that QE policy delays necessary structural reforms.

The great economic prosperity over a long period of time has led to an accumulation of enormous assets, to considerable prosperity in the economies of the industrialized countries. This is reflected in high, partly debt-financed holdings of stocks and bonds and other financial securities, real estate, and works of art. Property prices, share, and bond prices are volatile. They can rise quickly and may fall even more quickly. As a result, portfolio accumulation increases market risks in economies. As we know from the recent past, banking and real estate crises can quickly trigger global economic crises.

Economic crises threaten the very core of capitalism. If the economy flourishes, returns on equity r_e and profits Π are high and the accumulation of value stocks Σ, of economic wealth, is secured. In crises, these results, which are essential for the capitalist economy, are threatened. Faltering credit and profit flows with falling asset values can lead to the collapse of the financial market and thus to the collapse of the capitalist economy. As the recent crises show, central banks are called upon to intervene in the financial market to stabilize it.

The change in the economic process goes hand in hand with changes in state stabilization. The economy and stabilization influence each other. State intervention is changing from stabilizing the economy in the goods and labor market to stabilizing the instability of the financial market. This development can be traced in the transition from the Keynesian-influenced ISLM model to Minsky's new economic paradigm. The ISLM model offers the state two instrument variables to stabilize cyclical fluctuations: the effective deficit variable Df of fiscal policy and the less effective money supply M of monetary policy.

Fiscal policy directly fills the demand gap in the goods market with debt-financed expenditure Df. It thus supports aggregate output Y and the demand for low-skilled workers N, which is closely linked via the production function.

Without fiscal policy, workers would be the losers of cyclical fluctuations; losers of the market economy, which sometimes takes longer to rebalance from an imbalance. The Keynesian stabilization of the economy thus benefits the disadvantaged, the unemployed, and thus the poorer, in the first place. *Fiscal intervention is for the common welfare.*

Fiscal policy has been successful over a long period. This success nourishes public expectations that the government can correct market failures: the market mechanism of the product and labor markets can fail, and debt-financed fiscal policy can correct it. Politicians are accommodated by debt-financed expenditure policies. Unlike taxation, they do not have to burden citizens directly and convince them of the necessity of the tax burden. Deficit policy does not need to convince them of this. And they continue with fiscal policy, which at first sight appears to be cost-effective, because they see it as a proven means of economic growth.

In the meantime, the effects of the permanently applied deficit policy are obvious: it expands government activity, and in the long term, causes government debt and interest payments to rise. Like the private banks, fiscal policy drives debt financing and thus instability. With its indebtedness, it restricts its own ability to act and makes itself dependent on the monetary budget financing of the central bank. The expansion of debt D causes the wealth Σ to grow and, with its unequal distribution, inequality in wealth. And the state interest payments favor income inequality. Keynesian deficit policy has rendered itself ineffective and shifted the focus from the real economy to the financial market.

Minsky's new approach considers the changes in the economic process. Private banks are key players in this process, making the financial market the center of economic activity. Private banks channel the central bank money M into the economic cycle according to yield aspects. If there is no prospect of returns, the flow of money stops. In crises, the central bank must then take a variety of measures to improve the prospects for returns on equity r_e and profits Π. In addition, it must take measures to ensure that the value of wealth Σ does not fall. The ultimate goal of the pursuit of profit is to accumulate this value of wealth.

Private banks are central actors in the capitalist economy, and profits Π are at the heart of their economic activities. Consequently, Minsky bases his macroeconomic approach to the goods market on profits Π. They play a decisive role in the $\Pi-I$ and $P-\Pi$ interdependencies. The $\Pi-I$ dynamic reinterprets the IS relationship in the goods market and directs investment I toward expected future profits Π. Profits are generated by firms through a profit mark-up m on the production-determined variable labor costs NW of the less skilled workers N, $m = \Pi/NW$. In Minsky's price level hypothesis, this mark-up m determines the price level and thus the development of inflation and deflation.

Despite enormous central bank intervention, deflation threatens to exacerbate the recessionary forces in an economy still in crises. According to Minsky's price hypothesis, central banks can expand companies' scope for profit mark-ups in order to boost $P-\Pi$ dynamics and thus strengthen inflationary tendencies. According to the Minsky formula above, their success in doing so also depends on the $P-W$ and $P-A_p$ relationships. In the 1970s, Hayek blamed the first of the two relations, the wage-price spiral, for the inflation at that time. The economic constellation has changed. Globalization, together with logistics, puts pressure on the wages W of the less qualified workers N in the industrialized countries, which tends to favor deflation. Automation also has a deflationary effect by increasing labor productivity. In addition, the P−Π relationship is likely to become more relaxed, since a large part of the profits Π does not benefit the goods market but flows into the trading of stocks in the real estate and financial markets. This would require the central bank to counteract different deflationary forces in order to be successful. And deflation not only hampers the dynamics of the goods market, but can also put strain on the entire economy.

Inflation is likely to stay away in the circular economy à la Keynes. Because a lot of money, a lot of money from loans, flows into the trade of stocks, such as real estate, shares, and works of art, and as already mentioned, causes prices to rise there, sometimes drastically.

The profits Π include the salaries of highly qualified professionals and managers who are the real creators and marketers of new competitive goods on the world market. The distinction between executive and creative work, between low- and high-skilled workers, opens up a view of economic inequality, which has its origins in education. Rajan (2010) ties in with this in his analysis of the recent economic crisis. Former Fed chair Janet Yellen also shares this assessment, see Yellen (2014, pp. 1–13).

Central banks remain the main actors in times of crises. They now lack an instrument variable such as money supply M to boost the real economy. In addition, money supply-based approaches to fighting deflation are no longer effective. Their main focus is on the financial market and its stabilization. Instability stems from increased credit and market risks and the systemic risk generated by new financial innovations. These are exacerbated by the subjective risk behavior of market participants, as expressed in the Keynes-Minsky momentum.

Systemic risk is one reason why central banks are increasingly taking on private sector risks. And it must remain open whether the systemic risk will again threaten the economy in the next crisis, despite efforts to contain it through regulation, cf. the skeptical comments, in The Economist (2015a, p. 67).

As a result of the long-standing stabilization policy, markets worldwide depend on central banks, above all, on the monetary policy decisions of the US Federal Reserve—around 60% of world trade is conducted in US dollars and over 60% of the world's foreign exchange reserves are denominated in US dollars. After the financial crisis, the Fed is in the process of reversing its monetary policy and making it more restrictive again. Other central banks, in particular the European Central Bank (ECB), will not be able to follow suit so quickly or to the same extent. Here, in the sense of Rajan, a break will arise. With regard to the dependence of markets on central banks, the Economist states: "Central banks have done the lion's share of steering the global economy through the financial crisis. Markets everywhere depend on them more than ever. Should they appear to falter, they will face an enormous backlash", see The Economist (2015b). And for the global impact of Fed policy, see The Economist (2018b) and also The Economist (2018c). The latter emphasizes the Fed's global dominance and doubts that international cooperation will be possible in future: "The Fed acted as lender of last resort to the world, offering foreigners $ 1trn liquidity. Since then (2008), offshore dollars debts have roughly doubled". And further: "Finding ways to make offshore dollar finance safe, such as pooling dollar reserves among emerging countries, relies on international cooperation of the type that is fast falling out of fashion".

Like the financial crisis of 2008, the pandemic crisis of 2020 came unexpectedly. It poses a further challenge for state stabilization.

The EU stepped up its efforts and in the pandemic crisis of July 2020, launched an extensive and novel support program of €750bn, mainly to assist Southern Europe, Spain, and Italy. "It is the first time the EU as a block will issue bonds on a huge scale to back stimulus, spreading the fiscal risk among all member countries", notes The Economist, see The Economist: "The world this week", July 25th, 2020, 5th edition. With €390bn, a large part of the stimulus package will be distributed as grants. It is a new step for the EU and a further state intervention in the economy.

Similar state interventions can be seen worldwide. Tacitly the central banks are financing these interventions. "... central banks have created new reserves of money .... Much of this has been used to buy government debt, meaning that central banks are tacitly financing the stimulus", see The Economist: "Free Money. Governments can now spend as they please. That presents opportunities—and grave dangers", July 25th, 2020, 7.

A new quality is now also becoming apparent in the intervention, which we have already mentioned several times. Whereas in Minsky's approach to instability, the central banks still appear as "*lenders of last resort for private banks*", they now openly appear as "*market-makers of last resort for the whole economy*". The Economist, in the abovementioned issue, puts it in a nutshell: "In the old days, when commercial banks ruled the roost, central banks acted as lenders of last resort to them. Now central banks increasingly have to get their hands dirty on Wall Street and elsewhere by acting as mammoth "market-makers of last resort".

As "*market-makers of last resort*", central banks support uncompetitive companies, thereby increasing performance disparities between national economies. *Their intervention focuses less on innovation and more on preserving existing companies*. This is particularly true in Europe, where it is more likely to exacerbate the negative trend, see Sect. 2.13.2 "Globalization and economic change to the disadvantage of the old industrialized countries". The Economist points out: "Across the continent, suspended bankruptcy rules, tacit forbearance by banks and a flood of discretionary state aid risk prolonging the life of zombie firms that should be allowed to fail". And further: "If Europe sees the pandemic as a further reason to nurture a cozy relationship between government and incumbent business, its long-term relative decline could accelerate", The Economist: "Winners and losers", October 10th, 2020, 13.

5.2 On the Path from Crises with Old Methods to State Directed Economies

The heading does not refer to state capitalism as it is seen in China or the state as an entrepreneur, nor does it refer to sovereign wealth funds such as the Norwegian sovereign wealth fund, see The Economist (2016), which provides an overview of the most important sovereign wealth funds. Here the focus is on the state direction of the economy, the state direction of unstable economies. The effects of stabilization policies on instability, inequality, distorted markets, and intertemporal imbalance are of interest here.

In unstable economic processes, the most important thing is that the economy functions. The capitalist economy can only flourish if corporate projects are likely to generate profits. Low financing costs and low risks provide advantageous conditions for relatively secure profit expectations. Central banks create profitable conditions through their low interest rate policy and massive risk-taking. Ultimately, central bank stabilization leads to an improved profit situation for companies.

This instability, together with the weakness in growth, creates more risks in the economic cycle. Central banks are currently primarily responsible for stabilization. They intervene in the price mechanism that is central to the market economy. They cut central bank interest rates and make massive purchases of securities. They favor the expansion of credit. They increasingly take on corporate risks and support weakening states. In the increasingly dominant financial market, they override market forces, as we have described in Sect. 2.6.1, "Market equilibrium, price mechanism, competition, and profit".

In the absence of a viable concept, the central bank must intervene in the financial market in a variety of ways. The outcome is uncertain. Its actions aim at taking private sector risks, safeguarding asset values, and enhancing the confidence of market participants by structuring longer-term positive market expectations. The interventions, which are aimed at promoting return on equity r_e and the flow of profits Π and securing the wealth Σ, will primarily benefit the richer, the profit takers, and the owners. It thus promotes inequality. *The beneficiaries of state intervention are thus also changing.* For the Keynesian economic stabilization of the time favored the less well-off and lower paid workers N, they are now already losers of automation and globalization in the industrialized countries.

Although the stabilizing effect of central bank measures on the economy is uncertain in the long term, it is becoming apparent that central banks are in the process of gaining economic power and changing economic structures and mechanisms. There is a shift of power from private banks and from fiscal policy to central banks. Central banks are increasingly controlling the financial sector, becoming the main financiers of private banks and the states. They assume private sector risks and support asset values. They weaken private households' own provisioning. Ultimately, their actions generally increase instability and inequality, which, in turn, reduce social acceptance of the capitalist market economy. The Economist also sees it dwindling and blames bankers for the loss of acceptance, see The Economist (2014b, p. 64).

We can determine: The free market economy shows blatant weaknesses in crises which it cannot overcome on its own. It needs state support to do so. *The capitalist economy can no longer function without state support.* State intervention, for its part, increases instability and inequality and deepens the interdependence between market and state. The capitalist market economy needs a more pronounced social component as a counterweight to make the market economy more socially attractive again. The state can contribute to this by gearing its effective taxation more strongly to performance and by improving equal opportunities, for example, by structuring inheritance tax accordingly, cf. also the minority vote in the Federal Constitutional Court ruling on inheritance tax (2014).

In an article on the history of the development of the financial system, the Economist points out that, in a long process, it has become the task of the state to ensure the stability of the financial system and to assume risks there. And it is skeptical about the possibility of returning the risks and their costs to the private sector, see The Economist (2014a). The ECB is taking a further step in the direction of risk-taking, as it has committed itself to do everything possible to keep the euro community of states together.

The features of state capitalism are unmistakable. Financialization has interlocked the real economy with the financial economy, so that instability there, with its increased risk, the so-called "tail risk", can spill over more quickly to the real economy. The state will always be called upon to intervene in the economic process to stabilize it. It is under public pressure to take measures that will allow it to achieve the desired objectives quickly, but in a dynamic and interdependent economy that is constantly changing, where is the leverage to intervene in a targeted manner? It does not exist. The state would have to be able to assess the possible consequences of its interventions, for instance on instability and inequality, if it does not want to be surprised by unintended effects, but the basis for that is missing.

Economic inequality is seen as unjust, and this assessment will reduce the social acceptance of the capitalist system, the free market economy. Just as the growing interest payments of the continuing deficit policy, the long-standing support of the assets of the central bank will reduce the social impact of the transfer payments. The banking privilege of being able to profitably channel central bank money into the economy is also difficult to justify and accept in view of the changes in banking operations. While commercial banks originally took on and monitored lending risks, investment banks are now selling these risks through innovative securities, thereby creating systemic risk. Private banks make a profit in the first place and society has to step in when losses occur. And now central banks are taking on private sector risks in advance.

The capitalist economy is based on striving for profit, for assured prosperity, it is geared to making profit Π and to creating wealth Σ. It is based on the expectations of economic subjects that they will achieve material prosperity through their own individual efforts and that they will be able to preserve this prosperity for themselves and their families in the long term. Massive and mass disappointments of these expectations seriously affect a core component of the capitalist economic system. The stabilization of the US, the UK, Japan, and the euro zone, therefore, aims less at the "wealth effect" of consumption and more at securing these expectations, this trust in the future, which are so important for the functioning of the capitalist economy.

Markets, especially financial markets, are becoming increasingly dependent on central banks worldwide. In addition to the interdependence between flow and stock values, there is also an increased interdependence between central banks and markets. This threatens to create new distortions in the global economy. If the US economy recovers faster than the EU and Japanese economies—there is some evidence to suggest this—and if the Fed ends its low interest rate policy as the US economy recovers, new tensions will arise, particularly in the EU.

In particular, the widening of inequality caused by the state calls for a state correction. In order to reduce inequality, the state could reduce the tax burden on lower income earners and finance the growing state expenditure to a greater extent through an effectively progressive income tax. The state should ensure that controllable insolvencies mean that risks are once again borne more by the private sector. The EU Banking Union is the first step in this direction.

The preferential treatment of assets by the CB policy is also an argument for a more progressive inheritance tax. The resulting tax revenues, together with the additional revenue from a more effective progressive income tax, could give fiscal policy the much-needed room for macro-level intervention, for example, in the form of sovereign wealth funds such as the ESM fund. With this fiscal policy, which is once again taking effect, the state can specifically trigger the $\Pi - I$ dynamics on the goods market without having to intervene selectively in various ways in economic events.

The financial crisis has also led to innovations in the political sphere. It has given rise to new institutions in the euro area, first temporarily the EFSF and then permanently the ESM. And as the ESM continues to evolve, the question arises as to whether it can be developed into a powerful institution to successfully combat current and future instability. In any case, an expansion of the ESM opens up an opportunity for the further regulatory development of the euro zone.

The ECB has recognized that the euro countries lack a necessary common economic policy. With its OMT program, it is creating new economic policy facts, which, moreover, similar to the Fed in the USA, enable monetary budget financing of euro states. In the crises, the ECB has seized the reins of action. In accordance with the saying "necessité fait loi", it has autonomously expanded its competence, and for the time being, and at least in the short term, strengthened the cohesion between the euro states. It has filled a political vacuum. It has boosted confidence in the EU economy and pushed back the populists' emerging contradictory calls for simultaneous solidarity and sovereignty.

In the future, it is still desirable for the state and its institutions to be creative, because the unexpected will continue to happen. Dostojewski (1992, p. 130) refers to this fact: "... I knew that this was only theory and that in any case the most unexpected practice would appear before me". To react innovatively to unexpected events and to take society along on new paths is the political task of the future, which is a global and local one.

Given the crises and their consequences, a new approach is urgently needed. Following the financial crisis in 2008 and the pandemic crisis in 2020, central banks and fiscal policies are supporting the financial market and thus the expansion of credit financing. *Credit expands our current economic opportunities at the expense of future obligations*. Today we receive money to consume and invest. Tomorrow we have to pay back interest costs and the loan. This intertemporal exchange works if future earnings are sufficient to cover the cost of credit financing. This has worked for a long time in the past. Therefore, we have benefited from this advantageous intertemporal exchange and have been able to trust in the future.

The lack of interest payments by more and more "evergreening companies" is an indicator that future earnings will not be able to keep pace with today's financing costs. The future is clouded and with it our confidence in the future. *Government support for credit expansion will threaten the balance between today's spending and tomorrow's earnings. If confidence in the future dwindles, a serious economic problem will arise.* After all, as we have already mentioned in connection with Harari (2011, p. 344) trust is the base of modern economic activity. In connection with Government policy in the pandemic crisis The Economist speaks of a "zombification of Britain's economy, see The Economist: "The zombification of Britain", October 31st, 2020, 15–16.

In addition to instability, inequality, and distorted markets, it is, in particular, the intertemporal imbalance just mentioned that has left state intervention on the path of crises as a burden of the market economy. The intertemporal imbalance endangers a central pillar of the modern economy: *confidence in the future*. Confidence in the future cannot be allowed to dwindle. Its commitment to ensuring confidence in the future, therefore, remains necessary. The only question is in what form. Its old recipes no longer bear fruit. Thus, government innovation is desirable. In the short term, it can respond to the demands of many economists and cancel large amounts of debt to restore the balance between "much credit" and "fast growth". *But this is just curing of symptoms*. The state has to invent new ideas and society in democracies is open to them, as we recall in Sects. 1.7.2 "Reorientation of economic policy in democratically constituted states" and 2.14.2 "State, democracy, economy, society, and ecology".

Finally, let us place the current situation in the history of economic development in Chap. 2 "A review of the history of the economy and its concepts: change is a constant". In the early days of the gatherers and hunters, the *present conditions* determined economic activity, even at the beginning of the Agricultural Revolution. Gradually, the monetary economy developed, and with some delay, the credit economy. *And with credit, the view of economic activity turns from the present into the future*. If technical equipment in production brings in more today than it cost yesterday, then it is worth taking out loans for this equipment. If, despite the risks, the surplus yield is constant in economic expectations, then the credit business can flourish.

Credit plays a central role in Schumpeter's economic evolution. Entrepreneurs today dare to undertake considerable innovative projects that will reshape economic processes in the future. If the innovations bear fruit, the entrepreneurs can become rich. If not, they have failed and banks bear a large part of the losses. This is because innovative projects are usually debt financed and banks are the lenders. Therefore, according to Schumpeter, as we know, banks should monitor their lending thoroughly. Otherwise, economic development is threatened with crises. *Risks are borne primarily by companies and banks, so they remain mainly within the economy; they are enclosed in the area of the economy.*

According to Minsky, large-scale credit financing makes the economy unstable. As a result, the state is called upon to act in crises. Then the state also takes risks.

We also know that banks are creative in finding ways of getting rid of costly credit monitoring and making risks tradable. *As a result, risks no longer remain solely in the economy but are spread far outside the economy; now the risks are released. Ultimately, the society as a whole bears the risks.*

Central banks cannot control this development. On the contrary. They massively promote credit expansion and at the same time back unprofitable companies; they support "evergreening". In doing so, they disturb the intertemporal balance and undermine the foundations of the credit business. With international competitive struggle, intertemporal imbalance is becoming more accentuated in countries with pronounced "evergreening".

A rethink of central bank policy is, therefore, urgently needed. It can open up to the civil society and promote a knowledge-based society, which, together with innovative enterprises, can promote prosperity for society as a whole.

5.3 Reorientation of Government Economic and Social Policy

In the Keynesian approach, if the flow of money in the economic cycle dries up in the short term, the state should pump money into the cycle through additional demand. Or, as we have already expressed in Sect. 4.10.4 "Formal quantitative, qualitative analysis", the Keynesian approach is a paradigm which has been a central orientation aid for economic policy in industrialized countries. Keynes created the state as a compensatory agent: if economic players in the private sector spend too little, so that entrepreneurs cut back on production and lay off workers, the state should step in and close the spending gap in the cycle by generating additional demand. In this way, the state stimulates the demand for labor and thus reduces the scourge of unemployment, ultimately in the interest of the whole society.

As we also know, the idea of the state as a compensatory actor results from an isolated viewpoint, from a conditional viewpoint. It is conditional in time. The essential elements are, on the one hand, the idea that the economy is stable and is only out of balance in the short term, and on the other hand, the economic circumstances of the time. Inequality and debt have not yet weighed on the economy.

Continued Keynesian spending policies have pushed up public debt. The private sector debt level also continues to grow. Private banks are the main factor behind the general increase in debt. They increase debt financing, thus making the economy unstable. That is Minsky's message.

Under the changed circumstances, the state can no longer play the role of a compensatory player. It would then have to curb its debt financed spending policy in order to counteract the increased leveraged spending in the private sector. But an austerity policy would lead to undesirable tensions in society and the economy. The state must, therefore, leave it to the central banks to stabilize the economy. Their policies allow debt to rise further and promote long-term inequality. And under these conditions, it is difficult to imagine that fiscal policy can become effective again. The state must pay more attention to people in precarious living conditions; more general, it must pay more attention to the societal development.

One can be curious about how central banks will develop. In connection with e-banking, new perspectives are opening here. The innovative Swedish Riksbank is experimenting with e-money. It intends to give individuals direct access to the Swedish central bank by allowing individuals to open an account there. Direct access by individuals to the central bank would be revolutionary in several respects. It would make it easier for individuals to enter the e-banking market. It would weaken the privilege of private banks, which we have seen with the creation of credit in Sect. 2.8 "Economic evolution through innovation and credit creation (Schumpeter)", and the central bank would compete with private banks. The money in the central bank account would be safe and it would safely complement deposit insurance in private banking. Depending on its design, the state could use the central bank's private e-banking to stimulate demand in times of crises, a stimulus that fiscal policy is often denied due to over indebtedness. The Economist states: "Central bankers could be more confident in the stimulative effect of what Milton Friedman termed "helicopter money": distributions to the public of newly minted dosh". And further: "But used well, individual accounts could improve consumer welfare as well macroeconomic policy. It is a prospect that should interest", see The Economist (2018a).

Central banks have changed from "lenders of last resort" to "market-makers of last resort" and as such they leave behind distorted markets that no longer contribute to the common good in the sense of Adam Smith. In a weakened economy with crises, the state must intervene more and more, also to ensure the confidence of economic subjects in the future. The consequence is, as Huxley puts it, "a tendency toward statism", *a tendency to a centralized state government managing the economy*. Where is the way out of this impasse? The way out lies in opening up to society and strengthening it. In this reorientation, the central bank can find a new role as "*promoter of an autonomous civil society*".

Even companies are increasingly opening up to society. This opening is clearly visible in the development from shareholder value to stakeholder value. If shareholders have a primary interest in the return on their financial investment, stakeholders as owners, employees, suppliers, customers, and creditors have a much broader interest in the activities of a company. This broader orientation goes hand in hand with the increased openness of the state to civil society that is being propagated here.

In their new role, central banks would have to change their previous course in the long run. In their reorientation, they could support private economic subjects, citizens, with grants rather than with credits. In this way, they can ensure that a strong knowledge-based civil society can emerge, which can be a trump in economic evolution in the long run. This reorientation can result in an effective network of state, economy, and society, compare Sects. 1.7.2 "Reorientation of economic policy in democratically constituted states" and 2.14.2 "State, democracy, economy, society, and ecology". Now we can complete the fourth thesis in 1.8 "Key theses":

The close connection between the state and the economy must be loosened and the bond between the state and the society strengthened. Of particular importance will be the local level, where quality of local life can develop and where cooperation between knowledge-based society and innovative entrepreneurs can unfold to the benefit of the economy and the society as a whole, again to the benefit to the common welfare. A strong, self-reliant open society with great power of initiative may regain the trust in the future necessary for a promising evolution.

On the global level, the cooperative between the knowledge-based society and innovative entrepreneurs will foster competitiveness of the national economy. This cooperation not only contributes to the prosperity of the country, but also to an advantageous position in the international competitive struggle, which will be increasingly in demand in the future.

According to Iversen and Soskice (2019), the strength of the state is needed to restore markets open to competition, compare Sect. 2.14.1 "Democracy, capitalism and prosperity". As we know from Adam Smith, markets enable specialization and the development of talents through the division of labor and prosperity of nations. And here, nothing can replace a functioning market. It is, therefore, to be hoped that the market can function again with competition and that the Smith narrative of the "invisible hand" can continue to be relevant.

The reorientation of central bank policy can be a successful new beginning for state economic management, which is proving less and less economically effective and more and more harmful to society. In any case, it is worth an experiment. The new approach may turn out to be a workable state innovation. Much will depend on how the state will regulate the credit and grant system in the individual areas and how well the incentive and control mechanism will work in them.

5.4 Summary

Two narratives tell us about the common welfare. The Smith narrative lets the invisible handwork in the market for the sake of the public interest. In the Keynesian narrative, the state with its fiscal policy is the visible hand which intervenes in the economy for the common good.

Economic change and its continuing stabilization are associated with instability, inequality, distorted markets, and the threat of intertemporal imbalance. The threatened intertemporal balance "Much credit", "Fast growth" and "Great trust in the future" is the basis of the modern economy. The change is the result of a constant transformation, which is increasingly geared toward the future.

To make the future promising again, the state can realign its policies. It can turn its support to a knowledge-based society and innovative companies at a local level. In this way, the state can unleash forces of people at the local level who can take their affairs into their own hands at the grassroots level for the good of the community.

References

Baldwin, R.: The Great Convergence. Information Technology and the New Globalization, London (2016)

Bundesverfassungsgericht: Privilegierung des Betriebsvermögens bei der Erbschaftsteuer, Pressemitteilung Nr. 116/2014 vom 17. Dezember 2014, 1–4

Dostojewski, F.M.: Aufzeichnungen aus einem Totenhaus, München (1992)

Grant, J.: The Forgotten Depression, 1921: The Crash that Cured itself, New York (2014)

Harari, Y.N.: Sapiens. A Brief History of Humankind, London (2011)

Iversen, T., Soskice, D.: Democracy and Prosperity. Reinventing Capitalism through a Turbulent Century, Princeton (2019)

Koo, R.C.: Escape from Balance Sheet Recession and the QE Trap, Singapore (2015)

Rajan, R.G.: Fault Lines. How Hidden Fractures Still Threaten the World Economy, Princeton (2010)

The Economist: The Slumps that Shaped Modern Finance, April 12th 2014a, 47–52

The Economist: All it needs is Love. Capitalism's Reputation has been damaged by the Bankers, November 15th 2014b, 64

The Economist: Bank Resolution. Pre-Empting the Next Crisis, March 28th 2015a, 67

The Economist: With Great Power. Markets are Dangerously Dependent on Central Banks, September 5th 2015b, 64

The Economist: Sovereign-Wealth Funds, February 27th 2016, 77

The Economist: All the People's Money. Central Banks should Consider Offering Accounts for Everyone, May 26th 2018a, 70

The Economist: What Goes Around. The Fed should bear in Mind how Rate Rises Affect Global Markets – and Feed Back to America, June 16th 2018b, 66

The Economist: Has Finance been fixed? The System is Safer. But the Right Lessons have not been Learned, September 8th 2018c

The Economist: The World this Week, July 25th 2020, 5

The Economist: Free Money. Governments can now Spend as they Please. That Presents Opportunities – and Grave Dangers, July 25th 2020, 7

The Economist: Winners and Losers, October 10th 2020, 13

The Economist: The Zombification of Britain, October 31st 2020, 15–16

Yellen, J.L.: Perspectives on Inequality and Opportunity from the Survey of Consumer Finances, October 17th, 2014, 1–13